Sensory Futures

Sensory Futures

Deafness and Cochlear Implant Infrastructures in India

Michele Ilana Friedner

University of Minnesota Press
Minneapolis
London

The University of Minnesota Press gratefully acknowledges support for the open-access edition of this book from the Center for International Social Science Research at the University of Chicago.

Published by the University of Minnesota Press
111 Third Avenue South, Suite 290
Minneapolis, MN 55401-2520
http://www.upress.umn.edu

Available as a Manifold edition at manifold.umn.edu

ISBN 978-1-5179-1212-3 (hc)
ISBN 978-1-5179-1213-0 (pb)

A Cataloging-in-Publication record for this book is available from the Library of Congress.

Printed in the United States of America on acid-free paper

The University of Minnesota is an equal-opportunity educator and employer.

UMP BmB 2022

To my mother, Ann Rubin Friedner,
for all your hard work

To Saffron Orly Friedner Osborne,
for making me a mother

Contents

Note on Transliteration and Anonymization

I do not provide diacritical markings for spoken Hindi. I depart from technically precise transliteration in favor of readability.

I have anonymized all individuals and institutions, with a few exceptions. I do not use pseudonyms for government institutions such as the Ali Yavar Jung National Institute of Speech and Hearing Disabilities, the Indian Sign Language Research and Training Centre, and the All India Institute of Speech and Hearing. I do not use a pseudonym for Balavidyalaya or individuals associated with it, as it is a model program and known across India for its early intervention and training. Lady Noyce School is known by multiple generations of deaf adults and children throughout the National Capital Region. Finally, I name the four major cochlear implant manufacturers: Cochlear, Advanced Bionics, MED-EL, and Neurelec.

How to write of normal, normals, and becoming normal? Throughout this book, I place these words and phrases in italics or within quotation marks, and/or I leave them unmarked. I ask readers to forgive any inconsistencies and to see them as productive.

Sensory, Modal, and Relational Narrowing through Cochlear Implants

Becoming What?

During the summer of 2019, I met Neera, the first pediatric cochlear implant case in India. No longer a child, she was now a lively and warm young woman in her mid-twenties. While it feels strange to call her the first pediatric case, this is how I was introduced to her, and it was a significant fact: for Neera herself, for her family, for the surgeon who did the implantation, for the corporation that made the device, and for the Cochlear Implant Group of India, a professional association made up of surgeons, audiologists, and speech and language therapists. On the day of our meeting, I arrived at Neera's family's house before she had returned from work at an information technology company located on the outskirts of Pune. I chatted with her mother and father as we waited for her to arrive. When she finally reached home, expressing exasperation about the traffic on the roads, we launched into a negotiation about where each of us—Neera, her mother and father, and I—should sit on the two sofas and chairs in their living room. It felt like we were playing a complicated game of chess, trying to maximize lipreading opportunities for both Neera and me, although no one else in the room initially realized that I was concerned about where I would sit.

I finally said that I too needed to lipread, and everyone looked at me. "No!" exclaimed Neera's mother. "You have a hearing impairment too?" asked Neera. I explained that I had bilateral cochlear implants (I had mentioned this in my initial correspondence with Neera's mother, but I guess it had not registered). At that moment, Neera and her family expressed great surprise and peppered me with questions about how old I was when I had become deaf, when I had gotten my implants, when I had acquired language, and what my audiogram looked like.[1] Neera's mother said to me, "I should interview you now!" This was a scene that played out often during my research. For example, a research assistant and I talked to families in a hospital waiting room in Delhi, and my colleague ordered me, "Show them your implant!" Another time, I sat with the same colleague as she translated for me and a group of Tamil-speaking mothers of deaf children at an early intervention program in Chennai. During our conversation, she told the mothers that I had implants. They asked me questions, and one mother said that she was happy to meet me because she had never met an adult with a cochlear implant before, and she worried about what her child's future would be like. Her child was three years old and had recently been implanted. This mother's statement reveals a central theme and tension in this book: despite the increasing presence of cochlear implants, the futures of implanted children are unknown. What can an individual implanted child become, and to what extent are that child's current paths and future trajectories shared with other deaf people with or without cochlear implants?

There have always been deaf people in India, and deafness intersects with other important categories—such as class, caste, gender, and geographic location—to create different life trajectories. However, while I was conducting research for this book and learning about central and state government cochlear implant programs in India and the growing private cochlear implant market there, people constantly told me that cochlear implants have rewritten the script of what deaf children can become. Cochlear implants have inscribed (Akrich 1992) deaf children and their families, the state, surgeons, audiologists, and speech and language pathologists into roles that are different from those they previously occupied; for example, the state has become a sensory state, mothers have become therapists, and therapists have entered into international certification regimes. Through engagement with cochlear implants, these actors have become other than they were before. While becoming is often discussed in a hopeful and open-ended register, I see it as a pluripotent process that offers both possibilities and constraints.

In this book, I attend to *becoming normal,* specifically in relation to sensory normality. I argue that normalization leads to, and is a form of, narrowing. Becoming normal—a key promise of cochlear implant technology—constrains people's sensory, modal, and relational engagements. Normative sensory configurations and communicative practices based on listening and spoken language are the desired outcomes after cochlear implantation. These desired outcomes are tethered to ideas and ideals about a "right way" to sense, communicate, and relate to others. The Indian state, families of deaf children, medical professionals, and educators, among other stakeholders, increasingly expect that these normative outcomes will occur. They work to foreclose other outcomes for deaf individuals, such as becoming sign language users or orienting to others through vision and touch. As cochlear implants become more ubiquitous in India, sensory, modal, and relational possibilities for deaf children and those with whom they engage diminish. Sensory normality, as a desired goal and outcome, results in a contraction rather than an expansion of ways of engaging with the world.

Disability is a privileged site of engagement and intervention for the Indian state, and the central government's cochlear implant program is the state's most expensive intervention and investment in individual children. This expense is notable in that while the state constantly seeks ways to maximize the health of its citizens on the population level in order to increase productivity and independence, cochlear implants are an investment in individual children, and they represent a belief that such children can become normal through the implantation of a sense (of hearing). Because of cochlear implants, deafness, unlike other disabilities, is seen as malleable and fixable. Consider, for example, that in 2021, the chief minister of the state of Andhra Pradesh announced that because of cochlear implants, the state could become free of deaf people (Dara 2021). The fact that cochlear implants are so attractive—and the Indian government is working to manufacture its own indigenous implant—demonstrates a commitment to forms of normative becoming as well as a conviction that such becoming is possible through intervention in and on an individual body and sense.

A surgeon at a prestigious government hospital in Delhi told me, "The cochlear implant is the best solution that we have right now for disability." In speaking about "disability" broadly, the surgeon was pointing out the particular potentiality of deafness in relation to other disability categories. The surgeon's comments highlighted that cochlear implants are especially appealing because the "solution" they offer is that they activate the potential to become normal. In doing so, they activate (and deactivate) the potential of specific sensory, modal, and relational configurations. They also activate the potential of the state to expand its reach into the body and senses through its relations with multinational biotechnology corporations.

One of the first questions Neera asked me after we figured out our seating arrangements was which cochlear implant processor I had. She wanted to know which corporation made my implant (there are four major multinational cochlear implant manufacturers operating in India, three of which make devices that have been approved by the United States Food and Drug Administration). We learned that we both had implants made by a company named Cochlear, but that the implant processor model I had was two generations newer than hers; she had the Nucleus 5 and I had the Nucleus 7. Neera asked me how the N7 differs from the N5 (as they are called). Neera had "upgraded" to the N5 after previously using older versions of the processor; her parents had taken out a loan to purchase it. Neera's initial questions were not so surprising, given that cochlear implant manufacturers often use the language of "family" when discussing their recipients and attempt to create brand loyalty and identity through marketing and by hosting exclusive events; Neera and I thus discovered that we were in the same family, albeit of different generations.

Neera's implant and surgery had been purchased on the private market (and not through a government program) in 1999, when Neera was three years old, after her parents had taken her to specialists and spiritual healers around the country. Neera's mother read about adult cochlear implantation in an Indian newspaper and contacted the reporter for more information. Subsequently, she reached out to surgeons and to Cochlear. Because their daughter was the first pediatric case in India, Neera's parents were operating in uncharted waters. Neera's mother's family members asked her why she was so anxious to implant Neera and whether she was treating her daughter like "a guinea pig." However, Neera's mother insisted that she had to do everything possible for her child. The family purchased the implant—the processor and the internal components—directly from Cochlear, and a family member traveled to Bangalore to pick it up from the distributor there. Nowadays implants are sent directly to approved surgeons, or, in the case of government programs, they are shipped to a central distribution point and then sent out to hospitals. In addition, Cochlear and two other cochlear implant manufacturers have actual brick-and-mortar headquarters in India.

A brief interlude on what a cochlear implant is: Unlike a hearing aid, a cochlear implant bypasses many parts of the acoustic hearing system and electronically stimulates the auditory nerve in order to produce hearing. A cochlear implant has two main parts: a surgically implanted component

This poster, produced by the Cochlear corporation and displayed at a cochlear implant surgeon's clinic, depicts a family tree connecting Indian children who have received Cochlear's implants. The caption above the tree reads: "United by Sound, Connected by Cochlear." While this poster focuses on Indian children, Cochlear, like other manufacturers of cochlear implants, emphasizes that recipients of its implants worldwide are members of a family or community. I too am part of a broader Cochlear family tree. Photograph by author.

(the internal part), in which the most significant element is the electrode array inserted in the cochlea, and an external processor. The battery-operated processor is typically worn behind the ear and has a cable with a magnet in it that communicates with a receiver. The receiver transmits sound information to the electrode array. Each electrode stimulates a specific frequency range in the cochlea, which then stimulates auditory nerve fibers associated with that frequency. Adjusting to implant hearing takes time and work. Two to three weeks after the electrode array is inserted, an audiologist activates the external processor using proprietary software. The audiologist then adjusts the settings for each electrode and creates a range of hearing between a threshold level (the least amount of electrical stimulation possible) and a comfort level (the loudest sounds that the person can tolerate). This is called "mapping" the implant. The goal of mapping is to optimize the implanted person's access to sound by adjusting input to the specific electrodes. As the person becomes accustomed to the implant, the map needs to be adjusted, and typically the person will return to the audiologist frequently after the initial activation and mapping. Most people who receive implants can expect to have a stable map established by eight to eighteen months after activation.

As cochlear implants travel—from manufacturers' international head-quarters to their Indian locations and then to surgeons and hospitals, and on to the implant users themselves—so do people and forms of expertise. Becoming an implant user ties the user and the family to specific locations geographically, technologically, sensorially, and emotionally. Internationally, these locations include the headquarters of cochlear implant manufacturers in Australia, Austria, France, and the United States. They also include the schools and clinics where therapeutic methods originated in Australia, England, Canada, and the United States. In India, these locations are cities such as Mumbai, Delhi, Chennai, and Pune, although increasingly, cochlear implant surgeries are performed in smaller cities and towns, often as part of central and state government capacity-building efforts to develop cochlear implant infrastructure. Despite this expansion in surgical locations, however, it is often difficult for families of deaf children to find qualified audiologists, speech and language pathologists, and cochlear implant distributors outside of major Indian cities.

Neera's family had initially planned to have her surgery done in Chennai by a well-known surgeon because they believed that he had the most experience. However, a Mumbai-based surgeon had recently completed the necessary number of adult implantations to qualify to take on pediatric cases, as per Cochlear's rules. (The corporations that make cochlear implants have established rules about how many adult implant surgeries surgeons must perform before they are permitted to operate on children. They also require initial pediatric surgeries to be done under the guidance of mentor surgeons.) Since Mumbai was closer to Neera's family's home, they went to him—much to the disappointment of the surgeon in Chennai, who wanted the honor of doing the first pediatric surgery. Because Neera was the first pediatric case in India, a representative from Cochlear's Australian headquarters traveled to Mumbai to monitor the surgery (Cochlear had a significant stake in Neera's surgery, her implant's subsequent activation, and her re/habilitation, given the corporation's desire to grow its presence in India).[2] Neera's family then had to figure out how to get Neera the follow-up therapy she would need.

Since Neera had been lipreading for three years prior to her implantation, focusing on audition was difficult for her. A speech and language therapist suggested that in order to force Neera to use her auditory sense and listen, her family should stop speaking Marathi and instead speak English without allowing Neera to lipread.[3] Neera's two sets of grandparents thus learned a new language to communicate with her.[4] Neera's mother told me that Neera initially hated not being permitted to lipread and that she would often fight with her and demand to see her lips. Although Neera was the first pediatric implant recipient—the term used by cochlear implant corporations to refer to implant users—her family's story of traveling long distances and adopting new communication practices is one that I heard echoed throughout my research.[5]

A year earlier, in July 2018, I met seven-year-old twins who had recently been implanted in Bangalore. I went to their family's apartment, located down a small lane off the ring road of the city, and the twins showed me the huge cardboard box that their implants had come in, along with the cables, coils, and batteries required for the external processor to function. The twins had received processors made by the same corporation that made Neera's and my implants. Previously called the Special Processor for India and China, the processor model they received is now more neutrally called the CP802. Also distributed through government programs, the CP802 is an entry-level "basic processor" without noise-reduction programming or directional microphones. It is manufactured by Cochlear, which means the twins were part of the same family as Neera and I. The twins' surgeries and implants were paid for by family savings and funding from the hospital in which the surgery was performed. Theirs were the first cochlear implant surgeries performed at that hospital, and after successful completion, the hospital erected a giant billboard congratulating both itself and the surgeons involved. Meanwhile, when I met them, the twins had been sitting at home for six weeks; their external processors had been activated, but they had not been back to the audiologist for updated mapping. It was thus unclear how well the implants were working, since initially maps need to be adjusted frequently.

During my visit, the twins sat fiddling with their implants, wincing when the magnets attached to their processors touched their still-tender scalps, while their mother talked to them whenever she was able to pause in her significant housework routine. They had previously attended a school for deaf children where Indian Sign Language was (and still is) used. They had made great strides in learning ISL and were well liked by their teachers. One of the twins pulled out a school notebook, pointed to pictures in it, and used ISL to name the items depicted. We looked at black-and-white photographs of a hairbrush, a toothbrush, a mirror, and other household objects. He was eager to communicate, and these domestic pictures served as a scaffold. However, his mother, who had also learned ISL in her work as a substitute teacher at the deaf school, told me that she was no longer responding to the twins in ISL, only in spoken language. No one at the twins' former school thought it was a good idea for them to be implanted. Their mother too made it clear that she had yielded to pressure from her family to have the twins implanted (she was separated from the children's father and raising them on her own with help from her natal family). At the same time, she said that she and the twins had been subjected to mocking and disparaging comments at family functions and out in public, and she hoped that the implants would help to improve their experiences in such situations. She stressed that she was prepared "to do everything" to help her children succeed and that she was "going to work very hard," an especially poignant statement in light of her substantial household duties. As the principal at a school for deaf children pointed out to me, mothers in particular are expected to become "like cricket commentators" and talk nonstop with their deaf children.

Hierarchies of Signals and Technologies

I thought about the cardboard box that contained the twins' implants and supplies one frigid January morning in 2019 when I was out for a run in Chicago. This was one of my first runs after my second cochlear implant surgery and activation, my left ear this time, in December 2018. It was five months since I had last seen the twins. I was running, I was cold, and I was also angry. I was angry because I did not have any residual hearing left in my recently implanted left ear. I was no longer able to hear the low-pitched sounds of my child and husband stomping down the stairs in the morning. Previously, I used a hearing aid in my left ear and an implant in my right. I had utilized residual hearing, my hearing, that had been amplified by a hearing aid. This balance of implant and hearing aid, the mingling of different types of signals, made sense to me. I was indignant that during presurgery conversations, my surgeon had said that the hearing I had was so minimal, it was not really worth saving (residual hearing is often diminished or decimated entirely during cochlear implant surgery). Running along frozen Lake Michigan, I opted not to put my right processor on and was using only the left processor to train myself to hear from this newly implanted left ear. I ran by a colleague and stopped to chat. However, I could not follow the conversation and so quickly resumed my run. I had decided to get the second implant rather casually: my hearing aid broke and my health insurance would not cover a new one, but it would cover an implant, and I had met people who had "gone bilateral" and found it beneficial. My audiologist told me that I was a great candidate for a second implant. And more than a year later, I was "almost normal" during a sound booth test.

What is "success" with a cochlear implant, and what does it mean to have "normal" or "almost normal" hearing? Being able to hear, specifically to understand, speech on the phone is considered a prime indicator of success because there are no visual cues during phone calls. Another measure of success is being able to repeat words, then sentences, and then finally sentences accompanied by noise in a sound booth test. Take, for example, the commonly used AzBio Sentence Test, which evaluates speech recognition, first in silence and then in noise of either five or ten decibels.[6] The test taker sits in a quiet, and often stuffy, sound booth and listens to the disembodied recorded voices of American-accented men and women speaking in a conversational tone, uttering sentences such as the following: *I could hear another conversation through a cordless phone. You should be used to taking money from ladies. Hang the air freshener from the rearview mirror. You must live in a gingerbread house! The cat was born with six toes.*[7] These seemingly random and often ridiculous sentences are intended to test the listener's ability to hear without the help of contextual clues. The task at hand is to concentrate and repeat back what is said. The audiologist, sitting outside the booth and sometimes visible through a little window, counts how many words are repeated correctly for each sentence. Success consists of hearing within the "speech banana" of one's audiogram: this banana-shaped zone is the area of the audiogram where most speech phonemes are located, roughly between twenty and sixty decibels.[8] This does not include other sounds, such as the higher-pitched sounds of birds chirping, leaves rustling, and water dripping or the lower-pitched sounds of a vacuum cleaner, lawn mower, or jackhammer. It also does not include the sound of a person stomping down the stairs. The speech banana is a narrow slice of sound, sense, and sociality.

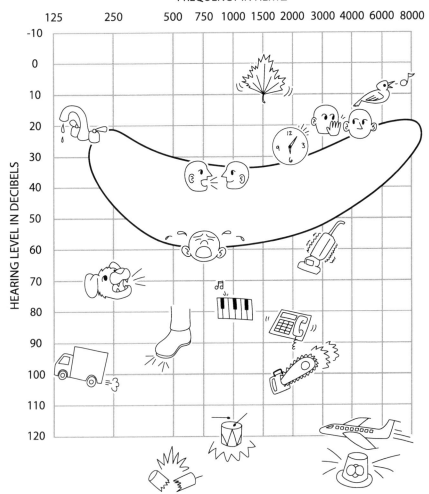

This audiogram shows the speech banana, where the phonemes of speech are located, and the locations of other common sounds. The goal of a cochlear implant or other intervention is to achieve hearing in the speech banana. Yet consider all the sounds—leaves rustling, people whispering, feet stomping, different kinds of music, firecrackers—that are not in the speech banana. There are many depictions of the speech banana, and cochlear implant corporations and early intervention centers often have their own proprietary versions, although the information included is the same. Illustration by Adrean Clark.

What kind of sensorium is this? I pose this question both literally and figuratively. Many attempts have been made to mimic what hearing with a cochlear implant and hearing loss in general sounds like, but what do these attempts actually mean, considering that brains adapt and adjust? These efforts to reproduce the experience of hearing loss and cochlear implanted hearing remind me of critiques of disability simulations in which nondisabled people attempt to experience what it feels like to embody disability through practices such as blindfolding, plugging ears, and using wheelchairs.[9] I am not interested in theorizing or describing what a cochlear implant sounds like or in drawing comparisons for a hearing audience. My least-favorite question as a deaf person, now an implanted deaf person, is "What do you hear?"

It is impossible to describe accurately or to theorize what the auditory experience of a cochlear implant user is, just as it is impossible to describe or theorize the embodied or sensory experience of impairment, or nonimpairment, more broadly, as Elizabeth Keating and R. Neill Hadder (2010) point out. Jonathan Sterne (2003, 13) argues: "If there is no 'mere' or innocent description of sound, then there is no 'mere' or innocent description of sonic experience." How, then, does one get at this experience? By showing an audiogram with its lines, *X*s, and *O*s? By waxing poetic with visual metaphors? By invoking sounds and trying to establish sonic commensurability? All of these possible explanatory endeavors foreground lack or deficit.[10] In this book I do not attempt to describe or theorize the hearing experiences of cochlear implant users, particularly in relation to sensory normality and its absence. I am, however, concerned with lack of another sort: the lack that stems from deep inequalities in how people hear with and experience implants, and the world, as a result of different iterations of technology, planned and geographically stratified obsolescence, and a growing private cochlear implant market.

The big box the twins received from Cochlear was different from the backpack the company provided for me. Their box was made of cardboard, with soft disposable plastic bags holding the contents, instead of durable nylon packed with reusable hard-plastic cases. And the twins received the CP802, while Neera had the N5, and I got the N7. At the same point in time, we all received different iterations of cochlear implant technology, undoubtedly because of the differences in our access to resources. Obsolescence also varies according to geographic location. In the United States, for example, the CP802 was never used, the N5 is now obsolete, and the N7 is the latest technology. In India, all three processors are currently being distributed, along with the Kanso, a new processor made by Cochlear that sits directly on the magnet location, with nothing behind the ear—it can thus be rendered almost invisible (it looks like a thick coin with a magnet attached). The Kanso is one of the most expensive processors on the market and is supposed to have the most advanced noise-cancellation technology; Indian audiologists consider it to be a "status symbol." What are the stakes involved when children like the twins in India are the recipients of cochlear implant technology that is considered obsolete in countries such as the United States and Australia? In this book I discuss hierarchies of sensation writ large and the ways that children and others who are implanted become subjected to these, as well as to hierarchies of technology development. There are also hierarchies of class, caste, gender, geographic location, and religion that play into how a child's potential is seen and activated.

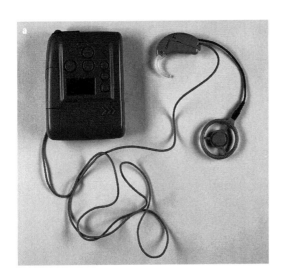

These three cochlear implant processors, all made by Cochlear, represent different generations of processor technology; with each iteration, the processor becomes more technologically sophisticated and less bulky. (a) Sprint, SP5 (1996). Photograph by Meg Lomax, Museums Victoria, https://collections.museumsvictoria.com.au/items/1446749. (b) Nucleus 6, Cochlear Americas, https://www.flickr.com/photos/cochlearamericas/34907729301/. (c) Kanso, Cochlear Americas, https://www.flickr.com/photos/cochlearamericas/34999520546.

Deaf (Dis)similitude and the Boundaries of Deaf Anthropology

In my book *Valuing Deaf Worlds in Urban India* (2015), I wrote about my first encounter with a deaf woman on a crowded bus, a woman who later became a friend. We signed "DEAF SAME" to each other across the bus, establishing that we were both deaf and therefore "the same." We never shared our audiograms or talked about the hearing aids or other hearing technologies we used. Rather, we focused on the fact that we were *deaf signers* with a shared interest in and commitment to promoting what my interlocutors called "deaf development," or more deaf-focused and sign language–based ways of being in and creating worlds. In that book, I analyzed how deaf people engaged in "sameness work" in which they actively minimized and circumvented differences—in age, class, educational background, and gender, for example—in order to foreground a unified sense of deaf sociality. It did not matter that some people were learning ISL as teenagers or young adults and that some people were fluent ISL speakers. What mattered was that people had the desire to learn ISL and that they endeavored to become a specific kind of deaf person invested in shared visions of deaf futures.

In contrast to that earlier work, here I explore the kinds of socialities that can exist around shared (desires for) normality. I attend to biosocial connections (Rabinow 2005), such as that between Neera and me, while also being mindful of biosocial refusals: a mother who wants her daughter to speak better than another deaf child; an early intervention program where deaf children become close friends, only to graduate and be told that they should interact only with "normal" children; an audiologist's insistence that no two deaf children ever have identical audiograms. Recall that Neera's mother asked me questions about my audiological and educational history. She asked for information about my age of diagnosis, when I first started talking, when I got my hearing aids and then my implants, and if I went to a normal school. She asked me for dates, numbers, and medical categories. (She may have enjoyed reading my audiology case file, if I had offered it to her.)

Later I learned that Neera and I had similar experiences in school relating to dismissive teachers and cruel classmates. However, Neera and her mother minimized these ambivalent or negative experiences. They instead focused on how well Neera did overall in school, how she did not use any accommodations in school, and how she was "like normal." As we ate dinner, however, Neera's mother talked about how she wished that Neera would continue speech therapy because she felt that her speech could be better, that she could become "more normal." And she turned to me and asked: "You are meeting so many implanted children around India, how does my daughter compare to them? How is her speech?" I politely declined to answer the question. But how to compare? I felt a sense of connection with Neera, and we listened carefully to each other, making sure that we could see and understand each other. These practices were outside the discussion of audiograms and speech clarity and gestured to a shared social and sensory experience in the world, even if we did not have the same sensory experience. (I also felt a sense of connection with Neera's mother, who did not seem all that different from my own mother.)

Much of the deaf studies and deaf anthropology literature has analyzed what is distinctive about deaf communities, socialities, worlds, spaces, and networks (Friedner and Kusters 2020). Some scholars have devoted their efforts to analyzing how deaf people orient toward each other—across difference—to create a sense of community predicated on sameness. In 1975, James Woodward made a distinction between *deaf* and *Deaf*, arguing that the former is a medicalized term while the latter marks someone as a member of a linguistic group. In 1980, Paul Higgins argued that membership in deaf communities is not ascribed but must be achieved through identification with other deaf people and participation in deaf community events (5–6). Whereas Higgins foregrounded that deaf people are "outsiders in a hearing world" who become members of a "deaf community," Carol Padden, also in 1980, introduced the concept of "deaf culture" to highlight that deaf people have their own social and cultural practices.[11] A focus on deaf communities and cultures—and other forms of deaf similitude—is an analytical and empirical move aimed at attending to, supporting, and perhaps bringing into being certain world-making projects, what Faye Ginsburg and Rayna Rapp (2013) call "disability worlds." However, what happens when there is a focus on "normal worlds," or desires to become normal, in these "disability worlds"?

Departing from the earlier deaf studies literature discussed above, I write about deafness without focusing on community. I avoid the concept of community in order to foreground differential sensory, social, and personal outcomes and the ambivalence, often rooted in a sense of comparative unease, that exists for implanted people and their families when they encounter each other. While individuals might share the same diagnostic categories, such as "severe to profound sensorineural deafness," there is

often variation in terms of age of onset, technology used, early intervention methods and duration, and family desires and dynamics. Families
considering cochlear implantation for a deaf child are told that they
should meet other families, usually handpicked "star cases," so that they
can see the difference between their child and the star cases. Audiologists
and speech and language pathologists engineer meetings between parents
in their waiting rooms. In particular, they want parents whose children
are not progressing or parents judged as not working hard enough to see
more successful children. But the waiting room is a (literal) site of tension, because not every child can become the same as the next. Despite the
omnipresent and proliferating discourses about potentiality and the possibility of becoming normal, there is also the specter of so-called failure and
the need for managed and modest expectations. This is why I was often
uncomfortable as I was conducting my research—I was frequently held
up as a model of what a "successful" cochlear implant user could become
in terms of listening and spoken language. That "compliment" that deaf
people have always found so disconcerting: "You speak so well!" How to
reconcile feelings of discomfort with the fact that a mother or family who
has worked hard to achieve that outcome might feel proud?

Disability and Deaf Rights Activism in India: Models in Flux

India has a vibrant and growing disability movement that comprises multiple groups such as nongovernmental organizations run by disabled
people, parents' organizations, direct service providers, and internationally funded charities. These organizations encompass many different perspectives, from a focus on basic needs and health to advocacy concerning
employment in multinational corporations and access to air travel. In 2016,
catalyzed by protests and activism that took place after the United Nations
Convention on the Rights of Persons with Disabilities was ratified, India
passed the Rights of Persons with Disabilities Act, a revision and update
of its first disability law, the 1995 Persons with Disabilities (Equal Opportunities, Protection of Rights and Full Participation) Act. Today, disability
rights activists routinely call on the state to increase accessibility in all aspects of life, from employment to education to recreation, and demands
for disability rights are ubiquitous.[12]

    The frame of disability rights encompasses a wide range of issues, in-
cluding advocacy for inclusive educational opportunities, sign language

interpreting on television news programs and at political events, nondiscrimination in employment, and the removal of architectural barriers in public and private spaces. In contrast to a focus on rights, the Indian state has traditionally engaged with disability as a category through the distribution of aids, appliances, pensions, and reduced-fare transit cards, as well as the establishment of reservations (quotas) in government employment and education; these efforts are aimed at maximizing independence and productivity while also showcasing the state's ability to provide for disabled people.

This focus on distribution, often glossed as welfare, is dismissed by urban-based disability rights activists and advocates as "charity," although rural disabled people stress that these entitlements are important and valuable for building and sustaining lives (Palaniappan 2019). India's central government cochlear implant program is the first initiative to include surgery under the Ministry of Social Justice and Empowerment's purview. The program is part of the Assistance to Disabled Persons for Purchase/Fitting of Aids/Appliances (ADIP) scheme. It is well publicized and often featured in the news media, as I discuss in chapter 1. Diverse actors see cochlear implants as manifesting different models of and approaches to disability and thus different relationships, responsibilities, and obligations.

Officials, activists, and researchers have strong perspectives on what constitutes a "charitable model approach," a "medical model approach," a "welfare model approach," a "social model approach," and a "rights-based approach" to disability. In practice, however, these models, approaches, and categories intersect and overlap (Staples 2018, 130). What kind of model and approach do people consider cochlear implantation to be? Is implantation an example of the medical model, in that it is an intervention that focuses on fixing an individual? The social model, in that it empowers individuals to participate in mainstream life? The charitable model, in that implants are seemingly gifted by the state? The rights-based model, in that implants enable individuals to exercise their right to maximize their health and well-being? (These are all arguments that I heard in the course of my research.) Implanting a sense poses empirical and conceptual questions around how the state approaches disability in general.

While Indian health researchers, government administrators, and some disability rights organizations see cochlear implants as a right, disability rights organizations have largely focused on advocating for the development and institutionalization of Indian Sign Language. The Delhi-based Disability Rights Group supported the Indian National Association of the

Deaf (not to be confused with the U.S.-based National Association of the Deaf) in its fight to establish a government-funded research and training center for ISL. As a result of lobbying by the Indian NAD, ISL interpreters have been engaged to interpret political speeches as well as spoken presentations at other events. There was also a (failed) campaign to gain recognition of ISL as an official language in 2018–19. While the Indian NAD initially was opposed to cochlear implants, as it explained in a position statement taken verbatim from a 1991 statement of the U.S.-based NAD, neither the Indian nor the U.S. NAD currently has an official position on cochlear implants.[13]

Although the Indian NAD has not adopted a public position against government-funded cochlear implant programs, many members of the organization, and deaf activists in general, decry cochlear implants, and there is lively traffic on social media describing medical complications associated with implantation and personality changes that can occur after someone is implanted. For example, one night in July 2018, deaf activists told me horror stories: a young man who could no longer smile because his facial nerve had been cut during implant surgery; a family who sold their land to implant a deaf son, and then the surgery was not successful; a young woman with chronic severe headaches as the result of implantation; and so on. These stories were in jarring contrast to the overwhelmingly positive coverage in the mainstream news media. Many of the horror stories were about adults and not children, an important fact, in that children are the dominant target of cochlear implantation and are seen to possess the most potential to become hearing and speaking. For deaf signers, deaf children are particularly important in that there is potential for them to become signers. Intergenerational transmission of language, values, and culture is an important concept and value within deaf communities. What kinds of intergenerational socialities (are imagined to) exist, and how often do deaf adults and deaf children actually interact in everyday life?[14] As children are implanted, mainstreamed, and discouraged from using gesture and sign language, their opportunities to interact with ISL speakers and other deaf people in general contract.

Children play an ambiguous role within disability rights movements in India and internationally, in that their voices are often mediated by parents, caretakers, or older disabled people and are not explicitly foregrounded.[15] Questions loom large about who decides for children and who can speak with authority for and to them. As scholars have noted, there is often tension between disability activists and the parents of disabled children about what is best for those children (and some parents of disabled children are also disabled and/or disability activists themselves).[16] What is often at stake are different teleologies: both parties have visions of what the ideal future might look like for disabled children and what these children should and should not become. Often, for families, the ideal future is one in which their children will become "just like everyone else" and they will "listen and speak as normal children do"; this future is predicated on sensory normality, or on getting as close to it as possible. In contrast, disabled and deaf activists' goal is for disabled and deaf people to reject normality and realize their disability or deaf identity, so that they can become part of disability or deaf communities.[17] I move away from sensory, communicative, social, and political teleologies in this book and do not say much about India's disability movements (except in chapters 1 and 4) because cochlear implants have largely not been "matters of concern" for such movements (Latour 2004). I do not attend to disability as an identity category and subject position from which to demand rights, although, as I note, the people I spoke with in my research often wondered what cochlear implants do to identities and abilities, especially in relation to asking for entitlements from the state.

To return to the examples of Neera and the twins (and see the Appendix for more cases), I argue that it is important to attend to their diverse sensory attunements and experiences. More than this, I want their futures to be (sensorially, communicatively, socially, and politically) open and not predestined.[18] In work on queer relationality, José Esteban Muñoz (2006, 677) foregrounds the role of "the receptors we use to hear each other and the frequencies on which certain subalterns speak and are heard or, more importantly, felt"; he pushes us beyond identity to the work of sensing in creating relationality. I examine how "receptors," in Muñoz's words, are socially and politically produced and, as a result, only certain "frequencies" are valued. How are touch, taste, vision, and other nonauditory senses fugitive forms of knowing, giving and receiving pleasure, and engaging that operate below the radar and beyond normative forms of recognition?[19] "Receptors" are produced through infrastructures. I attend to the multisensory, multimodal, and multipersonal processes by which specific kinds of signals are rendered valuable and transduced into meaningful forms of social connection as well as the sensory infrastructures that allow these transductions to happen.

Sensory Infrastructures

The Indian Sign Language Research and Training Centre opened its doors in 2015, and a handful of early intervention and educational programs around the country use ISL as a language of instruction. The revised 2016 Rights of Persons with Disabilities Act explicitly mentions sign language, an improvement on the 1995 act, which did not. However, at the same time that recognition and awareness of ISL is increasing, along with a limited infrastructure for training and employing ISL interpreters (there are currently very few ISL interpreters across India), a cochlear implant infrastructure is also growing rapidly. In 2012, Andhra Pradesh became the first state to offer a cochlear implant program, followed by Kerala, and in 2014, under Prime Minister Narendra Modi, cochlear implants were included in the ADIP scheme. Other states have since followed suit. Through the scheme, the Indian government is building sensory infrastructures that aim to produce normatively listening and speaking subjects.

I deliberately foreground the concept of infrastructure because the government administrators, public health officials, surgeons, audiologists, and speech and language pathologists I interviewed in my research talked about infrastructure constantly: the need for more infrastructure in the domains of newborn hearing screening, early intervention, surgical facilities, and listening and spoken language training. To them, infrastructure meant testing equipment, soundproof testing rooms, surgical operating rooms and necessary surgical equipment, auditory verbal therapy courses, auditory therapy centers with noise-canceling architectural features, transparent online platforms for registering for the central government cochlear implant program, and cochlear implant distribution and repair centers. This infrastructure is made up of visible, material, and often technical structures and institutions. Government officials saw the emergence and expansion of the central government cochlear implant program as an infrastructural project, designed to build and expand surgery and re/habilitation capacity and skill around the country. Indeed, infrastructure is mobilized as a means of asserting present or future modernity and benevolence.[20]

In this book, I explore the infrastructure associated with cochlear implants mentioned above, but I do not see infrastructure as solely material and technological. I think beyond the binary of visible and invisible infrastructure (Larkin 2013, 336) to consider auditory, tactile, and other sensory infrastructural forms. I also consider social and pedagogical infrastructures. I think of Lev Vygotsky's (1978) work on the zone of proximal development and the ways that therapists and families scaffold children's development by providing linguistic and social infrastructures through which children can communicate and engage with others; these infrastructures fix ideas of potential and provide children with paths toward becoming appropriately listening and speaking subjects.[21] Scaffolding imprints into and onto the senses through transitory and permanent forms of social and material infrastructures; it permanently molds senses, modes, and relations. Scaffolds create conditions for growth in specific directions, and capability and growth are normatively and prescriptively defined. Adults create conditions for children to learn by providing controlled and constrained communicative structures (Wood, Bruner, and Ross 1976, 90).[22] Vygotsky (1978, 86) notes: "The zone of proximal development defines those functions that have not yet matured but are in the process of maturation, functions that will mature tomorrow but are currently in an embryonic state. These functions could be termed the 'buds' or 'flowers' of development rather than the 'fruits' of development." In clinics, classrooms, and everyday life, parents work to maximize their children's potential development, specifically in relation to age-appropriate listening and spoken language skills. Parents are taught to structure communicative interactions as interpersonal infrastructure.

I attend to what I call *sensory infrastructures,* which include the technical infrastructures discussed above as well as authoritative, pedagogical, caring, and social relationships that occur around cochlear implantation, re/habilitation, and maintenance. Infrastructure works on and is worked on by the senses. Christina Schwenkel (2015) notes that "infrastructure, broken or not, often evokes a multiplicity of embodied sensations across the human sensorium." Catherine Fennell (2015, 32, 130) argues that infrastructures "press into flesh" and that, as a result of ongoing impingement, bodies are not "*infinitely malleable.*" Writing about Chicagoans living in public housing, Fennell analyzes how the conditions of such housing—temperature settings, smells, and the kinds of sociality enabled—result in certain bodily dispositions. How might we think about the ways that infrastructures produce, enable, and constrain the development of senses and the possibility of sensory experience? I go further than Schwenkel's seemingly already intact sensorium and Fennell's bodily dispositions to consider how infrastructure creates possibilities for the making of a sensorium.

Consider these three diverse spaces: a soundproofed early intervention classroom in which four deaf children with hearing aids and implants sit at a small table close together with their teacher while their mothers sit outside chatting; an air-conditioned therapy classroom, brightly lit and full of enticing toys, where a child sits between her mother and her therapist; and another early intervention classroom that is noisy because of a whirling fan, open windows, and concrete floors, in which many mothers and children sit together talking on mats in dyads, raising their voices to be heard above the others who are also talking. How are these spaces different sensory infrastructures? In the first and second settings, children are not allowed to look at their teachers or mothers to lipread and must use only audition. In the third classroom, mothers use visual and tactile cues in order to talk with and teach their children (and it might be too noisy to hear). Consider the infrastructures of urban primary school classrooms in India, where windows are open to honking traffic and fans click and whir as children sit on wooden benches, surrounded by fifty other children, while a teacher lectures or dictates. There are also classrooms in deaf schools in which there are fifty children, the majority without hearing technology, and a teacher who does not sign. What kinds of pedagogical, social, and sensory infrastructures develop in such spaces, and how do they create conditions for specific kinds of communication and relationality? Again, let us think about Vygotsky's "embryonic state," "buds," and "flowers"—what kinds of teleological becoming are enabled?

Multisensory and Multimodal Unruliness

I am inspired by Rebecca Sanchez's (2020, 272) statement that "deaf people's experience of sound is multisensory, multimodal, prosthetic, and interdependent." Deaf studies scholars and scholars of multimodality and translanguaging have recently called attention to deaf people's diverse semiotic repertoires and the ways that deaf people might, at any given moment, use a combination of resources to communicate: for example, they might mouth, speak, sign, gesture, and/or write. Scholars have stressed that deaf people are exceptionally skilled at communicating across linguistic difference because they have learned to work with multiple resources.[23] Similarly, disability scholars and activists who focus on autistic communication have called attention to multimodal communicative practices among autistic people, including typing, writing, facilitated communication involving the help of another person, gesturing, flapping, and stimming (Bascom 2012; Sequenzia and Grace 2015).[24] Indeed, Alastair Pennycook (2017a, 455) stresses that "language is part of a much broader set of semiotic possibilities." I think about communication beyond "language" and consider all the resources that people bring to the table in order to make meaning happen.

What is recognized as communication? How do we embrace communicative and sensory unruliness while also attending to hierarchies, power imbalances, and the different values placed on some modes of sensing and communicating? I discuss the ways that the senses are worked on according to different ideas of what an ideally sensing person is, or, specifically, an ideally sensing deaf person. At stake is the role of the senses, and the privileging of particular senses, in ideologies of "sense making" and the ways that certain senses are (not) permitted to (literally) make sense (Moriarty Harrelson 2017). As a result of cochlear implantation, therapeutic techniques have focused on one mode, listening and spoken language, and communication options have been segmented and placed along a continuum. Different communication options are categorized as listening and spoken language, sign language, cued speech, and/or total communication. These categories function as ideologically constructed ideal types. I stress that becoming multimodal is a fraught achievement, in that the senses, while always in relation, are often seen as in competition.[25]

I hold on to sensory difference—beyond and apart from the difference that culture and context make.[26] I analyze the kinds of social, political, and moral personhood that emerge when children are taught to orient toward sound and to become social through listening and speaking. I discuss developmental paths that are pluripotent and fraught with friction. Practitioners of auditory verbal therapy often stress that "deaf children must be forced to listen." This use of the word *force* points to the difficult labor of the child who must concentrate intently on listening as an AVT specialist repeats words and sentences again and again while covering her mouth or standing behind the child to prevent lipreading. (People I interviewed who attended AVT sessions as children constantly stressed the hard work required, although today AVT specialists often try to create more playful environments that might obscure the difficult work of listening.) In the case of deaf children learning to sign, there is a different source of friction: the fear attached to going off a path, trying to find sign language–based resources, confronting stigma, and generally going against societal expectations and sensory ideals.

One sultry night in summer 2016, I hung out with a group of deaf and hearing friends at the Indian Coffee House in New Delhi. A deaf woman, known for her assertive personality, turned to me and said, "You are half hearing, half deaf, half speaking, half signing; half half half half." I believe she said this with a bit of exasperation: she was unsure how to categorize me, and my halting ISL may have frustrated her. I do not think she meant what she said as a compliment; rather, it was her way of stating that I was not completely entrenched in one linguistic or social world (which is true for many deaf and hearing people); I was not whole, in her analysis of me. (Another interpretation is that I was more than whole at 200 percent!) In response to this provocative statement, I think about the ways that (some) disabled and deaf people experience their sensorium as complete, and I reject a focus on deficit or loss. In my case, all of those "halves" produce a sense of balance. People intersense (Howes 2006) and maximize their sensory potential in ways that might not be expected or desired, but they are never incomplete.[27] (I also recognize that there are other ways of being besides the binaries of half and whole, loss and gain, incomplete and complete.)

Dividing the senses into discrete categories is both an act of care and a form of violence, a way of both creating and inhibiting the wholeness of people's lifeworlds. I think about teachers in oral or aural schools pushing down the hands of deaf children when they gesture or sign as well as sign language teachers who prevent deaf children from mouthing. This is a relevant tangent: I also think about DeafBlind children in the United States and elsewhere who are prohibited from touching each other and who have been kept away from the importance of touch as a sense. I engage broadly with all of the senses that deaf people bring to bear on their experiences, and I argue for the importance of multisensory and multimodal engagement, or, following Margaret Mead, "total communication." Mead ([1964] 1972, 279) argues that the study of semiotics needs to be interdisciplinary and expansive; her push to study "total communication" in a total manner predates research on multimodal and multisensory communication approaches that have now come into vogue in attempts to analyze communication—including the nonlinguistic—and to attribute competence to communicative practices that were previously not valued or assumed to be deficient. Indeed, Michael Herzfeld (2001, 242) calls for

an anthropology that is "necessarily shot through with alertness to the entire gamut of sensory semiosis." I respond to that call.

Conducting Multisensory, Multimodal, and Multipersonal Research

I conducted much of the research for my first book in Indian Sign Language and with signing deaf people. In 2010, my right ear was implanted,
much to the disdain and chagrin of friends in Bangalore (many grimaced
when I showed them my implant after returning to the city to catch up). In
contrast, for this book, I foregrounded the perspectives of nonsigning deaf
people and their families, audiologists, speech and language pathologists,
surgeons, and government administrators.[28] I spent time in surgeons' offices, hospitals, audiology and speech therapy clinics, and with the families
of deaf people in their homes, in schools, and in early intervention programs. I endeavored to engage with these often power-laden perspectives
through modes that were not solely critical, because motivations, sentiments, and actions can be complex, multilayered, and ambivalent. To simply demonize or dismiss such perspectives would be to risk ignoring key
stakeholders in deaf life.

While I still see my ISL-speaking friends, almost all of the research for
this book was conducted in spoken language, another form of loss for me.
Most interviews with professionals were in English, although I also inter-
acted with families and observed consultations and therapy sessions that
took place in Hindi, Marathi, and Tamil. These interactions were sometimes translated on the spot by someone present, but I also recorded them
with consent in order to have them translated afterward. In therapy clinics,
I sometimes watched sessions through a hidden window or on a video system, after receiving consent from the families, in order to avoid distracting
easily distractable children. I was well aware that families traveled long distances for their audiology and speech and language therapy sessions, and
that the stakes could be high for a short session. Sometimes I was invited to
participate, and I clapped, sang, and talked during sessions. Audiologists
and speech and language pathologists warmly welcomed me to their clinics
and answered my questions patiently, sometimes taking the time to trans-
late for me, and they and the families present often asked me questions as
well. In surgeons' offices, I struck up conversations with people waiting for
their appointments and engaged in waiting room sociality.

There were also moments when my previous and current field sites came together. For example, I hired an Indian Sign Language interpreter to interpret for me from Hindi to ISL at a parents' meeting held by a non-governmental organization providing early intervention services and early childhood education. I asked the NGO's director for permission to bring the interpreter to the meeting, because he was adamantly against the use of ISL by the children with whom his organization worked. He was fine with the interpreter's presence, but he emphasized that the interpreter was there *only* for me. I also met speech and language therapists who used ISL with children, but "secretly"—they did not publicize this part of their practice.

There were also times when my implants gave me access, particularly to the Cochlear headquarters in Mumbai. I felt entitled to this access, since I have Cochlear's implants, and I insisted on having a photograph taken there with a life-size cutout of Brett Lee, the Australian cricket star who is Cochlear's "hearing ambassador." As mentioned above, families and therapists were eager to talk to me about my experiences with my implants and ask me questions about my trajectory. I often wondered if I would have been able to do this research if I did not listen and speak and if I did not have cochlear implants myself.

With Stephanie Lloyd, I conducted participant observation at the Alexander Graham Bell Association's 2018 annual symposium; we interviewed people together, attended the same and different panels, and constantly shared notes and perspectives. During the summer of 2018, I worked in Bangalore with a colleague named Sravanthi Dasari. Sravanthi and I were often together in noisy classrooms, where she could hear things that I could not. These moments of negotiated access revealed how anthropological work can be distributed, depending on the affordances of a site. In the summer of 2019, Deepa Palaniappan and I traveled together to Chennai, where she interpreted between Tamil and English. During one interaction I discovered that Deepa had told the mothers with whom we were talking that I was deaf and had cochlear implants: she turned to me and demanded that I show the mothers my implants. I was initially annoyed during such moments because I wanted to be the one to disclose, not her. But I came to realize that disclosure could be distributed too. As with Neera, I learned a great deal about children's and adults' cochlear implant experiences from other people, including the implantees' parents, spouses, surgeons, teachers, and therapists. Cochlear implants, or more specifically talk about them, necessitated different kinds of disclosures as well as proclamations about intimacy, care, responsibility, and connection.

The author stands in front of a cardboard cutout of Brett Lee, Cochlear's "hearing ambassador," in the Mumbai Cochlear headquarters. A placard next to the cutout (just out of the frame of the photograph) displays an inspirational statement by Lee: "I want to make sure that everyone has the opportunity to experience what I hear, whether that's the sounds of everyday life, the sounds of loved ones, or the sounds of cricket." Photograph taken by a Cochlear employee.

In 2018–21, Rajani Vaidya provided translations to and from English, Marathi, and Hindi in person and on recordings; she also conducted phone interviews. We often discussed the words and concepts used by interlocutors. In 2019, I traveled to Mumbai with Anjali Murthy, a former undergraduate student at the University of Chicago, for the Cochlear Implant Group of India's annual conference. There was no real-time captioning or interpreting at this conference, and I was the only deaf person present. Anjali scribbled or typed notes to me during presentations when I did not hear things, and we had long conversations in which we went over the presentations that we had seen together. I foreground the important role that all these women played in this research both to emphasize the multipersonal nature of anthropological work and to demonstrate that there is a becoming that takes place in the merging of different sensory perspectives.[29]

Ambivalent Objects and Modes

In addition to focusing on interdependence among people, disability studies scholars and lay disabled people have highlighted the role that assistive
technologies—white canes, wheelchairs, and prosthetics, among others—
have played in constituting, extending, and complexifying a sense of self;
for many scholars it is difficult to see where the self ends and assistive
technology begins (see Bateson [1972] 2000).[30] Such an approach looks at
assistive technology as extending the self and contributing to what Benjamin Bahan (2014) calls "sensory reach." Cochlear implants differ from
other assistive objects in that they are surgically implanted, they are bionic,
and the empirical and discursive boundary between person and device is
blurred: the implant is supposed to activate the brain's potential to become
a hearing brain and the child's potential to become a hearing child. In
popular media and scientific research, claims are made for how implants
produce specific kinds of "normally" sensing and acting subjects. According to this line of thinking, it is not simply that implants provide disabled
people with different possibilities for moving through and engaging the
world; rather, implants result in new sensory subjectivity. This resurfaces
questions around whether cochlear implants are tools, aids, or something
else entirely. Cochlear implants provoke difficult questions about the
boundaries between ability and disability, passing and becoming, and deaf
and hearing. They also ask us to consider what noise is, as well as what the
intended goal of hearing is.

I do not take a position for or against cochlear implants; rather, I look at
how they have become "domesticated" (Oudshoorn and Pinch 2003) and
how they create new imperatives for producing normative forms of sensory personhood as well as social, political, and economic ties. Cochlear
implants are more than just tools or aids and have the potential to both
transform the domestic and render domestication unruly. I ask: *What is
a cochlear implant good for? What kinds of sensory personhood does it produce? What kinds of sensory infrastructures exist in the realm of hearing and
deafness? And what kinds of sensory becoming and sensory worlds are at
stake?* I ask these questions in contrast to Deaf studies scholars, who have
mostly written about cochlear implants in a negative register. For example,
Paddy Ladd (2007, 3–4) writes that cochlear implantation is an example
of "neocolonialism"; motivated by economic profit, it imposes scientific
technology on and in deaf people. Similarly, Harlan Lane (2007, 59) argues

that cochlear implants are a means of controlling, medicalizing, and disabling deaf people, and that their use will lead to the "eliminat[ion] of Deaf culture, language, and people."[31] However, deaf communities' responses to cochlear implants have become more muted over time, perhaps as a result of the technology's ubiquity. Or perhaps deaf communities have simply become more ambivalent about implants.

I write about becoming normal—and about cochlear implants more broadly—with a sense of ambivalence as well. Neil Smelser (1998, 8) observes that "dependent situations breed ambivalence." Shortly after I got my first implant, someone asked me, "Do you not feel bad now, hearing all the things that you missed out on earlier?" I responded by trying to explain that no, rather than becoming aware of earlier loss, I actually felt like I had lost something postimplant. This loss exists at the same time as gain, as while I can now hear in the dark and do not need to lipread much when it is quiet, I am dependent on a multinational implant manufacturer, and an insurance company, for the maintenance of a sensory capacity. Ambivalence—as a mode and as a methodology—offers a way to traverse the space between loss and gain, ability and disability, independence and dependence, object and sense, and different values and interests. Ambivalence moves us beyond binaries, points to the limits of categories and classifications (Bauman 1991), and provides a way to move around the impasse created by moral imperatives (Kierans and Bell 2017). Indeed, as Kierans and Bell (2017, 37) write: "Ambivalence means that we have to accept that things are not readily clear, that we need to learn about the *conditions* under which something may get called an abomination or not, and about how people come to take up variable positions." Ambivalence also acts as an important response to technological imperatives and what Sharon Kaufman (2015, 131) calls the "changing means and ends of technology."[32]

Ambivalence offers a rejoinder to what Lauren Berlant (2011) calls "cruel optimism," the state of desiring something that is actually an obstacle to one's flourishing. I do not claim that cochlear implants are obstacles to flourishing; such a statement would ignore the many things I have heard about cochlear implants being life changing, as well as the fact that I myself have experienced them as life changing. As an implant user, I would find it problematic to argue against implantation. My own ambivalent experience, however, is one reason I would never tell families that they should not implant their children, although I would ask them to think expansively about "benefits" and "outcomes," as there is always a question of what might be lost in addition to what is gained.[33]

As I discuss throughout this book, the complex dependencies associated with cochlear implantation interpellate all stakeholders, including the state, multinational corporations, surgeons, and deaf children and their families: these dependencies point to the unfinished, anxious, and pluripotent aspects of becoming normal. If only these actors would or could express some ambivalence as well. I argue that it is important to consider how we live in ambivalent relationship to different paths and modes of becoming in the world—becoming normal is no exception. Because of desires for and pursuits of sensory normality, actors such as the state, therapists, and deaf people themselves, as well as their families, are becoming other than they have been. What, however, is lost, minimized, or constrained through such becoming? I hold on to ambivalence.

Disability Camps and Surgical Celebrations

Indian Disability Interventions and the Creation of Complex Dependencies

*How do the senses take form in broader political and economic formations?
How do particular sensory orientations contribute to forms of citizenship
and belonging, inclusion and exclusion, domination, security, state
policing, violence, or symbolic or psychological warfare?*

—Robert Desjarlais

Celebratory Cochlear Implants

DR. ANUP: So, we started, the first [cochlear implant] operation
was done on third of December 2014.

MF: Okay.

DR. ANUP: Third of December.

MF: Who was the surgeon, who did the surgery?

DR. ANUP: Wait, wait, wait. Why was it done on third of December? Why we did not start on any other day?

MF: Why?

DR. ANUP: That's what I am asking you.

MF: I don't know.

DR. ANUP: Okay, you must know. Third of December is International Day for Person with Disability all over world, including your country also.

Dr. Anup is the former director of the Ali Yavar Jung National Institute of Speech and Hearing Disabilities in Mumbai. He is an audiologist and speech and language pathologist in addition to a government bureaucrat and is known for being impassioned, especially when it comes to asserting his expertise. AYJNISHD is a national organization under the central Ministry of Social Justice and Empowerment that functions as a one-stop shop for deafness and hearing impairment in India. It offers educational courses in audiology, speech and language pathology, special education, and Indian Sign Language; performs hearing screenings and early intervention; conducts research on early intervention, speech and language pathology, and special education; and coordinates and distributes aids and appliances such as hearing aids and cochlear implants. As a government institute, it offers services for free or at prices that are much more affordable than those available at private clinics. There are regional centers under AYJNISHD across India (in the north, south, west, and east of the country) to provide comprehensive education, training, and coverage.

I met with Dr. Anup to learn about the central government's Assistance to Disabled Persons for Purchase/Fitting of Aids/Appliances scheme, which since 2014 has included cochlear implants, in addition to other aids and appliances such as hearing aids, canes, wheelchairs, scooters, and calipers. I had logistical questions about the ADIP scheme, but Dr. Anup in turn had other ideas he wanted to share, as can be seen in the exchange above. He wanted to stress that India's first central government–sponsored cochlear implant surgery happened on December 3, 2014, on International Day of Persons with Disabilities, an annual observance established by the United Nations in 1992. In doing so, he perhaps wished to make a broader point about the newfound place of cochlear implants within India's larger disability landscape and the trajectory of the work of the Ministry of Social Justice and Empowerment. (He was disappointed that I did not immediately pick up on the significance of the state's decision to schedule the first cochlear implant on that specific date.)

Dr. Anup had a view of how International Day of Persons with Disabilities should be celebrated that differed from the views of both Indian and international disability activists who advocate for disability rights as manifested in programs, policies, and infrastructure aimed at increasing accessibility in all aspects of everyday life.[1] To activists, accessibility means large-scale initiatives such as physically accessible infrastructure and transportation, equitable or preferential hiring practices, and nondiscrimination clauses in legislation, not individual aids and appliances. In contrast, Dr. Anup was celebrating a biotechnological and surgical intervention, in the form of a cochlear implant, on the first recipient, a carefully chosen two-and-a-half-year-old boy (also) named Anup. The Ministry of Social Justice and Empowerment had hoped to showcase "forward thinking" by first implanting a girl, but it failed to find an appropriate female candidate.

The second recipient was a girl, who "now fights with her mother, an excellent outcome," Dr. Anup told me. Anup, the first implantee, is "now going to school with the most normal speech, and the quality of the speech is just like us." (I am apparently included in this "us.")

A surgery to celebrate?[2] A celebratory surgery? A surgical assertion of the state's power?[3] It was difficult to wrap my mind around the fact that the central government's first cochlear implant surgery was performed on International Day of Persons with Disabilities. Dr. Anup was celebrating the Indian state's ability to restore or repair a deaf child's sense and make the child normal (in his words) through expensive foreign-made technology. This was an accomplishment that required the establishment of a cochlear implant infrastructure and ongoing acts of re/habilitation, maintenance, and repair. Lawrence Cohen (2004, 167) writes of surgery as a form of biopolitics: "We are awash in operations." He offers the phrase "operable citizenship" to theorize the relationship between undergoing surgery and donating and receiving organs (172); one becomes a state subject through going under the knife. Here, surgery catalyzes both the potential of the deaf child and the present and potential network of the state and multinational cochlear implant corporations.

In this chapter, I analyze the state's approach to disability, which has historically been based on distribution and entitlements. I take seriously that the distribution of aids, appliances, and pensions and the establishment of quotas in education and employment are no less important than the rights talk of disability rights activists. Scholarship on disability in India has largely focused on the contraction of the state as well as on the neoliberalization and privatization of disability-focused development.[4] In contrast to this literature, I examine the *expansion* of a specific state disability program and argue that the central government's cochlear implant program, and its pursuit of sensory normality for and on behalf of its citizens, reveals new directions for the Indian state in regard to engaging with disability and introduces novel assemblages of welfare, medicine, re/habilitation, and multinational capital.[5] The move from mass aiding to individual implantation marks a transition for the state and the corporation, from a performatively distributed external relation to a performatively implanted inhabitant of the body. Cochlear implants are a concretization of a new-found technocratic approach to disability that focuses on the individual and not the mass body. Cochlear implantation renders both the state and the corporation indispensable in that they are literally and materially implanted in the body. Implantation becomes a mode of presence (Fanon [1967] 1994, 121). The state gets under the skin in a targeted and individualized way.[6]

The conditions of possibility for getting under the skin have been sedimented through India's orientations and actions as a postcolonial state with a focus on population development and mass health. The Ministry of Social Justice and Empowerment enacts ideas of India as a developmental and welfare state in its distribution of aids, appliances, and pensions to people certified as disabled, and in its establishment of quotas for the education and employment of persons with disabilities.[7] The Indian state's orientation is an example of what Claire Laurier Decoteau (2013, 7) terms a "postcolonial paradox," which "entails a simultaneous need to respect the demands of neoliberal capital in order to compete successfully on the world market *and* a responsibility to redress entrenched inequality, secure legitimacy from the poor, and forge a national imaginary." Interventions are designed to make disabled individuals as productive as possible.[8] Cochlear implants are particularly appealing in this respect because they can ostensibly produce children who are sensorially normal. They also function affectively and promote ideas of a caring and benevolent nation-state.

Anxiety lurks around the edges of care and benevolence. Nancy Hunt (2016, 6) stresses that "moods matter," and I foreground anxiety as a mood here. According to the *Oxford English Dictionary,* anxiety is "worry over the future or about something with an uncertain outcome," and to be anxious is to "experienc[e] worry or nervousness, typically about the future or something with an uncertain outcome." Because cochlear implants come with uncertain outcomes, despite attempts to emphasize positive narratives and trajectories, they produce anxiety for all stakeholders. In addition, the complex dependencies that accompany cochlear implants introduce anxieties for all stakeholders, including the state, which must safeguard its substantial investment and materialize good outcomes, in the form of numbers of surgeries done and/or children's functioning. The shift from aiding to implanting is not only a story of neoliberal development and the expansion of state power through partnerships with multinational corporations. It is also a story of an intervention that renders the state, corporations, surgeons, and families anxiously dependent: the state wants to claim that its (very expensive) program is a success, corporations need their implants to be deemed successful in producing good outcomes, surgeons aim to develop reputations as cochlear implant specialists, and families desire that their children listen and speak and also worry about maintaining the devices. These are all uncertain and contingent outcomes, despite the anxious confidence performed by the state, corporations, and surgeons. As I discuss below, there are, however, certain and finished outcomes, such as those documented in *Guinness World Records.*

What could be problematic about the state providing poor children with a missing sense? While medicine in India has been rife with scandal, cochlear implants are seemingly a win for everyone, including and especially the state. Instead of scandalous publicity, cochlear implants offer both ethical publicity and affective "feel-good" publicity (Cohen 1999; Sunder Rajan 2017). Government administrators such as Dr. Anup and others to be discussed in this chapter claim that the state is eliminating disability through cochlear implantation because implants enable deaf children to listen and speak. They stress that cochlear implants instill sensory normality, and after implantation deaf children no longer need to attend separate schools, learn sign language, or use interpreters or other accommodations. Their logic is that sensory normality leads to independence. (These claims also function as performances of sorts, and in many cases I had to make decisions about whether to go along with them or demur, as I do not agree that cochlear implants eliminate disability.)[9]

The ADIP scheme started in 1981 with a stated goal to "assist the needy disabled persons in procuring durable, sophisticated and scientifically manufactured, modern, standard aids and appliances to promote physical, social, psychological rehabilitation of Persons with Disabilities by reducing the effects of disabilities and at the same time enhance their economic potential. Assistive devices are given to PwDs [persons with disabilities] with an aim to improve their independent functioning, and to arrest the extent of disability and occurrence of secondary disability. The aids and appliances supplied under the Scheme must have due certification" (Government of India 2017, 2). This stress on "due certification" reminds me of a comment made by Dr. Anup. I asked him which companies the ADIP scheme was using for sourcing hearing aids, and he replied: "We don't need a company, we need specifications." He continued by saying, "Human beings have a specification. We are not Indian or American, we are human beings." While I interpret this as a lofty statement about universal sensory needs and desires, in the case of cochlear implants, numerous people told me that the first set of specifications for the ADIP scheme was developed to privilege one manufacturer.[10] Multinational corporations were never far from the cochlear implant scene, in contrast to the manufacturers of other disability aids and appliances. And as I discuss in chapter 4, in fact specifications are not universal, and the cochlear implant technologies to which children have access differ widely depending on where their families are located geographically.

Many disability aids and appliances are produced by the Artificial Limbs Manufacturing Corporation, known as ALIMCO, located in Kanpur, Uttar Pradesh. The Indian government has boasted that the company, which started production in 1976, is the largest manufacturer of aids and appliances in South Asia (Government of India 2015). The aids and appliances, which are grouped by disability category on ALIMCO's website, are distributed through government agencies such as AYJNISHD and through nongovernmental organization partners. However, across class lines, disabled people routinely disparage the objects disseminated through the ADIP scheme, berating the clunky "one size fits all" wheelchairs with unsupportive seats and easily deflated tires, the heavy canes with insensitive tips, the rigid prosthetic limbs, and the nonindividualized hearing aids that always break.

In a report to the United Nations Committee on the Rights of Persons with Disabilities, an all-India coalition of disability NGOs and other organizations noted that aids and appliances are often sold for scrap metal (National CRPD Coalition–India 2019, 30). Middle- and upper-class disabled people have traditionally sought to purchase internationally produced aids and appliances, despite the heavy Goods and Services Tax placed on them. Disability activists have protested the levying of GST on disability-related objects, which they see as a particular form of cruelty. Cochlear implants are internationally manufactured and thus come with hefty GST. Indeed, in 2017, in an online petition directed to the prime minister, a mother of an implanted child wrote: "It's not a luxury sir; it's my Childs birth right to hear like any normal human being. Why should I be charged tax on a medical necessity?"[11]

In 2014, in response to negative perceptions and in a desire to technologically scale up under the "Make in India" campaign, the ADIP scheme began including "modern" and "technologically complicated" devices such as electric tricycles, smart canes, and digital hearing aids. The state also began planning to sell devices to neighboring and other developing countries. The Indian government's 2015 report to the United Nations Committee on the Rights of Persons with Disabilities noted that artificial limbs had been distributed to Iraq, Haiti, Pakistan, and Zimbabwe (Government of India 2015). Also in 2014, following the establishment of state government cochlear implant programs in Kerala, Andhra Pradesh, and Tamil Nadu and in the Indian Armed Forces' health services, cochlear implants were added to the ADIP portfolio for prelingual deaf children five years of age and below (exceptions are made for children up to six years of age) and postlingual children below the age of twelve who lost their hearing after the age of four or five. To be eligible, children cannot have additional disabilities.

To be eligible for a cochlear implant through the scheme, the child's family must have monthly income below Rs 15,000 (US$198). Partial inclusion in the scheme is possible for families with income below Rs 30,000 (US$396) a month. The government purchases cochlear implants from one of four major manufacturers through a competitive bidding process in which the contract is awarded to the lowest bidder that meets specification requirements. The four manufacturers are based in different geographic locations: Cochlear is headquartered in Australia, MED-EL in Austria, Advanced Bionics in the United States, and Neurelec in France. With the exception of Neurelec, the companies all have headquarters in India and employ Indian audiologists and speech and language therapists. These professionals provide support to the state for developing newborn hearing screening and cochlear implant infrastructures around the country; they also often conduct training for surgeons and re/habilitation workers in both government and private institutions, including in locations outside metro areas. In addition, they create branded re/habilitation materials to be used by therapists and families alike and provide help with troubleshooting devices. Thus, these professionals support the state, surgeons, re/habilitation professionals, and implant recipients and their families.

The cochlear implant is by far the most expensive device distributed through the ADIP scheme. The total package costs Rs 6 lakhs (US$7,934) and covers implantation, the external processor (which has a two-year warranty), batteries and replacement cables and coils, and two years of re/habilitation at an empaneled institute or provider.[12] By way of comparison, the second most expensive device under the scheme is an electric scooter that costs Rs 36,000 (US$476). According to ADIP guidelines, hearing aids for schoolgoing children can cost up to Rs 12,000 (US$157), while hearing aids for everyone else are covered up to Rs 10,000 (US$132), a significantly smaller financial investment than that for a cochlear implant.

In addition, because it involves performance of a surgery, the cochlear implant is a distinct kind of distributional object.

Promoting Surgical Cultures and Large-Scale Implantation

After meeting Dr. Anup, I set out to learn how cochlear implants came to be included in the ADIP scheme. I interviewed Alok Sharma, a former joint secretary in the Ministry of Social Justice and Empowerment. Sharma is an Indian Administrative Service officer who is much respected by both the mainstream disability community and re/habilitation professionals for his ability to get things done. He now works as a personal assistant to a state minister and did not have much time to spend with me (scheduling our meeting involved many phone calls). Fielding calls all the while and speaking rapidly, with minimal pauses, Sharma efficiently and energetically told me that the ADIP scheme was revised when the ministry realized that new technology was available and that the current level of funding per beneficiary was very low. The ministry sought out stakeholder participation, including input from the All India Institute of Medical Sciences, AYJNISHD, cochlear implant surgeons, cochlear implant distributors, and the Ministry of Health (there was no participation from signing deaf individuals or groups). Sharma continued: "And based on this stakeholder participation, we found out that if we do large-scale cochlear implants within the country, then the process of implementation of the cochlear implants will become popular, the cost of cochlear implants will come down—because it would get government supported." He stressed that bringing down implant prices was a service not just to India but to the world at large. He also said that as a result of "a transparent process using web-based platforms and application portals," "large-scale" cochlear implantation is now happening in India. He summarized his work as follows:

> We did three things. One, we brought down the prices of cochlear implants. We brought into India a culture of cochlear implants. We brought the culture of training the children, after the cochlear implants, with their parents. As well, we brought a culture of getting the doctors to do the surgery also. There are a large number of government hospitals which undertook the surgery. We empaneled the hospitals, we empaneled the doctors. All that also happened. So ultimately, it was an all-round process.

I discuss the "culture of training children and their parents" in chapters 2 and 3, but here I focus on "large-scale" implantation. The technology that Sharma emphasized—the purchase of expensive cochlear implants from multinational manufacturers, the use of web-based platforms, and the training of surgeons, audiologists, and speech and language therapists in the use of the latest technologies—represented a new frontier for the Ministry of Social Justice and Empowerment and the ADIP scheme in particular.

Sharma explained: "I feel that technology should be used in India. Our honorable prime minister has said that it all should be technology driven. And it should also be a make in India. I will be the happiest person if such instruments are made in India or maybe we find technology of our own which is cheaper, faster, better, and technologically more advanced." Abdul Kalam, India's former president and perhaps its best-known technocrat, spearheaded an initiative to develop an indigenous cochlear implant. Engineered by senior scientists at the Defense Research and Development Organization, the resulting implant is now in human trials. It will ideally cost one-fourth of the price of basic models currently on the market, although surgeons, audiologists, and speech and language therapists have professed skepticism about how it will measure up.[13] Still, interest in this indigenous implant surfaces constantly in conversations as a form of techno-optimism that more directly interpellates the state and highlights the state's desire to make cochlear implants available to all (*The Hindu* 2012). Both Sharma's reference to "the honorable prime minister" and the development of an indigenous cochlear implant channel salvation-oriented and nationalist sentiments, in that not only would deafness be mitigated, but the implant responsible would be developed and manufactured in India; hearing would be an Indian-made sense.

As Sharma noted, private and public hospitals all over India have been empaneled (enrolled) in the program to perform cochlear implant surgery. Surgeons at these hospitals are mentored by more experienced surgeons who are sponsored by cochlear implant companies, the hospitals, or the state. Audiologists and speech and language therapists have also been empaneled. Through the ADIP program, a cochlear implant infrastructure has emerged that includes both public and private clinics.[14] An audiologist in Chennai told me that before the ADIP program started, only very senior surgeons, audiologists, and speech and language therapists worked with implanted people, because at that time only a select number of wealthy people were implanted. With the emergence of government programs, however, the numbers of implanted people are increasing, and "everyone wants to be involved." Performing cochlear implant surgeries and working with cochlear implant recipients are considered prestigious professions, in addition to the material and financial benefits they offer.

The ADIP scheme's cochlear implant program has ushered in new technocratic processes through electronic platforms.[15] Every application for an implant is uploaded onto a central government site along with the required paperwork, such as audiograms, CT scan results, medical reports, disability certification, Aadhaar number, proof of income, and birth certificate. The documents are then reviewed at AYJNISHD in Mumbai by a central committee made up of the institute director (formerly Dr. Anup); the heads of the psychology, audiology, education, and speech and language pathology departments; and two consulting surgeons specializing in otolaryngology (also known as ear, nose, and throat, or ENT, surgeons). The program coordinator told me that cases are reviewed carefully and in a timely manner. However, debates occasionally break out in committee meetings over whether someone should be implanted or not. These debates often happen in relation to children older than five years of age. While the official cutoff age is five, it can take families time to learn about the scheme, get their paperwork in order, and apply. Thus, a number of the cases reviewed involve children above the cutoff age, and many surgeons, re/habilitation workers, and implant company professionals find these cases problematic, because the chances of satisfactory outcomes are said to decline as the child's age at implantation increases.

After someone is approved for a cochlear implant, he or she is placed on a waiting list, which—in the interest of transparency—is available for public viewing on the ADIP web portal. These waiting lists are also testament to the work of the scheme's administrators and affiliated surgeons, audiologists, and re/habilitation workers around India, and AYJNISHD regularly updates the numbers of surgeries performed and the numbers of hospitals and therapists empaneled.[16] As implants are delivered by the contracted companies, AYJNISHD slowly and incrementally sends them out to the empaneled surgeons and facilities. There is thus a question of what "large-scale" and "mass" mean in the context of such expensive distribution and surgical implantation. Despite the aspirations of Sharma and others, there is a limit on how many surgeries can be done and in how many bodies the state can materialize itself. There is also a limit on the nature and categories of relationships that can be formed, as discussed in the next section.

Recipients and Beneficiaries

In September 2018, after receiving permission from Dr. Anup to observe audiology and speech and language sessions in AYJNISHD's cochlear implant wing, I sat with two audiologists and two audiology and speech and language pathology students as they saw a steady stream of children coming for implant mapping and therapy. The cochlear implant wing was separated from the rest of the institute by a series of doors and a long hallway (I wondered if this was deliberate). Despite posters on the walls proclaiming the government's commitment to the latest high-technology interventions through the ADIP scheme, the wing still felt like part of a government institute. Names were entered into battered ledgers by hand, paper files were everywhere, therapy rooms were threadbare, and there were no fancy therapy toys in sight.

A mother and her son arrived without an appointment. They had taken an overnight train from Delhi because they suspected that the child's implant processor was broken. An audiologist used proprietary computer software to check the processor and confirmed that it was indeed broken, but thankfully, it was still under warranty. She recommended that the mother and son visit the Cochlear headquarters in the Bandra Kurla Complex, which was five kilometers and a world away in a posh multinational office park; there, hopefully, they would either be given a new processor or be able to have the broken one repaired. I was struck that a government audiologist was sending people to a private corporation; this situation clearly revealed the entangled relationship between the two as well as the limits of what the state could do. Since that time, the practice of sending families directly to the corporation has been ended; instead, the families must engage with a middle person, a licensed supplier. Too many families were showing up, materializing, at the corporate headquarters.

Government officials and ADIP program administrators label people who have received implants through the scheme as "beneficiaries," because, as an administrator told me, families "benefit" from the government program. At the same time, cochlear implant companies call implant users "recipients," both in India and internationally.[17] Unlike using the concept of "recipient" in reference to someone who receives a blood, tissue, or organ donation, labeling an implant user a "recipient" brings up questions about who the donor is and what forms of labor, transaction, and exchange are obscured. Implanted children and their families become both beneficiaries and recipients. Both terms, in foregrounding a (passive) gift relation, conceal that cochlear implants are paid for—by the state, by corporate social responsibility programs, or by private funding. Implants are purchased, not gifted, even if they are distributed as gifts through corporate social responsibility initiatives or through public relations events such as the celebration of a politician's birthday. As noted above, the central government program provides two years of support for batteries and parts. After two years, the children and their families must directly approach cochlear implant companies for repair services and accessories. While some states—namely, Kerala and Tamil Nadu—offer long-term support with maintenance, the families of children who receive cochlear implants enter into relationships of complex dependencies on multinational corporations, which is ironic given that these implants are meant to index a nationalist process.[18]

The stakes of being a dual beneficiary and recipient of a cochlear implant are different from those of being a beneficiary of government programs that engage in ongoing distribution of Indian-made aids and appliances. The state (re)distributes objects as they wear down or need to be replaced—or if there is a photo opportunity, a politician's birthday celebration, or an ordinary distribution camp scheduled. (Many of my deaf friends told me that hearing aids are given out "like candy" at such events.) In contrast, leading up to cochlear implant surgery and for two years following surgery, the state is present and materialized in the form of waiting lists, audit reports, and follow-up ledgers—but only for two years. Families return home after cochlear implant "switch-ons," which typically take place in audiology offices, with state-provided bulky bags and boxes emblazoned with the logos of the cochlear implant companies (see chapter 4). At the behest of the state, they bring the corporations home with them.

Deviating from the typical "switch-on" procedure, which occurs in a clinic, in January 2021 Andhra Pradesh's chief minister stood on a stage and appeared to personally activate the cochlear implants of small children who were recipients of his state government's scheme: the state here not only implanted but also activated the sense.[19] (I hope that some of the people surrounding the chief minister during the photo shoot were trained audiologists.) Implants materialize the state and multinational corporations at different points in time and in fraught ways.

While implant corporations benefit directly from sales of implants in the present, they also have perpetual and ongoing concerns about the future of implantation, a future that they need to secure by working in tandem with the state. These concerns map onto the following logic: "If outcomes are unsuccessful, if children do not start listening and speaking, both the state and the cochlear implant corporation look bad." A senior director of a cochlear implant corporation told me that his company was investing in infrastructure for newborn hearing screening and training for speech and language therapists in India, a gift to the state.[20] His logic was this: if the state and the corporation establish relationships with children at an early age and provide appropriate speech and language support, outcomes will improve; if outcomes improve, implants will look attractive and the market will grow. Implant corporations thus are dependent on their recipients' outcomes, albeit not on the recipients themselves. Implant manufacturers in India and internationally hold workshops, trainings, and events for re/habilitation professionals, surgeons, and recipients in efforts to bolster outcomes. The state and cochlear implant corporations are simultaneously donors and recipients and are interdependent. The implanted children and their families, however, are dependent.

Some surgeons hold on to the idea of cochlear implantation as a gift and argue that cochlear implant surgery is "not a surgery from which to make money," as a senior cochlear implant surgeon said at an annual conference held by the Cochlear Implant Group of India, or CIGI. Another surgeon brought this statement to my attention and told me that it annoyed him because he wondered if this meant that cochlear implants should only be given out as charity. If so, he continued, why are corporations profiting? Who should benefit financially from cochlear implants, and for whom is a cochlear implant a gift?

Cochlear implants were certainly a gift to and from India's first cochlear implant surgeon. Dr. Daisy Fernandez performed her first cochlear implant surgery in 1987. Dr. Fernandez told me multiple times that not only was she the first Indian cochlear implant surgeon, but she was also the first female cochlear implant surgeon internationally. She traveled around India and the world performing implant surgeries, accompanied by international surgeons. The popular press lauded her tireless efforts to give deaf people the gift of sound.[21] Because of her cochlear implant work, she was a recipient of the Padma Shri Award, one of the Indian government's highest civilian honors. In her advanced age, Dr. Fernandez established a charitable foundation providing cochlear implants to children, and when I met with her in her hospital office, she was seeing a steady stream of potential implant recipients. She now provides implants out of charity and conviction.

Cochlear implant processors, batteries, cables, and cords are often distributed as gifts. In August 2019, I sat in an auditorium at a Tamil Nadu state health office in Chennai with small children and their parents, waiting for a rehearsal for a celebratory function to be held the next day. At this function, politicians would distribute implant parts such as batteries and coils, and, in a few rare cases, new implant processors. I sat with a young family who had traveled by overnight bus to Chennai. Their four-year-old son's processor had fallen off during a scooter ride, and they were told that they would receive a new processor at the next day's event. I also talked with a woman whose daughter's implant battery had stopped charging. This particular distribution event was odd, because under the Tamil Nadu Chief Minister's Comprehensive Health Insurance Scheme, accessories and parts for cochlear implants are supposedly covered, although there is not yet a structure in place to ensure that families' needs are met efficiently. Families might wait months for parts or for processors to be repaired or replaced. Those at the rehearsal were waiting to receive something to which they were presumably entitled, but it was framed as a gift. Devices and parts, gift wrapped and distributed the day before a statewide election at a closed-door function, were material signs of the state's investment in and care for its disabled citizens (as well as part of an attempt to influence the outcome of an election). Notably, this event involved a small and carefully chosen group of children and families, in contrast to the "mega camps" discussed in the next section.

From Camps to Surgically Implanting a Sense

As discussed above, most of the disability aids and appliances in India have historically been produced in the country itself and are distributed through the Ministry of Social Justice and Empowerment. AYJNISHD and its nodal organizations hold camps in order to reach as many disabled people as possible, particularly those in rural areas; at these camps, screenings are conducted and disability aids are distributed. In scholarly writing and the public imagination, medical camps in India are strongly associated with the mass sterilization that took place before and during the Emergency under Indira Gandhi: they are spaces where people's capacities have been regulated or removed.[22] Jacob Copeman (2009, 18) notes that despite historical associations of camps with forced sterilization, members of India's lower classes see camps as opportunities for free medical treatment; camps also function as a "populist political instrument." Immunizations, eye exams, blood donation, blood pressure checkups, and hearing tests, among other things, take place at camps. They are spaces of distribution—of disability objects, medicines, kitchen appliances, and food, for example. Religious organizations, civic bodies, medical organizations, politicians and political parties, and individuals wishing to celebrate something hold camps. The distinction between commodity and gift (Appadurai 1986, 11) is obscured at camps. Cohen (2011, 125) points out that camps are associated not only with "the immediate, punctuated time of present emergency" but also with "the periodic and regular time of the civil gift"; he notes that medical camps "presume a mass population that chronically lacks both access to and information about appropriate health resources and that depends on the gift of these resources through a form—the camp—able to treat the mass in its entirety." Camps function both inside and outside everyday life, and they are a prime mode of engagement between the state and people, here specifically disabled people, albeit on different registers and scales. There are ordinary camps that do not receive much mention aside from brief notices in local newspapers and official government reports as well as so-called mega camps, which feature politicians or celebrities.

The state utilizes disability camps to demonstrate largesse and affection toward disabled populations through a form of engagement that I call "anonymous love," building on Lisa Stevenson's (2014) work on "anonymous care." By "anonymous love," I mean that disability has turned into an exceptional—even transcendent—category to be showered with affection and benevolence under the current government. This divine categorization resonates and articulates with Prime Minister Modi's divine derivation of authority. In December 2015, on the occasion of International Day of Persons with Disabilities, Modi announced in one of his regular addresses on his radio program *Mann Ki Baat*: "We see a person's disability with our eyes. But our interaction tells us the person has an extra power. Then I thought, in our country, instead of using the word *viklang* [disability], we should use the term *divyang* [a neologism that awkwardly translates to divinely abled or divine ability]." In renaming *viklang* as *divyang,* Modi has derived legitimacy and authority from postdevelopment and posthumanist channels. This focus on seeing and feeling disability differently functions as a form of governing through affect (Rudnyckyj 2011), which is why I call this anonymous love. Anonymous love sets the stage for spectacular bionic interventions such as cochlear implants, which, perhaps ironically, render deaf people normal and ordinary. Modi and the Bharatiya Janata Party, despite significant protest from disability activists, thus position disability as exceptional (Benton 2015) and above contentious politics, as well as above criticism and guidance from civil society and international bodies such as the United Nations.

Consider that in December 2019, Kashmir was under military occupation and significant violence was being inflicted on Kashmiri Muslims (both situations that continue today). Instead of, or in addition to, focusing on the state's removal of sensory capacities through targeted blindings, the media covered cochlear implant surgeries and the creation of sensory capacities (United News of India 2019). I look at these occurrences of sensory removal and benefaction relationally to argue that the state instrumentalizes cochlear implant surgery to create positive public sentiment. Feeling good about disability (or *divyangjan*) and feeling good about the state go hand in hand. In addition to a sensory state, the state is trying to become an emotional state, a state of mind. We could consider implantation a form of state violence, what Eunjung Kim (2017) calls "curative violence." While surgeons and the state approach cutting as a form of care (Plemons 2017), how are fantasies of capacitation directed at disabled people also a form of terror?[23]

Disability camps are crucial spaces for the performance of anonymous love through the ostensible capacitation of the body; such expansion exists in contrast to the forcible removal of capacities that took place at sterilization camps. In disability camps, disabled people are exceptional as a mass body to be intervened on through the performative distribution of objects and love. The performance is what is stressed, as in some cases disabled people receive empty gift-wrapped boxes, with the actual devices delivered only after the fact. Distributing objects demonstrates love and the materiality of state power. Through processes of enumeration—accountings of how many objects are distributed—disabled people are included in the nation. The people themselves are not counted, only the objects.[24] Even in the case of cochlear implants, which are individualized, the state focuses on numbers.

Let us turn to one mega camp. The grandest (and most publicized) camps are held in Prime Minister Modi's home state of Gujarat or in his constituency in Varanasi, Uttar Pradesh. These camps are often set up with a goal of breaking a record in relation to disability and getting the new record published in *Guinness World Records*.[25] At the camp held for the prime minister's 2016 birthday celebration, in Rajkot, Gujarat, three world records were broken: one for the largest number of disabled people lighting diyas, or oil lamps, simultaneously; one for the largest number of disabled people assembled to make a wheelchair logo or image, which said, "Happy Birthday PM"; and one for the most hearing aids disseminated in eight hours (Times News Network 2016). In addition to these record-setting events, which were heavily photographed and featured in the media, consider the discussion of numbers and other records broken in the following official Press Information Bureau (2017) release:

> At Rajkot Camp aids and appliances to the tune of Rs.11.19 Cr. were distributed among 17589 divyang beneficiaries including 3000 beneficiaries who have received aids and appliances from the State Government amounting to Rs.1.53 Cr. So far it is the biggest camp in the history of the country in terms of the number of beneficiaries in a single camp for distribution of aids and appliances. Earlier similar mega camps involving the Prime Minister were conducted by the Department of Empowerment of Persons with Disabilities at Varanasi, Navsari & Vadodara in the year 2016 benefiting about 10000, 11,000 and 10,500 beneficiaries respectively.
>
> During the event 90 motorized tricycles, 1960 tricycles, 1541 wheel chairs, 77 Cerebral Palsy (CP) chairs, 2896 crutches, 3095 walking sticks, 529 Braille cane, 112 rolators [*sic*], 162 Braille kits, 732 smart canes, 214 smart phone with screen reader, 68 daisy players, 20 ADL kits for leprosy cured, 2206 digital hearing aid, 1101 artificial limbs and callipers, 4416 TML kits and 73 laptops for person with intellectual disability were distributed among various classes of Divyangjan as per their need. The State Government on their own also distributed devices for rehabilitation and empowerment of persons with disabilities to 3000 divyangjans.
>
> Two Guinness World Records were created in connection with the event. On 28th June 2017 a Guinness Book of World Record was created in the category of highest ever participation of 1442 persons with hearing impairment in a sign language lesson at a single venue while performing our National Anthem. Previously, such a record was hold by Taiwan (China) with participation of 978 persons with hearing impairment. The participants of this

historic record repeated their performance in front of the Hon'ble Prime Minister today. Second Guinness World Record was created in the category of highest number of Orthosis (Calipers) fitted to 781 mobility impaired persons on a single day.

In addition to the above two Guinness Book of World records, another new "World Book Record" has also been created in the category of World's Largest Disbursement of Aids and Appliances for Persons with Disabilities (Divyangjan) at a single venue in one day involving 17589 persons with disabilities (Divyangjan).

At a mega camp in Rajkot, Gujarat, disabled people simultaneously lighting oil lamps set a new record to appear in Guinness World Records. Manufacturing such camps, records, and inspiration is a performance of anonymous love. What is not evident is the boredom, hunger, and general discomfort of those gathered to make this record. Image from Twitter.

These numbers, captured for posterity or until the records are broken, do not capture the long wait times, boredom, and hunger that participants experience while waiting for politicians and other benefactors to arrive at camps, nor do they reveal that in many cases, the objects distributed at camps are inappropriate or ill fitting. Children are given adult wheelchairs in which they cannot safely sit (they sink into oversized demonstrations of state largesse), and hearing aids are distributed without being programmed to meet the children's specific audiograms.[26] These objects are often ultimately sold, disposed of, or repurposed as scrap metal. (In contrast to these objects, cochlear implants are surgically implanted devices that cannot be discarded.)

The administration keeps close tabs on the number of distributed objects as evidence of its commitment to disabled people. An Indian Sign Language interpreter who regularly interprets for Ministry of Social Justice and Empowerment functions told me that it is easy to interpret at these events. Officials' speeches usually consist of an overview of how many aids and appliances have been distributed, how many ISL interpreters have been trained, and how many words are now included in the ISL dictionary; the only thing that changes is the numbers. Occasionally, however, there are mishaps, such as when Minister of Social Justice and Empowerment Shri Chand Gehlot announced during a speech: "1700 visually impaired children have been treated with Cochlear Implant Surgery

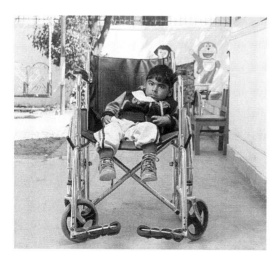

A disabled child sits in a large and inappropriate manual wheelchair after attending a camp at which wheelchairs were distributed in honor of a politician's birthday. Here the chair functions as an oversize demonstration of state power, and the child sinks into the outsize generosity of the state. Photograph by Manik Mandal.

A tweet from the Ministry of Social Justice and Empowerment's Accessible India campaign handle announces that 1,200 cochlear implants have been given to children, "all of whom can hear now." What about the surgery and re/habilitation process? How is the campaign so confident that these children can now hear? Minister Gehlot appears to be placing a hearing aid, not a cochlear implant processor, on this young woman's ear. Image from Twitter.

and almost all of them are now leading a normal life" (Press Information Bureau 2019).[27] According to government logic, disability categories can be intermixed and intermingled, as, after all, all disabled people are *divyangjan,* or divinely abled people. What is important here is the number 1,700, which actually refers to the cochlear implants and not the children, and the unmarked category of *divyangjan.* This is a form of governmentality that attaches to objects and not to individuals or communities (see Gupta 2012).

Numbers versus Outcomes

An anxious matter of concern: Is implantation the desired outcome in and of itself? How is an implanted sense quantified and qualified? Different stakeholders negotiate what a cochlear implant outcome is and should be, and there is much talk about outcomes as an unspecified category. Stressing the importance of outcomes as something other than the number of implant surgeries done is also a way of distinguishing oneself from and critiquing others who focus on numbers as outcomes. In October 2019, I met with a senior administrator implementing the ADIP cochlear implant program. A former special educator, he anxiously commented that upper-level administration officials were breathing down his neck and demanding to know why more cochlear implant surgeries were not being performed. These officials told him that in previous years, the number of surgeries performed had been greater. He said that these officials treated cochlear implantation like a "*mela* [festival] or camp."

When I asked how many surgeries had been done, he asked an assistant to bring him a memo containing this information, and then, dramatically switching tone to a more official register, he read out: "This year until October 2019, we have performed 266 surgeries under the ADIP scheme and 31 surgeries using corporate social responsibility funds. 297 surgeries have thus been done since October 5th. 121 children are waiting for surgeries. 291 are waiting for approval. 309 have incomplete applications."[28] The administrator stressed that because he had been a special educator, he cared about outcomes, and not the numbers of surgeries performed—although he did not elaborate on what he meant by outcomes. Unlike other state actors who saw implanted children, typically carefully chosen star cases, only at *melas,* he engaged with families and actually saw cochlear implants in action. He was anxious about the state's anxiety about numbers.

Cochlear implant surgeons are also concerned with numbers, often for reasons similar to the state's, in that doing more surgeries bolsters their legitimacy, prestige, and appeal. During interviews and informal meetings, surgeons often immediately announced to me how many surgeries they had performed. It is also the norm for them to showcase their numbers of surgeries when they make conference presentations to other surgeons and cochlear implant industry stakeholders. One surgeon pointed out that for the surgical community, "it is a numbers game" in which surgeries are performed and then performatively discussed. Another surgeon told me that many surgeons say "right and left how many implants they have done. So and so says: 'I have done 1,000 implants, I have done 500 implants,' and so on, but they are not talking about outcomes." She added, "Show me one of these 1,000 children with implants who talks!" This surgeon specifically wanted "outcomes and not numbers." Echoing cochlear implant corporation concerns, she commented that "people are going to stop trusting the technology because they're only going to see poor outcomes." She then critiqued the ADIP scheme for its singular focus on numbers and said that the government does not "take care with the rehabilitation process"—an important critique that I return to in chapter 4. I was struck by the almost universal scorn and derision toward the central government program among the attendees of the 2019 CIGI conference, the majority of whom were from the private sector. It was fashionable to critique the program's failure to provide re/habilitation and replacement parts post-surgery. However, the ADIP program enabled many surgeons to become cochlear implant surgeons and created an implant infrastructure in India; the scheme rendered discussions about outcomes possible.

The flashpoints in discussions around outcomes are age of implantation and re/habilitation pathways. Surgeons, audiologists, and speech and language pathologists complained that the ADIP program allowed children up to six years of age to be implanted. In contrast, they pointed out, the Kerala state program covers children only up to age three, which is why outcomes in that state are so good. However, at the same time, both government and private surgeons are eager to do cochlear implant surgeries and to increase the numbers of surgeries performed. One surgeon told me, "Everybody wants to jump on the cochlear implant train." Surgeons' desires for higher numbers are also motivated by their wish to develop relationships with implant manufacturers; the more implant surgeries they do, the greater the incentives they receive from companies in terms of financial rewards, training, and opportunities to be mentor surgeons. Manufacturers do not provide implants to a surgeon until he or she has performed a set number of surgeries under a mentor surgeon (surgeons are thus also benefactors to each other). After demonstrating competence, a surgeon can obtain implants directly from the companies; the prices that surgeons pay for implants are not publicly available, and there is much speculation about distribution networks and how much of a markup exists (Nagarajan 2017a).

Further complicating the idea of a finished or final outcome, cochlear implantation challenges the logic of "camp time," "surgical time," and "project time" in that auditory performance will ebb and flow over an implantee's lifetime, depending on mapping, re/habilitation, and cochlear implant maintenance.[29] There are surgeons who perform outsize and long-term roles in their patients' lives. Relationships are another kind of outcome and a reminder that critiques of medicine need to be nuanced. Dr. Meenu Parel, a Pune-based surgeon, stood up at the 2018 CIGI conference and proclaimed that surgeons who perform cochlear implant surgery are responsible for their patients for life. At the CIGI conference the following year, Dr. Parel talked about the importance of long-term planning for cochlear implant patients, including plans for handing over their care as a surgeon ages and retires from practice. Dr. Parel monitors her patients' therapy sessions, and patients return to her clinic for processor repairs, accessories, and upgrades; at her outpatient department meetings, one can often find families who have returned to ask about replacement parts or processors as well as for more general life advice. Dr. Parel established a cochlear implant team consisting of speech and language therapists, audiologists, and a social worker at a Pune hospital. She stresses the importance of comprehensive care over the long term. "Care" here means many different things—care during surgery, care for the re/habilitation process and outcomes, care of the device, and care for the child and the family.

While the political and financial outcomes associated with cochlear implants might be clear(er), experts have not decided what constitutes a successful outcome for a child beyond the generic "The child will talk." At the 2019 CIGI conference, one of India's leading audiologists interrogated a panel of other audiologists about how they evaluate outcomes. She asked what measures they used, specifically mentioning the Meaningful Auditory Integration Scale, the Speech Intelligibility Rating Scale, the Categories of Auditory Perception Scale, and the Parents' Evaluation of Aural/Oral Performance of Children.[30] These measures depend on parent accounts or test listening skills and speech production, usually in sound-proof settings, and ignore the role of context and the diverse settings in which children find themselves. Pisoni et al. (2008, 54) note that because "the field of clinical audiology is an applied science drawing knowledge and methods from several different disciplines, no common integrated theoretical framework motivates the choice of specific outcome measures and tests, interprets the results and findings, provides explanations, or makes predictions." I saw this lack of a dominant framework on display at the CIGI conference as different audiologists and therapists discussed the varied outcome measures they used. There was, and is, an avalanche of (talk about) outcomes (Hacking 1982). (Families often choose surgeons, audiologists, and speech and language therapists based on these professionals' advertised outcomes, and surgeons, audiologists, and speech and language therapists often compare their outcomes and speak negatively about the outcomes of their peers.)

There is also the long-term and population-level outcome that government officials and surgeons speak of: "eradicating deafness," in their words. This outcome, of course, depends on the success of the individual-level outcomes discussed above, albeit over the long term. (Medical and audiology research studies about cochlear implant outcomes in India generally have not looked beyond a period of two years postimplantation, and the ADIP scheme does not have a mechanism for maintaining contact with implant beneficiaries beyond the two-year period after implantation, if even that.) In an interview, a surgeon responsible for starting a state cochlear implant program told me that since cochlear implantation now exists, the state could conduct newborn hearing screening in earnest to identify deafness as early as possible. He said: "We can do that now because we have a cochlear implant program. Otherwise it would be criminal, you know, picking up a child and not doing anything about it." (He did not consider hearing aids or teaching a child and family sign language to be "doing anything.") This surgeon insisted that his state would become "deafness-free" by the year 2025, meaning that deafness would be corrected in those born deaf. He stressed too that categories of targeted recipients were expanding, and he had set his sights on older postlingual deaf people: "So here is a situation in which we have a solution in our hand, and then we are looking for the problem."

As 2025 was fast approaching (six years from the time of our interview), I wondered exactly when this surgeon thought deafness would be eradicated. Would this happen at the time of implantation (which is what government accounting privileges, with its focus on numbers of implants performed) or would it be post-re/habilitation? And when would re/habilitation actually be completed? Some families finish their allotted two years of therapy under the ADIP scheme and cannot afford additional therapy; other families live too far from therapy centers to receive regular therapy at all. A well-respected auditory verbal therapist in Delhi told me about ending a child's therapy sessions because the child was listening and speaking at age level and no longer needed therapy; she declared this child a successful outcome. However, surgeons and other therapists commented that such success is difficult to maintain: a drop in performance often takes place once children enter higher grades of study and language becomes more complex. Outcomes are never concretized and always need to be maintained.

Surgeons and other professionals sometimes take unexpected turns to adjust or remedy poor outcomes. Dr. Praswant Bal is a savvy foreign-educated Bangalore-based surgeon who performed surgery on older children who did not become listeners or spoken language users. He did this both through the private market and with NGO funding. In order to rescue his outcomes, and perhaps his reputation, Dr. Bal created an app for mobile devices that allows deaf children to learn sounds (not language) by seeing immediate feedback on their production. Children using the app look at the screen and practice pronouncing "ma," "ta," "pa," and other sounds, and the app tells them if and when they are vocalizing these sounds properly. According to the app's brochure, the premise is that if the brain receives sound in a visual format, then it is able to develop "near normal speech." The brochure claims that in trials, "completely deaf and mute persons" have learned to utter eight sounds in a matter of weeks.

Dr. Bal's project has since been funded by the central government: it fulfills the state's desire for innovative and technological projects that utilize existing infrastructure and are "make in India." A state government was excited about the project and permitted a pilot in deaf schools in the state, in which the children used instruction time to practice uttering sounds. According to Dr. Bal, officials in the state's Ministry of Social Justice felt that hearing aids (as distributed through government programs) were not successful for obtaining good listening and spoken language outcomes, and they were interested in whether his app could maximize outcomes. This brings up questions about what it might mean to privilege the production of sounds over learning language and subject content—perhaps in Indian Sign Language.

Dr. Bal was uninterested in ISL, insisting that it could not be used to communicate effectively in the world. He was also unconcerned about a deaf school using instructional time to teach sounds instead of language or academic content. He instead focused on feedback from parents who were ecstatic that their deaf children were uttering the sounds "Ma" and "Pa," and termed the first time that parents heard such sounds "switch-on moments." His use of this phrase brings to mind well-circulated "switch-on moment" videos of cochlear implants being activated, although in such videos we ostensibly see deaf children hearing (and not speaking) for the first time. What is switched on or activated in these moments of uttering sounds, and for whom? Dr. Bal seamlessly remade himself as a technology entrepreneur and easily received funding—for an app that teaches deaf children how to utter sounds. (If only it were that easy for deaf people to obtain funding and choose new paths.)

Camp, Surgery, Re/habilitation, Relationships: Building an Infrastructure

To further examine the relationships among surgeons, corporations, and the state, I turn to the experiences of Dr. Reetu Murthy, a surgeon in Bangalore who was previously a faculty member at a medical college focusing on routine otolaryngology care. I discuss Dr. Murthy's experience at length because her zeal for cochlear implant surgery and her close relationship with the state are both remarkable and ordinary. After Dr. Murthy first observed cochlear implant surgery performed around 2013 at her medical college, she left her job and devoted herself to developing a cochlear implant practice. She saw her practice as remedying the work of other intervention programs—namely, hearing aid distribution programs—that failed to benefit deaf children. Dr. Murthy's efforts overlapped temporally with the rollout of the ADIP program, and she performed the first ADIP surgery in Karnataka, where she was also instrumental in setting up a state cochlear implant scheme.

In a meeting in her sunlit and cheerful clinic featuring a playground in the lobby and colorful posters from cochlear implant companies, Dr. Murthy told me that she initially thought cochlear implant surgery could be performed only by very senior surgeons. However, after encouragement from a senior cochlear implant surgeon who agreed to mentor her, she resigned from her position at the medical college and opened a private practice with a re/habilitation team consisting of an audiologist and a speech and language pathologist. She saw what implants could do, and, because she "needed patients and needed implants," she commenced a mission to "mobilize patients." Accompanied by an audiologist, she visited deaf schools in Bangalore, hoping to give presentations about cochlear implants to the students' parents, but the schools would not allow her to do so, or, if they did, the parents did not come. She also visited different institutes in Bangalore and Mysore, where she was met with suspicion and resistance.

Dr. Murthy was finally able to do a few surgeries: one patient was a recently married man who used his dowry payment to cover part of the costs, with his employer and a loan paying for the rest; another was the child of a cook, for whose surgery Dr. Murthy sought funding from the Prime Minister's National Relief Fund. She also implanted the child of a nurse who had assisted her with an earlier cochlear implant surgery. When Dr. Murthy visited this child's school, she observed that all of the students were wearing "useless" hearing aids distributed by an NGO. She told me that hearing aids are distributed, they break, and then they are distributed again. This cycle, she stressed, is financially wasteful as well as unhelpful to children.

Dr. Murthy became adept at seeking out funding through government programs and private donors, notably through corporate social responsibility initiatives and the Prime Minister's Fund. At this point, the ADIP scheme began, and Dr. Murthy became frustrated because she was not getting patients, even though she had raised funds and implants had become free for certain populations. Finally, she went to the state health minister and showed him a video of an implanted child who could listen and talk. She related their conversation to me:

> "Sir we want to do a camp with the government in a rural place.
> If there is a camp in the government's name, people will trust it.
> If I say, I'm doing [a] camp and I am going to operate and give
> [a] free implant, parents may not trust me. So let us do it through
> the government." He said, "Sure, but you will have to do it in my
> constituency because I know the people and how to get the work
> done." I said, "Okay." This was the first time I heard the name of his
> constituency. . . . We said, "*Theek hain*" [okay].

The health minister's insistence that the camp be held in his constituency points to the political nature of camps and disability distribution processes in general. Dr. Murthy organized the camp at a primary health center in the health minister's constituency, which was no easy logistical task. She had to arrange for CT scans and MRIs in addition to hearing tests, and she knew she had to ensure that all needed tests could be performed in one day, so that children would not be lost to follow-up. She reached out to medical colleges with the health minister's assistance and acquired full teams of anesthesiologists and radiologists. She gave detailed instructions about the specific images she wanted from the radiologists; as she told me, "Why waste time and resources to do a full MRI and CT?" The minister also offered the help of Anganwadi and Asha (community child-care and health) workers who would transport children to and from the camp and ensure the presence of two hundred to three hundred children. Dr. Murthy called on her senior mentor to accompany and support her.

On the day of the camp, a routine was established. First, each child had a basic audiology exam. If hearing loss was suspected, the child was sedated and underwent a brain-stem evoked response audiometry test. If hearing loss was diagnosed, the child underwent an MRI followed by a CT scan. After these tests, the child recovered for an hour and was sent home. In a day, Dr. Murthy's team found forty children eligible for implants through the ADIP scheme. (They also found other children and adults with hearing loss who were ineligible because of age requirements; they were sent for hearing aids.) In discussing the uniqueness of her camp and its deviation from typical camps, Dr. Murthy pointed out that there was a "food issue": the children and their families expected food, since it was a government camp and many had come from far away. However, sedated children cannot eat, and so food was not distributed, only the possibility of a cochlear implant. This tension in the structure of the distributive process, between food now or expensive biotechnology later, reveals the novelty of cochlear implants in that they are not distributed in the moment, in the current structure of the camp. Camp space and time are stretched.

Dr. Murthy's team remained in this rural setting for three days because they were afraid to lose these hard-found children to follow-up. In describing her thinking at the time, again Dr. Murthy stressed: "Since it was through the government, on that scale, people will trust you. They didn't think that we were doing something wrong or anything." The day after the testing battery, the team called all of the eligible parents to ask them to attend a counseling session about cochlear implants and to request their signatures. The families were told that the surgery would take place at a government hospital in Bangalore. Dr. Murthy then uploaded the forty files into the ADIP system for approval by the AYJNISHD central committee. As she said: "We did the camp for the poor children. Nobody was ready to go anywhere and do camps. They were sitting in their places and taking all the rich patients. We went to the rural place, we did the camp. We picked these children up from the grassroot level." While Dr. Murthy's comments might seem self-righteous, that she personally recruited patients through rural camps is noteworthy, although many of the audiologists and audiology students I spoke with discussed their participation in camps with excitement and a sense of adventure; they saw such camps as opportunities to seek out patients as opposed to waiting for them to arrive on their own.

Dr. Murthy received one of the first batches of implants through the ADIP scheme, twenty-five in total. Since she was no longer affiliated with a government hospital, she was given an honorary appointment at a Bangalore government hospital so that she could perform the surgeries. This was much to the annoyance of some hospital employees, who felt that she was encroaching on their territory, although Dr. Murthy eventually became a mentor to a surgeon at this hospital. She told me that the hospital staff was resentful of her ability to commandeer resources and rooms, but she remained unfazed. As she described her attitude to me: "Nothing doing, the government has given me twenty-five implants and I need to finish these in one month so that I can get more. The more I finish, the more implants I get, and the more children who get implants." Patients were given travel fare to Bangalore, and Dr. Murthy and her mentor surgeon took over two operating theaters and operated side by side, doing six implants a day, until they had done all twenty-five. Dr. Murthy was worried about operation failures, because it would take only one to derail her practice; she thus took "special care" with these first implant cases.

The children were discharged a day after their surgeries. Activation took place three weeks later in Mangalore, close to the health minister's constituency and an overnight bus ride from Bangalore. Dr. Murthy and her team subsequently traveled to Mangalore every month to conduct follow-up care, mapping, and therapy. However, problems arose: they were in Mangalore for only one day each month, few qualified staff were available there, and the central government took a long time to pay for services. Dr. Murthy returned to the health minister and asked for a Karnataka state scheme. The minister was sympathetic and told her to write a scheme, which she did, using funds from the National Health Ministry's Rashtriya Bal Swasthya Karyakram program, which focuses on early detection and screening for health problems and disabilities in children, to create the Shravanadosha Mukta Karnataka (Deafness-Free Karnataka) program. The Karnataka program mirrored the ADIP scheme, except that the cutoff age for implantation was six years, and the program covered travel fare to and from surgical and re/habilitation centers as well as lost wages.[31]

Dr. Murthy found an ally in the health minister. Similar to other surgeons I interviewed, she stressed the role of interpersonal connections and the work of individual government bureaucrats who appreciated the impact of cochlear implants, like Joint Secretary Sharma discussed above. Dr. Murthy's extensive endeavors to find potential government beneficiaries and implant recipients through visiting schools and other institutions, setting up a camp, and even writing a new government scheme shed light on the difficulty of accomplishing what Sharma calls "large-scale" implantation and demonstrate that cochlear implant distribution processes and infrastructure are quite complex, contingent, and precarious. Dr. Murthy currently has a thriving private clinic and is taking increasingly fewer ADIP-funded cases. She also has a more expansive view of success and outcomes, in that she is implanting children with multiple disabilities as well as older children—two populations whose precarious outcomes might bring down the reputation of implants, as I often heard in my research.

What a difference timing and the proliferation of cochlear implants make. While Dr. Murthy's early experience as a pioneering surgeon involved actively seeking out patients, my discussions with audiologists and speech and language therapists at government institutes in Delhi and Mumbai about the current state of the ADIP scheme reveal different and more ambivalent trajectories. Between working with a steady stream of families and overseeing student practitioners, state-employed audiologists and speech and language therapists told me that they feel powerless in relation to families requesting implants through the ADIP scheme. Families assert that it is their right to apply for the scheme, making statements such as "Government is providing this scheme for people like me," "Government is doing this for us," and "I am eligible for the scheme." Families often insist on forgoing hearing aid trials in favor of cochlear implant surgery as soon as possible (perhaps because they are aware that hearing aids provided by the government are a significant step down from cochlear implants and/or because they have read or seen positive media coverage of cochlear implants). As one audiologist stressed: "We cannot say no to people for implants because it is a government scheme that they are entitled to. We are a government office, and if we refuse to give someone an implant, they can file a complaint against us or accuse us of looking for bribes." To put it briefly: "We are government, we cannot say no." What else, besides yes or no, could be said here?

In this chapter, I have traced how the state produces presence and materializes itself as a welfare state through the ongoing distribution of disability aids and appliances. In contrast to previous forms of distribution, the distribution of cochlear implants has resulted in the state venturing inside the body and acting on and in individuals in targeted ways. The state becomes a sensory state in its attempts to produce sensory normality. Cochlear implants ostensibly produce capacities and make children normal. In addition to becoming beneficiaries, children who receive cochlear implants become recipients, a category and relationship that they and their families are initially unaware of entering into. In the process, cochlear implant manufacturers become providers of state infrastructure, and surgeons become cochlear implant surgeons. Cochlear implants also offer new possibilities for government administrators, surgeons, re/habilitation workers, and families to reinvent themselves, although this reinvention is fraught, produces anxiety, and involves complex dependencies in which all stakeholders are potentially imbricated.

The question of what could be problematic about the state providing poor children with a missing sense takes on a more ambivalent valence when one considers these complex dependencies and the unfinished nature of implantation, contrary to what government administrators, cochlear implant corporations, and some surgeons insist. In the following two chapters, I focus on what happens after surgery. I argue that implantation is only the beginning, and that becoming normal through cochlear implants, despite state discourse, is an anxious, long-term project that lasts a lifetime and produces multiple unknown outcomes along the way.

2

Becoming Unisensory

Creating a Child's Social Sense through
Auditory Verbal Therapy and Total Communication

> *To say that perception is shaped by culture and that society regulates how and what we sense is also to say that there is a politics of the senses. Our ways of sensing affect not only how we experience and engage with our environment, but also how we experience and engage with each other.*

> —David Howes and Constance Classen

> *Now, there are a bunch of children who are implanted very early and who have had the benefit of intensive rehabilitation very young. And when I say very young, I'm talking under the age of three. They learn to become confident of their hearing and begin to use their hearing as their primary sense, and not vision as a primary sense, for communication— these kids as they grow older, we see them being wonderfully verbal. And more important than wonderfully verbal, they are very auditorily dependent, you know, they would react to sounds like you and I will do in the sense that if they don't hear they are uncomfortable, and they want to hear better.*

> —Dr. Rashmi, professor of audiology and speech
> and language pathology in Chennai

Auditory Dominance

In September 2019, I sat with Zahra, one of India's most widely known practitioners of auditory verbal therapy, in her large and airy clinic space surrounded by gardens in central Mumbai, swatting at mosquitos as we chatted. Zahra is universally respected in India and held up as an example of a top-notch AVT specialist; many surgeons, audiologists, and speech and language pathologists commented on her excellent listening and spoken language outcomes with deaf children. Zahra cannot, however, officially call herself an auditory verbal therapist because she has refused to become certified by the Alexander Graham Bell Academy, the international AVT certifying body based in the United States. I asked Zahra why she had not sought certification and she scoffed, insisting that she did not need a piece of paper to prove her worth as a therapist. Indeed, she had been a practicing therapist long before the certification came into being. Zahra first learned about AVT more than thirty years ago from a visiting Australian AVT practitioner, one of the many "experts" who traveled to India to teach different re/habilitation methods. At that time, before cochlear implants had become widely available, she had been working with a small group of children out of her house, and she did not know if the method would work. All she knew was that she wanted to teach deaf children to listen and speak.

One day, Zahra was in the middle of a lesson with a child. A friend stopped by to visit, and she turned her attention to her friend. However, the child kept talking, even though Zahra's friend was also talking. Zahra asked the child to stop talking in deference to her friend. The child replied: "No, *you* stop talking. I was talking first." Zahra knew at that moment that AVT was working for this child because she was appropriately social. The girl knew how to take turns, and she responded confidently and independently (although her sassy comeback might not be universally appreciated). For Zahra, "success" was not only about developing a child's ability to utilize listening and spoken language but also about developing a *social sense*—which for her and other AVT practitioners hinged on the development of a sensorium in which audition is the dominant sense. Audition *first,* and then everything else will follow. "Everything else" means interacting through listening and spoken language, engaging in dyadic turn-taking, and maintaining a contextually sensible conversation through speech. The goal is to inhabit the world in a way that is effortlessly and normatively intelligible to others.

AVT is a set of principles and a methodology focused on maximizing deaf children's ability to relate to the world through audition. It entails ensuring appropriate auditory technology (often called sensory aids) such as hearing aids and cochlear implants, minimizing visual cues, modeling "natural" and "social" turn-taking and conversation, and maximizing parental involvement. Therapists stress that children and families must start

AVT as early as possible, ideally before the age of three, with increased age correlating with decreased outcomes, although different therapists have varying perspectives on who is "too late" or "too old" (or "too disabled," with other disabilities besides deafness affecting outcomes). AVT is not speech therapy in that it focuses on maximizing a child's ability to use audition and not on speech per se; listening is emphasized before speech, a point that AVT practitioners stress constantly.

I attend to the development and proliferation of AVT as a specific therapeutic method with great purchase in cochlear implant infrastructures; I interrogate what kind of sensing subject AVT aims to produce as well as the linguistic, semiotic, and sensory ideologies with which it is bundled. Historically and currently, speech and language therapists, audiologists, families, and manufacturers of hearing aids and cochlear implants have argued that AVT is successful in creating "auditorily dependent" and "wonderfully verbal" children, as evidenced in the quotation from Dr. Rashmi above. In AVT circles, a hierarchy of sensing exists: value is placed on having an auditory brain, being an auditory person, and minimizing visual language and communication; the ultimate goal is sensory normativity.

Again, AVT is not speech therapy: speech therapy often invokes strongly negative feelings in sign language–speaking deaf adults (and in AVT practitioners as well). In the realm of deafness, anthropologists, neuroscientists, and other scholars have criticized speech therapy's failure to produce adequate language development and socialization and have pointed to the continuing dominance of such therapy as evidence of oralist (valuing spoken language) ideologies.[1] Unlike speech therapy, AVT is seen as unleashing and cultivating potential through its work on the brain and the senses (although, as with speech therapy, there is always the risk of failure).

Cochlear implants provide new opportunities for producing ideal sensory subjects and sensory infrastructures predicated on listening and spoken language. AVT principles and methods are key to this production, and one cannot discuss cochlear implant outcomes without also talking about AVT's role in these outcomes. AVT has brought into being new conceptions of the senses, the body, and language: it depends on the division of the senses into discrete entities and the creation of communication, modality, and sensory categories that are ideologically and hierarchically arranged. AVT practitioners play what Ludwig Wittgenstein (2009) calls "language games," and they also play sensory games and modality games, in that they have created and compartmentalized sensory, modality, and communicative categories.

As with cochlear implants, the emergence of AVT in India involves a "global re/habilitation community" organized around seemingly universalized principles and the production of an unmarked normal sensing subject. While there are only five certified AVT practitioners in India at the time of this writing, AVT has oversize importance in cochlear implant circles and is constantly discussed by implant manufacturers, surgeons, and speech and language pathologists as a "best practice." (In addition to the five certified therapists, there are many practitioners in India like Zahra, who adhere to AVT principles and methods without being certified.) AVT certification and its possibility have brought new forms of internationally recognized expertise and prestige into re/habilitation circles in India.

In this chapter, I move from the United States to India and in time from the 1930s to the present, although other countries, notably Australia and England, have their own AVT pioneers and histories; there are Canadian, British, and Australian actors in the story I tell here. I traverse these spaces and times in order to flesh (or sense) out how deaf children's senses are conceptualized. At stake is the value placed on the creation of a specific sensorium and sensorial way of being social. I end with a call for recognition of the value of multisensory and multimodal orientations and communicative practices—as well as the importance of attending to signals that are not just auditory. I argue for the importance of thinking about the affordances of all kinds of sensory signals and for a "social sense" that does not just emerge through listening and spoken language. In making this argument, I join with scholars of autistic sociality and communication and disability studies scholars who have labored to expand conceptions of communicative competence and ways of being social.[2]

Producing a "Normal Five-Sensed" Child

In November 1974, John Croft, the father of a then nine-year-old deaf child named Rose, wrote a passionate essay titled "The Third Way." He argued that the contentious debate between oralism (a focus on promoting spoken language for deaf children) and manualism (promoting signed language for deaf children) obscured the existence of a *third category and movement,* which he called "auralism."[3] Croft (1974, 1), an education professor as well as the parent of a deaf child, argued that both oralism and manualism are imperfect, in that neither method can "teach an individual with only *four* senses how to compensate well enough to compete successfully in a world where others have *five*." In contrast, Croft explained, auralist methods create "hearing-deaf" children who become "functionally mildly hard-of-hearing" through the training of their auditory sense (1). According to Croft, aural children can have conversations through walls, use the telephone, and hear their teachers regardless of where they are in the classroom. They do not need to read lips during spelling tests and can watch television. Aural children experience "five-sensed normality" (Croft and Croft 1978). What is required for "five-sensed normality" is a constant focus on audition, "until *listening* becomes as much a habit as looking, and feeling, and smelling, and tasting" (Croft 1974, 3).

In some ways, Croft's admonitions and his concern with categories were ahead of the times, or at least we might initially think so. The principles and methods that he advocated are now called auditory verbal therapy, although at the time they were not gathered under any specific approach or name. Croft often discussed his own family's experience with Rose in his writings and speeches. Rose's hearing loss was not discovered until she was two years old. As a result of this so-called late diagnosis, her visual sense had a two-year "head start." To counteract this, Rose's family focused entirely on her auditory channel to make sure that it did not remain "deficient" (Croft and Croft 1978). When Rose was diagnosed, the doctor who examined her did not say that Rose could not hear. Rather, he said that she "does not appear to be *using* any hearing. Therefore, after providing proper amplification, we must begin immediately to teach her to listen" (Croft and Croft 1978, 2). Rose learned to listen through weekly therapy sessions with an AVT pioneer and by working extensively with her mother.

As Croft (1974) reported, whenever Rose's mother or neighborhood children played with her, they did so in a way that encouraged her to use her hearing, rather than use her eyes to lipread (I wonder how Rose's family monitored the neighborhood children). Rose was always in a "normal" classroom without accommodations, and her school records did not mention her deafness. She was permitted to hear "only normal sounds" and to "imitate normal speech" (Croft 1977, 4; Croft and Croft 1978, 5). Rose wore her binaural hearing aids from morning to night. A broken hearing aid was quickly repaired or replaced; she never went even three hours without a well-functioning hearing aid (Croft and Croft 1978). Throughout all of this training, her listening ability improved and her aided audiogram climbed up the chart. At the age of seven, Rose reached the borderline of "normal hearing at some frequencies" (Croft 1977, 3). According to Croft (1977, 2), his daughter and others like her are "hearing-deaf children" that have been a "remarkably well-kept secret."

During the summer of 2019, I talked with Rose through a complicated setup of FaceTime, a CapTel phone (a landline phone with a small screen on which Rose could read what I said, as my speech was typed into text by a remote captioner), a Bluetooth hearing aid–compatible headset, and the occasional writing on paper held up to the screen. During our call, Rose told me that she learned as a child to "anticipate hearing," which I took to mean that she became oriented toward sound. Growing up, she watched *Sesame Street, Mister Rogers' Neighborhood,* and the evening news, where she enjoyed Peter Jennings's and Ted Koppel's voices; she found closed captioning distracting and unenjoyable when it became available (this is the opposite of my experience—I loved closed captioning). As a child Rose repeatedly had to listen to and identify the sounds of dogs, cars, cats, and airplanes, among others, as part of auditory training. However, she was not complaining and was proud to identify as an "auditory verbal person" and a "five-sensed person." Rose's parents wanted her to see herself as a hearing person first and a deaf person second; she said that they were successful.

Rose felt that her listening ability was still improving because of the way she had been trained to attend to hearing. She shared an example from her high school graduation ceremony, where, as a result of unusual grade point average calculations, there were many valedictorians and salutatorians. As she sat bored in the audience, various classmates were called to the stage and recognized as valedictorians and salutatorians; she heard those same words again and again. On the car ride home afterward, she complained to her mother about the many valedictorians and salutatorians. Rose's mother expressed surprise to hear Rose pronounce these two words properly, as she had not been able to do so previously; she was able to pronounce them now because she had heard them over and over. Rose also told me about visiting a Mexican restaurant where she was able to pronounce a Spanish word after hearing it for the first time, offering this as further evidence of the fact that her auditory ability was still malleable and developing because of her rigorous childhood training.

At the end of our phone call, Rose said that, unbeknownst to her mother, she does lipread. When I asked why reading lips was so fraught, Rose told me that during childhood therapy, her therapist stood behind her and did not let her read lips. In a follow-up e-mail, Rose wrote: "AVT emphasized on LISTENING with our brain so anything to distract the use of 'listening' like lipreading can degrade the quality of your 'listening' muscles. So naturally lipreading was frowned upon. However as we get older our 'brain' is kidnapped to think and process many other things besides 'listening' so lipreading has become a supplemental support to the 'listening.' However it can overpower the listening component." I am struck by the hostile language of kidnapping here and the need for a constant focus on audition, even in the midst of other life events. Laura Mauldin (2016) calls this "precarious plasticity," the idea that there is always a risk of becoming visual. Even as an adult, Rose worries about her listening ability becoming overpowered by vision.

Rose's words mirrored those of her father. In Croft's essays and speeches, audition and "five-sensed normality" are contrasted with a deaf child's tendency to become visual. Croft's writings and speeches emphasize a battle between audition and vision and the need for vigilance to ensure that the visual sense does not win out. Crucially, and departing from the well-trafficked fight between oralism and manualism, this focus on audition adds something new to the mix—auralism. Mauldin (2016, 138) writes: "The therapeutic culture surrounding CIs [cochlear implants]—and especially the neuropolitical aspects of it—maps onto long-standing educational divides and serves to rearticulate past arguments for oral education in more sophisticated technoscientific terms." More than this, it is important to consider the epistemological and ontological foundations of *audition as a way of life*; these underpinnings do not map onto the manual/oral debate and predate the emergence of cochlear implants—although cochlear implants offer new and unprecedented conditions of possibility for creating auditory children.

Unisensory

Rose's therapist was an early auditory verbal therapy pioneer before the method was known by that name. Referred to in different circles as the unisensory approach, acoupedics, auralism, the auditory approach, the acoustic method, and natural language, what is now called AVT was originated by three women: Helen Beebe, working in Pennsylvania; Ciwa Griffiths, working in California and New York; and Doreen Pollack, working in Colorado.[4] Trained in the 1930s and 1940s, all three traced their genealogies back to the same forebears: Austrian physicist Emil Fröschels, who developed the chewing method to help with stuttering; Viktor Urbantschitsch, an Austrian otologist who proposed theories of psychic deafness and offered up auditory gymnastics; and Henk Huizing, a Dutch otologist (Estabrooks et al. 2016; Goldstein 1933; Power and Hyde 1997). Helen Beebe's archives at Penn State University contain letters written in the 1960s–70s between Beebe (note that she was affectionately called by her last name by those around her), Griffiths, and Pollack discussing their passion for their shared method and their sorrow that it was not universally known and valued.

Their method stressed that most hearing-impaired children, even those who are profoundly deaf, have some residual hearing that can be capitalized upon. Making the "maximum use of residual hearing which most have" requires that the child be "bathed in sound" and "surrounded by people who believe he hears," as Beebe wrote on undated index cards.[5] These three women, with their backgrounds working in deaf oral schools, were not satisfied with the ways those schools depended on visual methods such as lipreading. They also firmly believed that deaf children should be mainstreamed. In her elegant handwriting, Beebe wrote on a notecard a quote attributed to Alexander Graham Bell: "The best school for the deaf is the one with only one deaf child." On another notecard, she recorded the observation that mainstreaming "can make the difference between a 'deaf' child and a normal child with hearing impairment." This note makes it clear that Beebe believed that a child (like Rose) with a hearing impairment could become normal, depending on the kinds of sensory habits developed.

In a 1976 essay titled "Deaf Children Can Learn to Hear," Beebe wrote:

In a unisensory program intensive auditory training means developing the use of amplified hearing to its maximum potential. Even *profoundly deaf children* can learn to hear. They can be brought to the point of handling conversational speech—repeating and discussing a story through hearing alone. They are not allowed to rely on lip reading until they are hearing oriented. Eventually they become multisensory. . . .

In early training we know that the child with one sensory receiving modality intact (sight) and one impaired (hearing) will rely on the easier modality and so we force him to listen and hear by preventing him from watching the speaker's mouth. If our goal is to provide maximal use of residual hearing, he must be *forced* to hear enough to stimulate the motor speech center of the brain and to appreciate what hearing and discrimination can do for him. (241–42)

Beebe, like other AVT practitioners, was vigilant about intrusion from visual input and strongly believed that children could become hearing only if they were "forced" to use whatever hearing they had; this was the way to maximize potential. Only after becoming unisensory can a deaf child become multisensory. I also flag Beebe's mention of the brain, which has come to occupy a significant role in shoring up the importance of creating auditory dominance in current AVT discourse (see Mauldin 2016; see also chapter 5 of this book).

Beebe's unisensory approach, as established from the 1940s onward, called for early detection of hearing loss, appropriate binaural amplification (a new practice at the time, as previously children were fitted with only one hearing aid), intensive auditory training, a chewing approach that focused on making children aware of their chewing motions in order to develop natural voice quality, one-on-one therapy, educational placement with hearing peers, and full family involvement. Part of Beebe's private clinic in central Pennsylvania was devoted to a model demonstration home, the Larry Jarret House, where families could stay for a week at a time and learn techniques for working with their children at home. Families from across the United States traveled to the clinic to receive instruction from therapists on how to maintain constant interaction with children during domestic activities (as I discuss here and in chapter 3, domestic spaces were key for utilizing and practicing AVT techniques). The Jarret House was also a demonstration space where visitors from near and far could witness the unisensory approach in action.

AVT's formal beginning dates to two conferences on the auditory approach held in Pasadena, California, in 1972 and 1977. At the first conference in 1972, Beebe, Pollack, and Griffiths met in person for the first time. In 1978, the International Committee on Auditory-Verbal Communication was formed as a section within the Alexander Graham Bell Association for the Deaf and Hard of Hearing (known simply as AG Bell).[6] One AVT practitioner and expert trainer I spoke with told me that the use of *auditory* in the therapy's name is self-evident, while *verbal* was chosen to mark AVT as separate from oral therapeutic approaches, which do not require hearing. There are nonhearing and nonlistening oral deaf people, who, according to this trainer, often have exaggerated and artificial "deaf speech."[7] In 1985, an AVT certification process was proposed, as practitioners wished to differentiate their methods from those of other approaches (such as the auditory oral approach, which allows visual cues) and to have a credential that recognized AVT mastery.

In 1987, the International Committee on Auditory-Verbal Communication left AG Bell and formed an independent group called Auditory Verbal International. The members of AVI left AG Bell out of frustration that the association was not supporting auditory verbal approaches. In their eyes, AG Bell focused on oralism but not auralism. Many practitioners involved in AG Bell used visual-oral methods in residential and other deaf schools. There was also pushback against AVT from oral deaf adults who had not learned through audition (and who might have had "deaf speech," in the words of the above-mentioned practitioner and trainer). AVT as an approach, especially its focus on mainstreaming, was threatening to administrators, teachers, and former students at schools for the deaf. Ironically, while these schools have largely focused on oral education, AVI saw them as "too visual" and having too much in common with proponents of sign language. In addition, AVT practitioners mostly worked in clinics and thus differed from therapists, teachers, and administrators in school-based settings.

AVI offered its first AVT certification examination in 1994. In 2005, after struggling financially and logistically, AVI reintegrated with AG Bell. Currently, the AG Bell Academy for Listening and Spoken Language oversees the AVT certification process (Estabrooks et al. 2016).[8] At the time of this writing, there are approximately one thousand certified AVT practitioners internationally, with most concentrated in countries in the global North. The official designation for a credentialed AVT practitioner is Listening and Spoken Language Specialist Certified Auditory-Verbal Therapist (LSLS Cert. AVT). Another available credential is that of Listening and Spoken Language Specialist Certified Auditory-Verbal Educator (LSLS Cert. AVEd). The former is the credential usually sought by therapists who work one-on-one with children and families, while the latter is intended for those likely to work in schools.[9] The latter certification, according to a prominent AVT practitioner, is controversial because a fundamental premise of AVT is that deaf children should be mainstreamed (recall the quote above attributed to Alexander Graham Bell and singled out by Beebe). The AG Bell Academy, through its certification authority, has control over who can call themselves AVT practitioners or say that they are "doing AVT." Therapists without AVT certification often stress that while they are not certified, they do use AVT principles and methods. They might also call themselves auditory verbal habilitationists or practitioners of auditory-based therapy.

Certification requires a degree in a deaf education or re/habilitation-related field, mentorship by a current certified LSLS AVT professional (which the potential AVT practitioner might pay for), and successful completion of an examination administered in either English or Spanish at a licensed testing center. Once certified, AVT practitioners must abide by the following ten principles, as stated by the AG Bell Academy:

1. Promote early diagnosis of hearing loss in newborns, infants, toddlers, and young children, followed by immediate audiologic management and auditory-verbal therapy.
2. Recommend immediate assessment and use of appropriate, state-of-the-art hearing technology to obtain maximum benefits of auditory stimulation.
3. Guide and coach parents to help their child use hearing as the primary sensory modality in developing listening and spoken language.
4. Guide and coach parents to become the primary facilitators of their child's listening and spoken language development through active consistent participation in individualized auditory-verbal therapy.
5. Guide and coach parents to create environments that support listening for the acquisition of spoken language throughout the child's daily activities.
6. Guide and coach parents to help their child integrate listening and spoken language into all aspects of the child's life.
7. Guide and coach parents to use natural developmental patterns of audition, speech, language, cognition, and communication.
8. Guide and coach parents to help their child self-monitor spoken language through listening.
9. Administer ongoing formal and informal diagnostic assessments to develop individualized auditory-verbal treatment plans, to

monitor progress and to evaluate the effectiveness of the plans for the child and family.

10. Promote education in regular schools with peers who have typical hearing and with appropriate services from early childhood onwards.[10]

Consider, in particular, the third principle, which calls for hearing to be the "primary sensory modality," and the sixth principle, which calls for listening and spoken language to be integrated into "all aspects of the child's life." Engagement with the world is supposed to occur through audition. AVT professionals now "guide and coach" parents just as much as they work directly with children. This novel focus on parents differs from the work that the early pioneers did with deaf children in that therapists now model techniques for parents, instruct parents in what to do, and help them develop listening and spoken language–rich activities to do with their children at home. As I discuss in chapter 3, this focus on coaching parents has particular ramifications for deaf parents who are considered not appropriately sensible or social because they cannot use listening and spoken language themselves as well as for any parents who are overworked and overwhelmed.

In June 2018, I sat in a packed, heavily air-conditioned conference room at an AG Bell annual convention held at a five-star resort in Arizona. Audiologists and AVT practitioners, including a few therapists from India, were listening to Carol Flexer, a leading figure in AVT. Flexer resembles a preacher with her animated demeanor and use of chants and repetition, all oriented toward the importance of the brain. She led participants in a call-and-response chant: "The ears know nothing, the eyes know nothing, and the nose knows nothing. It is the brain that knows everything." She stressed that deaf children have hearing brains. They have doorway problems and need "doorway devices" such as hearing aids or cochlear implants to help access the brain. Children must wear doorway devices from the earliest age possible, and the brain must be stimulated during every waking hour. As Flexer and Ellen Rhoades (2016, 24) have written: "We hear with the brain; the ears are the *doorway* to the brain for auditory information. Consequently, hearing loss is primarily a brain issue—not an ear issue."

In contemporary AVT worlds, a deaf child is a child with a hearing brain and a closed doorway to that brain. This concept of "closed doorways" reminds me of the oft-cited statement attributed to Helen Keller: "Blindness separates us from things, but deafness separates us from people." For AVT proponents, deafness is not only a "closed doorway to the brain" but also a closed social doorway between people, because communication and sociality can take place only through listening and spoken language. Listening and spoken language are thus instrumental for developing a social sense and participating in the world. The workings of the brain are ultimately exteriorized and socialized in that families must learn, scaffold, and perform ("guide and coach") appropriately social and communicative behavior, as outlined in the principles of AVT, to unleash the brain's potential.[11]

The senses are scaffolded and isolated into what Caroline Jones (2005, 389) calls a "modernist sensorium," and there is a manufactured war between hearing and vision. For example, in an AVT handbook, Flexer and Rhoades (2016, 30) provide "important definitions" for the concepts of "sensory deprivation," "sensory compensation," "sensory competition," and "sensory dominance." These concepts are often discussed in the context of a battle between vision and audition and the need to avoid visual dominance (also see Mauldin 2014, 145). Where are the other senses and how might we take a more cooperative view of the senses working together? In response I argue that we must sensorially stretch the social beyond a binary between vision and hearing and examine how the social can be produced and inhabited in diverse and expansive intersensory and multisensory ways. I am referring here not to what Maurice Merleau-Ponty (1962) calls the prereflective unity of the senses, but rather to the ways that different senses can be cultivated or constrained. Unity is not prereflective or presocial.[12]

Modality Continuums

To be sure, AVT is not the only method used to achieve listening and spoken language results. Therapists, families, and older deaf adults in both the United States and India told me about techniques that involved visual and tactile cues: focusing on a therapist's lips, feeling throats for vibrations, vocalizing onto feathers, and forcing air out of one's nose and monitoring the sensation, among other things. (These techniques are typically not romanticized or thought of nostalgically; I too have memories of throat vibrations and articulation exercises during my weekly speech therapy sessions.) With improved hearing aid technology and the normalization of cochlear implants, therapists stress that now it is easier than ever before for children to attain good listening and spoken language outcomes through unisensory approaches, especially when the children are implanted at a young age. Many multisensory techniques have gone by the wayside.

Janet, an American therapist who works internationally, told me: "Children hear so much more now. It used to be that with profoundly deaf children, they really relied on their eyes because they only got a very narrow part of the speech spectrum with their profound hearing loss. And you could develop wonderful speech and language through that very narrow bit that they got. But it was hard work. And you did kind of have to force it a bit, because they were very visual." While therapists constantly told me how much easier their work has become since the advent of improved technology, it is clear that more labor has been foisted onto families (particularly mothers).[13] Increasingly, audiologists and therapists argue that there is no reason why a deaf child diagnosed early enough should not have access to listening and spoken language—although there is always the lingering question of what to do with older children.

Similar to Wittgenstein's (2009) "language games" and the accompanying sensory games and modality games in AVT worlds, AVT practitioners speak of communication options, communication opportunities, and communication outcomes. Options are evaluated according to whether they are more or less auditory or visual and the kinds of outcomes they produce. The AG Bell website lists and describes "four primary communication outcomes, each tied to an approach to language": listening and spoken language, cued speech/language, American Sign Language/bilingual-bicultural, and the total communication method.[14] While AG Bell addresses these as four distinct and differentiated options, practitioners often speak of a "communication continuum" or a "communication spectrum," although this spectrum is made up of bounded categorical approaches to communication. *(How can there be only four ways to communicate?)*

While AVT practitioners and many families of deaf children strive for what they call the "gold standard of listening and spoken language," what happens on the ground—in clinics, schools, and homes—is not bounded, and an array of senses, modalities, and ways of being social exist. People might be aural and oral, and also use some gesture and sign language, for example, or they might do something else entirely. Outcomes can never be preplanned or guaranteed, despite the clear categories and labels that have been set up for different therapeutic and communicative approaches.

In India, neither cued speech nor the bilingual-bicultural approach was in use at the time of my research, although educators and deaf activists had been advocating for a bilingual-bicultural approach. In addition, "total communication" was an amorphous, catchall category. I had many conversations with therapists in India and the United States in which we confused ourselves about what different techniques entailed: What does it mean to be "auditory oral," "auditory aural," and/or "auditory verbal"? When is lipreading permitted or not? How do you know when someone is lipreading or what senses a person is using to communicate? Communication can escape categorization.

But how to talk about "oral failures," or, in this case, "aural failures"? Janet told me that she advocates for AVT practices to be "diagnostic" and for therapists to evaluate children each time they see them while also having three-month, six-month, and long-term goals. She stressed that there is no such thing as a "failed AVT child." She said that some children simply need "something else": "I think in AV[T] we see that the full communication continuum is essential. Every communication method must be a choice. And in AV[T] if a parent chooses spoken language we start at the far end of the continuum and diagnostically assess the child. And if they're not making the progress they need to, we keep moving along the continuum as far as we need to until that child's rate of progress is appropriate." According to Janet, sometimes children just need "information in a different way." Janet's focus on choice ignores the power- and value-laden terrain and the fact that many families are not presented with any choice—as I saw firsthand with families with whom I worked. There was no "something else" for them. In addition, Janet's ostensibly diagnostic and scientific approach prevents AVT from ever being a failed method.

While Janet stressed that children never fail, I am reminded of a story that I heard more than once while visiting an institute in Kerala that offered both early intervention programs in listening and spoken language for small children and university-level courses taught in Indian Sign Language. The institute was starting a bilingual early intervention program in which it would teach ISL as a first language in which to then teach reading and writing in Malayalam. The program coordinator told a mother of a deaf child that her son was not successful in the listening and spoken language early intervention program and that she recommended transferring him to the bilingual class. Upon hearing this, the mother fainted (or at least that is what multiple people told me) because she was so distraught about her son learning ISL and not spoken language (also see Friedner 2018).

As David Howes and Constance Classen (2014, 5) write: "Equally significant to the ways in which the senses are practiced are the ways in which a society decides that they should *not* be used: when and what we must *not* see, or touch, or taste." There are distinct sensory politics and ideologies at play here. It might seem that a focus on the brain, what Elizabeth Fein (2020) calls the "neurodevelopmental turn," renders the terrain apolitical, as deaf children ostensibly have hearing brains and are harnessing their potential to be auditory. These neuro-claims, however, are politically fraught despite the fact that neuroscientists conducting brain research do not make any normative claims about any particular configuration of the sensorium being more or less optimal.[15] In AVT circles, a normative value is placed on audition above all else. Ideological claims are made that audition is the "fastest sense" and that auditory dominance can result in improved academic performance (Flexer and Rhoades 2016, 24, 29). These references to speed and performance also point to the importance of functioning optimally within capitalist systems (Malabou 2008; Martin 2007). And let us not forget that the channeling of potential occurs through exteriorized social, familial, and educational scaffolding; the work of "forcing" a child to hear happens in the domain of therapeutic and everyday life.

AVT in India

As noted above, there are currently only five AVT practitioners in India, although there are therapists working toward certification and others who hope to become certified in the future. Certification is an achievement and a class, educational, and linguistic privilege, because of the foundational training in speech and language therapy required, the monetary expense, the time and mentorship required, and the fact that the certification exam is administered only in English and Spanish. As one certified therapist in India told me, having AVT certification opens doors to domestic and international conferences (such as the one mentioned above) and to consulting, as well as to membership in a global AVT community. Two of the certified therapists currently operate their own clinics, two are employed by a cochlear implant manufacturer, and the fifth runs a parent advocacy organization; all conduct short-term AVT courses and trainings around the country, consult with other clinics and practitioners, and give lectures. They also mentor other potential AVT practitioners and conduct remote or video sessions with families and deaf children in other countries.[16] When I visited the two therapists with their own clinics, the cochlear implant company posters on the walls and the abundant (often imported) toys and books throughout made me think I could be in a U.S.-based clinic. At the same time, I was aware that these were only two of many clinics in India, and that, for the most part, these therapists served both carefully chosen and self-selected elite and upper-class families (although one therapist worked with a foundation that provided free implantation to children below the poverty line).

As more children and adults in India become implanted, AVT practitioners and cochlear implant corporations stress that additional AVT specialists are needed. Current AVT practitioners have been lobbying the Rehabilitation Council of India for an AVT course, and a cochlear implant corporation is currently working with the Ali Yavar Jung National Institute of Speech and Hearing Disabilities to run an AVT diploma course. There is an ongoing debate in professional speech and language therapy circles about who has sufficient skills and training to work with implanted children and whether the existing audiology and speech and language pathology curriculum, which includes multisensory approaches, is sufficient. AVT expertise is surrounded by much gatekeeping and boundary policing. For example, at the 2019 conference of the Cochlear Implant Group of India, a certified AVT practitioner chided another therapist who was not certified for saying that she practices AVT with children.

In addition to policing each other and staking out a unique professional space of their own, AVT practitioners express frustration with surgeons and audiologists, who, they claim, do not value them. Speech and language therapists do the most important work with families and children on their cochlear implant journeys, these therapists argue. The often-repeated mantra is that surgery is 10 to 20 percent of the work of implantation, and the rest of the work is therapy.[17] An agitated therapist stood up in the Rehabilitation Hall at the 2019 CIGI conference and said: "The surgeons need to be in here listening to these presentations. They need to see how important our work is and not just focus on numbers of surgeries done." (Only one surgeon attended sessions in the Rehabilitation Hall, which was the conference's smallest and most sparsely attended presentation room; the largest and most crowded was the Surgical Hall, followed by the Audiology

Hall.) I mention this therapist's sentiment to point out the larger terrain of contested skill in which AVT practitioners and other therapists work. AVT practitioners told me that they must work constantly to prove their value to surgeons and families, especially because they have made large financial and time commitments to an international certifying body, charge higher fees than many other therapists, and run specialized practices.

In addition to critiquing surgeons for not valuing them, AVT practitioners differentiate themselves from speech therapists. For example, a certified AVT specialist named Aruna criticized current Indian therapy practices by stressing that speech therapists in India focus only on speech, not language. She said that therapists teach children as if they are parrots, drilling them to repeat words.[18] This is something that mothers might do as well and that AVT practitioners try to rectify: in an AVT session in Mumbai that I observed, a therapist worked with a mother of a three-year-old boy who was recently implanted. The therapist wanted to make sure that the mother was not instructing her child to repeat words. The mother had been saying, for example, "Say pencil," or "Say giraffe." The therapist told her that this practice was not helpful to her child; instead she should have "natural conversations" with her child in which they take turns talking.

Aruna told me that she teaches language through AVT principles, in contrast to what she considers to be "drill-based" and "unnatural" speech therapy.[19] She "stimulate[s] the auditory brain, at least for children under five," because "audition is the only modality through which fluent and perfect speech can develop." In addition, children older than three who are "habitual lipreaders" can be made into auditory listeners through techniques like the "auditory sandwich," which involves first speaking without letting the child see your lips, then repeating and allowing the child to lipread, and then "closing" the sequence by saying the same thing with only audition again.[20] This method uses carefully scaffolded and hierarchically organized sensory sequencing—listening before seeing and then listening again—in order to create appropriate sensing.

Aruna said that the most important part of her job is helping children become appropriately *social.* Similarly, another AVT practitioner, emphasizing the social work that she does, said that she teaches children not only language but also conversation. In her words: "A lot of these children have the language, [but] they don't have the conversation, they don't have the conversational skills, they don't have the social skills." Social skills are defined as engaging in dyadic turn-taking and in contextually sensible and linguistically expansive conversation. AVT practitioners in India and elsewhere stressed that the children with whom they worked were not only age appropriate in their general knowledge, language, and social skills but often ahead of their peers—all of the therapy had paid off.[21] AVT is thus envisioned as creating highly social and intelligent children. However, speech, specifically nondeaf speech, is still the goal. (Aruna was particularly concerned with ensuring that children did not have "deaf speech" or "deaf accents.") What about other parts of the brain and forms of life more generally that are not stimulated?

Aruna became an AVT professional through her personal journey with her deaf son. After he was diagnosed, she toured different centers and educational institutions across India. She was unsatisfied because she did not meet deaf children with "good speech" or who were using the latest hearing technologies. Aruna learned about the well-known correspondence course offered by the John Tracy Center, through which she received a curriculum in the mail, and she attended one of the center's international summer clinics in Los Angeles.[22] She also spent thousands of dollars purchasing every book available from AG Bell. She was excited to learn about cochlear implants, and her son became one of the first implanted children in India at the age of two. Aruna's primary goal is to teach parents to work with their deaf children, and she does this in her cozy and cheerful clinic full of imported books and toys; she does creative art projects with the children and hosts music sessions for them as well. Because her clinic is full of multisensory endeavors, whenever I visited I was always taken aback by the constant return to audition.

I frequently asked therapists about isolating audition. On one hand, therapists were quick to tell me that during typical conversation we use all of our senses. As one of them put it, "When we sit together and talk, we look at each other, we use all of our senses." On the other hand, therapists emphasized that such conversation cannot happen automatically with deaf children: they need training to become five-sensed (to use John Croft's words). Initially, then, the therapist must focus solely on audition. Other senses can be engaged only once the child is "confident" in audition and the therapist is certain that the child depends on audition and has a robust "auditory system."[23]

However, this privileging of audition is the goal only for children who are young enough and do not have other disabilities. One therapist told me that for children with multiple disabilities she makes "concessions": she makes her lips "available to the child and will sit facing the child." Concessions and reliance were two concepts that therapists used to discuss visuality. Why not think instead about the affordances of different communication modalities and look at multisensory engagement positively? Indeed, in their work on normative communicative engagement, Elinor Ochs, Olga Solomon, and Laura Sterponi (2005, 560) point out that "communicative habitus is not neutral with respect to its influence on children's development, in the sense that habitus does not necessarily maximize communicative potential." What are some other means of cultivating potential and reimagining communication?

While I sat with Zahra in anticipation of an Indian Independence Day celebration at her center, a ten-year-old girl in a flowing orange dress and green-and-white barrettes came over to her to say hello and to ask why Zahra was not wearing any orange, white, or green clothing, as everyone had been told to dress in the colors of the Indian flag. Zahra gently turned the child so that she was facing away from her and leaned over to speak into her ear. She said that she had forgotten to dress up, and she asked the girl if she was going to sing the national anthem as part of the celebration. She held the girl's waist tenderly and spoke warmly. When I asked Zahra about how she communicated with the girl, she said that the girl could hear across the room, but she had always liked physical contact. She had insisted on sitting on Zahra's lap when she first attended the center as a small child. As she grew, she became too heavy for a lap, but she still needed touch, Zahra said. Here a touch served as an anchor, under the radar, as a supplement to audition, another form of engagement, or a means of cultivating potential, depending on how you look at it. Touch, as Erin Manning (2007, xv) argues, can be a form of relational worlding: "The proposition is that touch—every act of reaching toward—enables the creation of worlds."[24]

Six Sounds

Use of the Ling Six sound test is an important practice in AVT clinics and educational spaces, as well as in domestic settings. During this test, performed by a therapist, teacher, or parent, the child's back is turned to the speaker, so that the child cannot see the speaker's mouth. The speaker utters the following phonemes one at a time and waits for the child to repeat them back: [m], [ah], [oo], [ee], [sh], and [s]. These phonemes broadly represent the speech spectrum from 250 to 8,000 hertz and thus target and include low-, middle-, and high-frequency sounds. These sounds represent what is known in audiology and speech and language pathology worlds as the "speech banana" (as described in the Introduction) and encompass the frequencies of everyday speech and talk; this spectral range is the same as that tested by conventional audiometry. The Ling Six sound test is both diagnostic, in that it can identify whether assistive devices such as hearing aids or implants are working, and pedagogical, in that it aids in the child's detection, discrimination, and identification of speech. If a child can listen to and repeat the Ling Six sounds, this demonstrates that the auditory sense is primed and that the child is ready to listen.

I sat in early intervention classrooms in India where teachers called children up to the front of the room one by one to sit with their backs to them while they uttered the Ling Six sounds. I also observed children collectively reciting the sounds back in singsong cacophony. I visited clinics where therapists sat next to children, albeit carefully positioned so that the children could not see their mouths, and recited the sounds. It was easy to tell which children were new to the practice because they appeared unmoored: they tried to turn around and look at their teachers or therapists to read lips or seek assurances about whether their utterances were correct. In response, the teachers gently turned their heads back away. Children who were familiar with the Ling Six sounds were confident and repeated them effortlessly.

One Sunday afternoon I sat with a young boy and his mother as the mother and I talked about the work that she was doing to raise her son, specifically the work of talking to him constantly. She asked me about my earlier visit to her son's school, and I told her that it was interesting to see teachers doing Ling Six sound tests individually with children while the other children sat and gestured (quietly but noisily) with each other. She interrupted my observations to stress the importance of the Ling Six sound test, noting that she did it daily with her son. She called her son over for a demonstration, and he sat on the floor in front of us with his back to us. She said the sounds softly and he repeated them, with a smile on his face. He then wanted to give a friend sitting with us the same test, and he had her sit in front of him while he said the sounds—"mmmmm," "ahhhh," "oooooh," "eeeee," "shhhhhhh," and "ssssssss"—and she repeated them. This was all done with smiles and laughter (it was a performance).

The work of mastering and repeating these sounds has become a meaningful communicative practice and routine, a familiar ritual, that binds this mother and son together.

This mother had learned that the Ling Six sound test is a way to check that her son's hearing aids are working and that the hearing aids, child, and environment are interacting. She said that her son's listening to the six sounds and responding to them establishes that communication, teaching, and learning can begin. While she did not talk about this process in terms of signals, the Ling Six sound test detects whether auditory signals are being transmitted and received. It does not measure the emotional quality of these signals or the roles of other pathways and motivators in facilitating these signals. For example, in Zahra's conversation with the young girl, her gentle and loving touch might have helped the auditory signal reach the girl's ears.

How might we think of the role of emotion and desire in enabling the transduction of waves into the sounds that become the Ling Six sounds and communication in general? As Stefan Helmreich (2015, 226) states: "Transduction is the result of *work,* of labor that, when done well, produces a sense of seamless presence, presence we should not take for granted but rather should inquire into as itself a technical artifact." In this case, mothers do the difficult work of uttering and repeating these sounds while children labor to detect, discriminate, identify, and comprehend them; nothing about this process can be considered, in Helmreich's words, "seamless." The process itself is an example of what Jonathan Sterne and Tara Rodgers (2011, 48) term "signal labor." Neuroscientists have recently argued that deaf children and adults do additional work, or engage in increased listening effort, to receive what have been called the "degraded" or "impoverished" signals transmitted to them through hearing aids or cochlear implants.[25] According to this research, deaf children and adults work harder than nondeaf people to process information, and they need to recruit greater cognitive resources. Signal labor, indeed.

Carina Pals, Anastasios Sarampalis, and Deniz Başkent (2013, 1075) state that "listening effort can . . . be defined as the proportion of limited cognitive resources engaged in interpreting the incoming auditory signal. It has been suggested that the presence of noise or distortions in a speech signal increases cognitive demand and thus listening effort." I am not interested in claiming that deaf people with hearing aids and implants work through degraded signals (that is deficit framing). I am, however, invested in analyzing the stakes of the additional labor required and the way that a focus on audition assumes that there is only one signal or stimulus deserving of attention. AVT practitioners stress that noise is anything other than the target stimulus, which is speech.[26] Who decides what the target stimulus is? Noise is considered to be "antisocial" and a threat to the dominant social order (Novak 2015, 126); it gets in the way and obstructs the signal. However, we might also consider how noise offers up different social and relational cues as well as access to different signals. Marie Thompson (2017, 3) argues that noise is "a productive, transformative force-relation and a necessary component of material relations." There is no signal without noise.[27]

The Hand Cue

According to AVT practitioners, visual noise interrupts or prevents the reception of the auditory signal. Rose Croft's therapist did not stand in front of her and often walked around during their sessions. Two of Beebe's former students told me that Beebe did the same during sessions, and sometimes Beebe instructed them to face the wall so that their backs were to her. Beebe was strict, they said, and this was an example of "tough love."

When therapists and parents cover their mouths with their hands while speaking with deaf children to foreclose the possibility of lipreading, this is called the "hand cue." One does not just obstruct one's mouth: one uses a flat hand, angled slightly away from the mouth, and at least a few inches off the face, in order to minimize sound interference. On blogs and in chat rooms, therapists and parents discuss how to perform the hand cue properly: Should the hand be angled at forty-five degrees or ninety degrees? How far from the mouth should the hand be? Other ways of preventing lipreading include holding a book or a screen of some kind in front of the mouth, as well as the "natural" techniques of "visual distraction" (holding up stuffed animals, for example) and "joint attention" (focusing the child's attention on toys, books, or other objects rather than on the speaker).

While sitting in waiting rooms or in therapy sessions, I often saw mothers covering their mouths or tilting their heads away from their children. Sometimes their actions were obvious, but other times they were more subtle—a hand on a cheek, cupped fingers over a mouth. During a therapy session, the therapist and parent sit alongside or slightly behind the child and not across from the child, in order to minimize the possibility

A woman holds her hand in front of her mouth to perform the hand cue, a practice used to prevent deaf children from reading lips or attending to visual cues. The hand cue is well known as a symbol of AVT practice, although increasingly therapists engage other methods, including holding screens, books, or stuffed animals in front of their mouths or employing visual distraction techniques such as focusing the child on a toy or another object or person. These techniques are seemingly more "natural." Illustration by Adrean Clark.

of lipreading or other visual cues. The hand cue, when used in its simplest and most obvious form, prompts the child to begin "listening." It functions like another popular cue: pointing a finger at an ear and commanding the child to "Listen!" As Talbot (2016, 12) notes regarding the hand cue: "Children quickly learn that when the adult's hand is in place, they are expected to be listening. You may see the young child start to cover their mouths as they talk in the early stages of Auditory-Verbal Therapy." Children addressed in this way will do the same, as they see it as the appropriate way to engage with others.

The hand cue is designed to "integrate the five senses" (Rosenzweig 2011). According to this sensory ideology, isolation results in integration. However, I do not see what is sensorially evocative or social about covering one's mouth. Critics of this method argue that it obstructs or impedes sound from reaching its recipient, it is unnatural, and it is socially awkward; this concern about "social awkwardness" is compelling because AVT practitioners stress that they teach children to be social participants.[28] Covering or obstructing one's mouth when talking can be a barrier to joint attention at the same time it is ironically supposed to signal that it is time for listening and speaking. And thinking about signals, the hand cue also impedes other kinds of multisensory, multimodal, and multipersonal communication. Why not increase sensory input and signals all around? How might children benefit from multiple forms and modes of signals, especially considering that these children work through degraded auditory signals? AVT practitioners typically do not discuss deaf children's and adults' signal labor (Sterne and Rodgers 2011) or their greater cognitive load and effort.[29]

Stripes

In September 2018, I attended a training conducted by Purnima, an Indian AVT specialist. The training was for audiologists and speech and language pathologists in Delhi, and it included a discussion of an AVT case, which Purnima stressed was not a "star case." She introduced the case as follows: The child was two years old. Her parents wanted her to learn English and eventually attend an English medium school, although their primary language was Marathi. However, the mother's English was "not natural and the father did not speak English at all"; in pointing this out, Purnima was also indirectly providing the information that while this family was middle-class, they were not part of the English-speaking elite. When the girl's mother sang "Twinkle, Twinkle, Little Star," she sounded artificial and rocked her arms from side to side, giving visual cues. Purnima thus suggested that the family switch to their mother tongue, Marathi, which "provided a full language environment." ("Full" is an interesting choice of adjective.) According to Purnima, switching to Marathi

fulfilled the principles of AVT in that language should be natural, meaningful, and relevant. With Marathi, the child could communicate with her
grandparents at home in their joint family household. In addition to hearing loss, the child had seizures and facial dystonia. Purnima had contacted
the child's neurologist to learn about the seizures; Purnima stressed that
her work also focuses on the brain, and she emphasized her role as a health
professional and team player. In order to pay for the child's cochlear implant and surgery, the family sold their house and all of their gold. The
mother said that she would need to buy gold for her daughter's marriage
in the future, but she preferred to spend money on a cochlear implant now.
(A cochlear implant now would ostensibly make it easier for this mother
to find a good husband for her daughter in the future.) Purnima also told
the mother not to work outside the home for three years, or "there would
be no hope for the child." The family's long-run developmental trajectory
was thus abandoned in favor of the child's development in the present.
Slowly, Purnima said, "the child started becoming normal."

After giving us this case context and details, Purnima showed us a
video of a session with the family. In the video, we saw the girl's mother,
Purnima, the girl, and her father (in that order) sitting on one side of a
small wooden table in a cozy therapy room. There were bright pictures
behind the table, a tablecloth and a pitcher of water on the table, and toys
on the floor in various bins. First the group discussed who wanted water
and who would pour it. Then they examined a bin with plastic animals and
discussed the animals they saw. Purnima planned to introduce the topic of
"stripes" in this session. Before the session, she called the father to tell him
to wear a striped shirt, and she too wore stripes. (The mother did not own
a striped shirt.) During the session, Purnima pointed to the striped shirts,
and a "natural" discussion about stripes took place.

Throughout her running commentary to us as we watched the video,
Purnima stressed how much planning goes into lessons; nothing is done
without premeditation. Lessons are carefully tailored to the family (and
not just to the deaf child's brain), with specific activities and goals documented in lesson plans. Her goals for this lesson were to expand the child's
language and move her from one-word to multiple-word responses, to encourage her to use social communication such as "please" and "thank you,"
and to introduce "stripes." Purnima finished this overview of her lesson by
telling the therapists present, "In the past, we did therapy in very difficult

situations. Your situations are much easier." She said that today's therapists have better technology, more sophisticated toys, and less noisy rooms. Just as deaf children have access to better technology, so do AVT practitioners. Her implication was that there is no excuse for not attaining a listening and spoken language outcome.

In a forty-five-minute session I observed with a different therapist in Mumbai, a three-year-old boy, his mother, and his grandmother were invited into the therapy room after they had taken turns knocking on the therapy room door. This activity was designed to demonstrate sound detection. After settling around a small table and starting with the Ling Six sound test, the therapist playfully read a picture book about jungle animals with the child and then facilitated a sequential ordering exercise with cards featuring pictures of a boy with balloons that are subsequently popped. In a final activity, the child was given a doll to place in different positions, such as sitting, eating, and sleeping. Throughout the session, the therapist patiently explained to the child's mother what she was doing and why. Every activity had a goal. The therapist was working on audition with the book about jungle animals; the card sequencing was for cognition, vocabulary, and emotions; and the positioning of the doll was to teach verbs.

The AVT sessions that I observed were happy, playful, and engaging. A young adult told me that he loved therapy as a child because adult attention was showered on him and he was able to play with toys and read books. A U.S.-based AVT practitioner stressed that she wanted her therapy sessions to be the highlight of the children's week, and that she measured success initially by whether or not the children and their families were smiling during sessions. However, despite the existence of toys, books, creative projects, and enthusiastically inflected speech to anchor, contextualize, and animate these literal "language games" (Wittgenstein 2009), multiple modalities are not permitted in most AVT sessions. Despite the nurturing and lighthearted manner that permeates these sessions, in which work and play are intertwined (Goodley and Runswick-Cole 2010) and "magical and pretty worlds" are created (Mattingly 2010, 209), there are hard boundaries around what is acceptable in terms of communicating and relating in AVT sessions. It is also difficult for me to fully be at home in a space where lipreading is considered taboo, where such a signal—and form of connection—is blocked. I have a vivid fieldwork memory of an AVT session in which an animated therapist spoke but also gestured. The five-year-old boy with whom she worked had eyes that darted constantly to look at her hands, seemingly searching for a meaningful signal.

Everything

I contrast these AVT sessions with another session I observed, also with a three-year-old child who had recently been implanted, this time in Pune. The therapist was a young woman named Tanima who worked with a large caseload of deaf children from all over Maharashtra. Mothers and their children arrived at the clinic for their therapy appointments after long bus journeys. The stakes were high, in that if the child was tired or hungry, the forty-five-minute session would not go well. In this session held in a small, brightly lit therapy room, Tanima perched directly in front of the child, who sat in an old-fashioned wooden high chair. The girl's mother was positioned next to Tanima, and two young interns sat next to the girl. When I arrived, the group was reading a picture-book story about a bear participating in different activities of daily life, from getting dressed to brushing teeth to playing with friends. The child looked sleepy and distracted. Tanima worked to engage her by constantly talking to her in an animated and enthusiastic way, showing her the pictures in the book and moving her hands to touch them, and gesturing. After reading the book, Tanima, the interns, and the girl's mother asked the girl to pass them objects in front of her, and when she did, they said, "Aacha!" (Good!) and used a hand gesture. The session included touching, gesturing, miming and mimicking, looking at pictures, talking, and listening. I was struck that Tanima sat directly in front of the girl, made eye contact, and actively manipulated her hands, trying to get her to communicate. She was like a marionettist in her work to animate the girl, although the goal was for spoken language to emanate from the girl herself without facilitation or prompting.

When Tanima and I discussed her creative use of different modalities, she said that she just "knew" what to do in the moment and that she was not following a method. Tanima had been exposed to a stream of international visitors sharing AVT and other auditory therapy methodologies, many of these visits sponsored by cochlear implant companies. Tanima said that she "learned many approaches from different people . . . but we do whatever the child needs." The claim of providing "whatever the child needs" was something I heard from other therapists as well. They criticized what they called the elitist bias of AVT and stressed their desire to do whatever it takes to allow communication and development to happen. State-employed therapists in particular stressed that they could not focus only on AVT because, unlike therapists who can "cherry-pick" the families with whom they work, government therapists must work with all families. These therapists discussed the importance of "total communication," a term often used to refer to the use of gesture with some Indian Sign Language lexicon as well as visual and tactile modes of communicating. Many AVT practitioners, surgeons, audiologists, and others speak of "total communication" as negative, sloppy, and unrefined, an approach of last resort. In this conception, total communication is not language, and it certainly is not listening and spoken language. However, there are other ways of defining total communication.

According to Mervin Garretson (1976, 89) and Lionel Evans (1982, 21), total communication is a philosophy and not a method; it is meant to be flexible and person centered. It does not map onto manualism or sign language; rather, it combines "aural/oral-manual modes according to the communicative needs and expressive-receptive threshold of the individual" (Garretson 1976, 89). More than this, total communication supports "the moral right of the hearing impaired, as with normally hearing bilinguals, to maximum input in order to attain optimal comprehension and total understanding in the communication situation" (Garretson 1976, 89). Total communication draws upon speech, sign, gesture, finger spelling, pantomime, drawing, writing, and touch—it can involve all modalities, and it is designed to meet the needs of deaf people (and presumably all people), whatever they might be (Evans 1982).[30]

This approach articulates with Margaret Mead's ([1964] 1972) use of the concept of "total communication," which she introduced in a conference presentation titled "Vicissitudes of the Study of the Total Communication Process." Mead stressed the importance of attending to and valuing multimodality across the disciplines and called for a more nuanced study of communication beyond linguistic utterances. With this in mind, it makes sense that those focused on auditory verbal approaches would be critical of total communication as a philosophy and as an approach, as it expands how we think about communication beyond language. Total communication could also be considered an example of what Pentcheva (2006, 631, 650) calls synesthesis, or "consonant sensation," situations in which "sight, touch, hearing, smell, and taste are engaged simultaneously." If listening is supposed to be a (unisensory) way of life, total communication functions as a threat, as does the potential unruliness and nonnormativity of a multi-sensory and multimodal approach.

I hold on to the concept of total communication as a provocative and aspirational philosophy because it opens up possibilities for communicating outside of standard categorical statements about what communication is and is not. I do not know how it would unfold as a systematic method, but I imagine that it would draw upon what Charles Goodwin (2017) terms "co-operative action" and what Mara Green (2014b) conceptualizes as people's moral orientation and attunement toward making communication successful. Total communication as analytic and approach resonates with recent work on multimodality in deaf studies and sociolinguistics. Annelies Kusters et al. (2017) call for attention to deaf people's diverse semiotic repertoires as a way to depart from an approach that sees languages as bounded and unimodal systems. Instead, they argue, people bring a multiplicity of modes with which to communicate. As they note, "Blommaert and Backus (2013) explain that 'A repertoire is composed of a myriad of different communicative tools, with different degrees of functional specialization. No single resource is a communicative panacea; none is useless'" (222). The idea that no single resource is a panacea is important to consider in light of the value focused on listening and spoken language. Indeed, as Kusters et al. observe, attending to semiotic repertoires enables "a *holistic* perspective, taking into account inequalities and power differences by paying attention to hierarchies of resources, and to lack of accessibility to resources" (228). I share their concerns with the ways that semiotic resources are differentially valued in the creation of communication—and communication categories—and I am also concerned with sensory access (also see De Meulder et al. 2019). Additionally, I am interested in destabilizing the value affixed to different sensory modalities and the creation of distinct sensory repertoires and hierarchies of the senses.

The immense diversity of semiotic and sensory repertoires is left out in the binary created between manualism and oralism, the focus on aurality as unisensory and unimodal, and the creation of neat communication categories along a continuum. I am reminded of deaf educator Patricia Scherer's (1972, 553) statement during a heated debate at the 1972 AG Bell conference between educators and researchers advocating for total communication and those supporting oralism: "I like to present 'total communication' for deaf children as the English language on the hands, on the lips, supported by residual hearing, supported by everything that is needed to assure the communicator that he sends a clear message to the receiver. During this act of communication, the child is observed and he tells you how he needs to learn language. You must then respond to him in the channel or the way that is best suited to meet his particular and specific needs." Later in the debate, Scherer concluded: "'Total communication' for me breaks down the barrier of deafness because it is simply . . . 'the reaching out of one man's soul to another'" (560). I see this statement in contrast with AVT practitioners' above-discussed concerns with closed doorways to the brain.[31] What about other doorways and paths?[32]

Recall Tanima's approach to therapy, which involves doing "whatever works." Similarly, consider comments made by a cochlear implant surgeon named Dr. Swarnad, who runs a series of early intervention programs, a school for deaf children up to six years of age, and a training program for mothers of deaf children throughout Maharashtra and Goa. Initially during our first meeting, he emphatically declared that his programs were "purely AVT. We only use AVT in our schools. Our children need to listen and speak." However, a short while later in our conversation, he changed his tune. He said: "Actually, I am going to tell you something that you probably do not want to hear. There is a Sanskrit word and concept called *sahishnuta*. This word means 'many paths.' Indians, we pray to Krishna, we go to church, we go to the mosque, we do everything. The same we do for communication in our school. We use total communication, whatever works." While Dr. Swarnad invoked a romanticized vision of Hindu forbearance and tolerance, I hold on to the importance of attuning to a child or person and being open to different senses and modalities. A focus on becoming auditory prevents such attunement and openness.

Ultimately, as Ochs, Solomon, and Sterponi (2005, 548) argue, "the habitus of a speech community may poorly serve the communicative development of the child, yet mature speakers may find themselves at a loss to improvise alternative strategies and persist with their default child-directed communicative practices." In the next chapter, we move out of the clinic to early intervention and pedagogical spaces in which families (particularly mothers) want to do everything possible. They are, however, instructed by professionals to limit, rather than stretch, their communicative practices and to exclude different senses and modalities. They are discouraged from "improvis[ing] alternative strategies" or orienting through total communication. Yet they find ways to make communication happen. Despite instructions or their absence, mothers and children work through diverse signals and engage in signal labor (Sterne and Rodgers 2011). They intersense and orient toward each other in multisensory and multimodal ways, creating infrastructures of care.

3
_____

Mothers' Work

Intersensing and Learning to Talk like a Cricket Commentator

> *To intimate is to communicate with the sparest of signs and gestures, and at its root intimacy has the quality of eloquence and brevity. But intimacy also involves an aspiration for a narrative about something shared, a story about both oneself and others that will turn out in a particular way.*
>
> —Lauren Berlant

A Mother's Sense

On an unusually warm and sunny day in February 2019, a colleague and I chatted in a coffee shop in New Delhi. We sipped *kanji,* a fermented carrot juice that is a winter specialty, and talked about early intervention and education for small children with cochlear implants. My colleague, who runs an early intervention and education program for deaf children in Delhi, commented, "The problem with so many approaches now to early intervention is that mothers are no longer mothers, they are forced to become therapists!" We then looked at our glasses and thought about how the juice—its color, flavor, texture, and consistency, as well as the glass tumbler that held it—would turn into a teachable object in an interaction between an imagined mother and her implanted child. The idealized mother-as-therapist in this moment would talk to her child at length about this glass of *kanji.*

The small act of drinking and savoring this special winter delicacy would be stretched out as an opportunity to teach vocabulary and new concepts. We speculated that the mother would tell the child that the tumbler is made from glass and that glass is fragile, that carrots are an orange vegetable grown in the soil in Punjab, what it means that the carrots are fermented, and that the drink is both spicy and sweet, among other things. We could have gone on and on. Our café conversation resonated with a discussion

I had with a mother in Delhi who narrated the process and aftermath of having her small daughter implanted. This mother told me about how she had to completely transform her mothering practices: "Now I am a speech therapist, a teacher, and a special educator as well." In her statement, meant to be humorous, like the discussion between my colleague and me, there was a realization that mothers are required to play multiple roles in interacting with, teaching, and caring for their deaf children. Drinking juice is never just drinking juice.

In this chapter, I move out of the clinic to think through what a seasoned deaf education teacher in Mumbai told me: "Mothers need to be like cricket commentators, they need to speak about everything they do and see. When at the market, they must constantly talk about the fruits and vegetables they are looking at, and if a potato is dirty, for example, they must point this out. It is not like with hearing children who can overhear things. You must tell a deaf child everything." Scholars of childhood in India have argued that Indian children often learn from each other during play rather than learning from adults. Scholars also point to the role of distributed parenting and caring, and stress that it is rare for Indian mothers and children to form exclusive communicative dyads.[1] Children often learn through overhearing; as Veena Das (1989, 270) observes, in Punjabi, there are two distinct verbs: *kehna,* to tell someone something, and *sunana,* to cause someone to overhear. She notes: "It is not a single imperative voice that the child hears in Indian society but a multitude of voices" (279). What happens when mothers and children are supposed to be together constantly and the children do not hear a multitude of voices, but instead orient solely to the voices of their mothers?

Cochlear implantation—and working with deaf children in general—introduces new ways of relating to children through language, specifically through the need to narrate and stretch out everyday words and worlds, using the ordinary and the domestic as spaces of language development. Mothers focus on the senses, and on sensory attachments and attunements, as cultivated through ongoing talk and choreographies of attention (Tulbert and Goodwin 2011); they do this while making tea, taking walks, and washing floors, for example. They scaffold everyday life in a manner that dyadically binds them and their children to each other in intersensing ways.[2] Brendan Hart (2014, 288) studied parents of autistic children in the United States and Morocco, and found that they establish practices through which they make their children's actions and words intelligible.

He terms this "joint embodiment," which he defines as "an improvised social choreography whereby parents and child prompt each another verbally, gesturally and physically as they together move through the social world." What is at stake is how mothers and children sense together.[3]

I attend to joint embodiment, specifically the ways in which mothers intersense with their children and engage in anticipatory sensing in order to facilitate their children's sensory engagement with the world. The methods and principles of engagement that I observed in the mothers I interviewed were not based on auditory verbal therapy (as discussed in chapter 2), at least not all of the time. Instead of adhering to a unisensory approach focused solely on listening and spoken language, the mothers engaged in therapeutic and everyday talk that was frequently multisensory and multimodal, often to the dismay of authoritative figures. I focus on the everyday stretching of the social through linguistic, sensory, and multimodal communicative processes in educational spaces in which deaf children and their mothers spend time.

By "stretching the social," I mean that mothers actively work to find and create opportunities to be social with their children, in ways that transcend a focus on a single sense and that at times go against the grain of what therapists and early intervention teachers and experts advise. Stretching the social also means that mothers actively work to produce a social world in which their children are valid and valued sensing participants. Mothers attempt to scaffold their children's senses and attend to a variety of signals, beyond the auditory, to include these in daily life. While in some cases mothers focus on listening and spoken language outcomes, or have been taught to attend to them, multisensory and multimodal communicative practices and nonlinguistic forms of care also loom large.

The surgeons, therapists, audiologists, and mothers I spoke with stressed repeatedly that there are two "senses" at stake: the child's auditory sense and also the ostensibly intuitive and "natural" sense of the mother. These two senses are expansive: outside of AVT spaces, the auditory sense often includes lipreading, reading, and memorization. The maternal sense includes learning how to be an outspoken and articulate mother, in addition to a speech therapist, teacher, and special educator, as we saw above. There is tension here, as the founder of a well-known early intervention program told me: "It's really the common sense and the wisdom of a mother. More than any scientific qualification." The boundaries between what is "natural" common sense and what is considered to be "scientific practice" are often blurred, and there are times when mothers are asked to resist doing "what comes naturally," like snuggling with their children, sitting face-to-face with them, or communicating with them nonverbally. Mothers are required to learn what is natural from experts, and in the process, they have to second-guess themselves. The auditory and maternal senses, while seemingly innate, must develop together relationally through "hard work." This work involves creating and participating in sensory infrastructures that are social, pedagogical, therapeutic, and technological. Mothers and their deaf children thus engage in processes of becoming both who they already are and something new. They do so in relation to each other, in a jointly embodied and intersensing way.

In the discussion that follows, I move between two early intervention and educational programs, one in Chennai and the other in Bangalore, both started by mothers of deaf children. Focusing on mothers' and children's experiences, I draw from interviews and time spent with mothers who attended these programs with their children and/or visited them for instruction and guidance. I am not interested in adjudicating or evaluating these programs; both produce important and valued relational infrastructure for mothers and children. These are just two of many programs in India, and mothers and children often cycle through multiple centers and draw on different therapeutic approaches, practicing what Siri Mehus (2011) calls "semiotic bricolage." "Sensory bricolage" might be another term to describe these practices.[4] Each program has its own approach, often guided by a particular sensory ideology, although the ultimate goal of all programs is for children to develop "language," whatever that means. Reaching this goal typically involves a focus on listening and spoken language, sometimes incorporating lipreading, gesturing, tactile stimulation, reading, writing, and sign language. As discussed in chapter 2, there is a complex classification system and set of values attached to different modalities. My point is that these spaces are messy in terms of the modalities and pedagogical approaches employed, despite what administrators might say.

Hard Work

Many of the therapists, clinicians, teachers, and administrators with whom I spoke had steadfast ideas about how mothers should communicate with their deaf children. They critiqued mothers' inability to speak nonstop with their children and the fact that the mothers were often shy, quiet, and un-educated. (Sometimes they criticized both parents, but typically mothers bore the brunt because fathers were seen as responsible for earning money.) Mothers, according to the professionals, needed to be taught how to relate to their children differently and appropriately. Forget about warm cuddles, making nurturing meals, or simply being in proximity—what is important is *to talk.* An audiologist and speech and language pathologist in Delhi told me about a conversation she had just had with young parents as they left her office carrying their deaf child: "When the mother was about to leave and she got up, that's when I told her that from now on you have to start speaking with the child. Whatever you are thinking, whatever you are doing, whatever you plan to do, all that has to become verbal." Mothers are supposed to talk about ordinary everyday activities, such as chopping vegetables, packing a suitcase, and drinking milk, so they do not need any specialized knowledge. They must, however, learn how to talk, and to talk constantly.

In addition to honing their abilities to become "natural" mothers, mothers must negotiate the fact that a deaf child does not have only one age, but instead occupies multiple ages simultaneously. One of these is the child's chronological age. Then, after receiving hearing aids, the child has a "hearing birthday" and a hearing age. After implantation, the child also has an implanted age. The child's hearing and implanted ages inevitably lag behind the chronological age because the child's listening and spoken language ability has not (yet) developed. More than this, a cochlear implant surgeon told me that, in fact, the "child is hearing mother's voice in the last three months of the pregnancy. So a deaf child is already twelve weeks deaf by the time [the] child is born." Based on this surgeon's assessment, a child also has a "deaf age" that starts before the actual birth. Deaf children are therefore behind before they are born.[5]

Mothers, and families in general, are thus oriented to both normative developmental time and an alternate chronology in which they hope that their child's hearing age will eventually "catch up" with the child's chrono-logical age—an achievement that depends on the mothers' "hard work" (in Hindi, *mehanat*). Because of these multiple ages and birthdays, mothers are required to care for children who are simultaneously different ages. I met a mother with a three-year-old child who was also a newborn in hearing age. Similarly, another mother had a five-year-old child who was simultaneously a two-year-old in hearing age and a six-month-old in implanted age. For mothers, negotiating these different ages takes great skill and flexibility.

Mehanat is a concept that came up often in Delhi and other Hindi-speaking locations when parents, again particularly mothers, spoke about all the time and talk they put into their deaf children. When I asked a therapist in Delhi what *mehanat* means, she shared with me an expression,

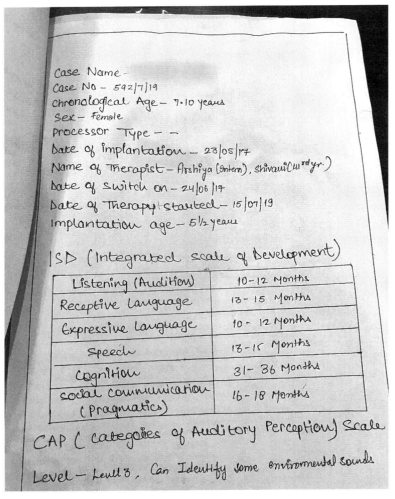

A page from a child's case file shows that the child is multiple ages at once. The child's chronological age, implant age, and ages on various developmental scales are noted. Families, specifically mothers, are expected to attend to their children's multiple ages. Photograph by author.

"Mehanat ka phal mitha hota hai," which translates to "Hard work bears sweet fruit." The hard work, she said, is figuring out how to give your children complex instructions that they will understand; finding ways to teach them to identify different fruits, vegetables, and other objects; reading stories with them; and looking at pictures or experience books and discussing them. Hard work literally results in sweet fruit, or at least naming the fruit. While *mehanat* is a concept used widely by parents to talk about the work they do in raising their children (those with and without disabilities), it has specific stakes in regard to deaf children in terms of these children being both "behind" their appropriate hearing age and malleably open to intervention. As professionals constantly stress the urgent need for early intervention and the existence of a critical period, parents feel a great deal of pressure to work hard *now*.

In July 2018, I attended a parents' function at an early intervention NGO in Delhi that was run by a passionate older man with an adult deaf daughter. The director, known to everyone as Sir, began his lecture by talking about how "HI [hearing impaired] children" are not the same as normal children in terms of how they acquire language. Their hearing birthday is when they get their hearing aids or implants. He said that parents and families must do *mehanat*. Parents must talk to their child about everything—clothes, food, seasons, holidays—and they should make a book with pictures and words to teach their child. About books in general, he said, "You must read the same book again and again and go through the story again and again." The director stressed that *mehanat* should not be done only by mothers: "Fathers have the same responsibility too, it does not only fall upon the mother. Parents must sit and teach their child for two and a half hours in the morning and one hour in the evening." A father timidly interrupted Sir's lecture to interject that he left for work at 5:30 a.m. Sir replied, even more animatedly, that the man should wake up at 3:00 a.m. to teach his child. "The full family needs to be involved in the hard work."

In the midst of his speech, Sir glared at parents who arrived late and asked them, "Why are you late for your child?" Noticing parents who were not taking notes, he asked, "Why aren't you writing things down? You should bring a notebook and write all of this down." The main point of his talk was that "HI children can be like normal, it is just that they cannot hear." He spoke about his daughter, who "is 100 percent deaf but can talk like a normal person." This director's focus on sitting, reading, and teaching was an outlier in the therapeutic and pedagogical worlds in which I spent time; most therapists, schoolteachers, and administrators with whom I met stressed that such a pedagogical focus would be boring for the child and would not be natural. Additionally, the three and a half hours of talk that Sir recommended would not be considered enough, and his comment that "HI children can be like normal, it is just that they cannot hear" would not be acceptable to AVT practitioners, who would argue that these children can become normal and can hear. I focus on Sir's admonitions because of the temporal, logistical, and pedagogical pressure he placed on families.

Mehanat does not mean hard work just in the sense of laboring and toiling; it also connotes work that is virtuous, upstanding, and morally good. Someone who is *mehanati* (hardworking) is industrious and teachable, capable of improvement. The goal of performing *mehanat* is to produce a valuable outcome, although parents and re/habilitation practitioners emphasized that the process is also important. Returning to the idea that someone who is *mehanati* is a teachable person, I stress that it is primarily mothers who are malleably learning to modulate their talk and ways of relating to their children. They are cultivating their maternal sense as well as their children's auditory sense. I recall the words of a mother in Mumbai who told me that she was "blabbering her heart out" with her son. While this is a colloquial and loving phrase, her words obscured the work that she put into communicating with her child and the ways that "blabbering" demonstrates love and care. Among other things, she labeled all of her household objects, created an experience book containing pictures of important people and activities in their family, and talked with her son constantly about daily life. She had been trained to do this by various re/habilitation professionals, and then she worked with her son. She is now a therapist herself, working with other mothers and children. A number of mothers told me about learning an entirely new language, typically English, with which to communicate with their children. In one case (as described in my Introduction), an extended family spoke Marathi with a deaf child, allowing her to lipread. After the child was implanted, the family was instructed to use only English and not to let the child see their mouths; the elderly grandparents also learned English so that they could communicate with the child. This work of the grandparents was considered true *mehanat*.

Consider Imran's family, with whom I spent time in Delhi and whose case I discuss at length in chapter 5. When I met him, Imran was twelve years old, although his birth certificate indicated he was ten. He and his family lived in a village that was a five-hour journey from Delhi. He was implanted in Delhi when he was five years of age, after his family struggled to cobble together the needed money. Before his implantation, Imran had not learned how to listen and speak with hearing aids. After a few weeks of therapy following the implantation surgery, Imran's family moved back to the village, where Imran attended the village school. There, he was told to sit in a corner and did not develop listening and spoken language. The family moved to Delhi when he was ten, after relatives told them of an NGO in the city that would provide therapy. Imran started receiving therapy from the NGO, and his parents enrolled him in a government school, using his altered birth certificate to claim he was two years younger than he was. This cheerful, intuitive, and snuggly twelve-year-old shared a classroom with much younger children, most of them seven years of age. At that point, however, Imran's hearing age was at most four years. Like other deaf children, Imran occupies multiple ages at once, and in his case there was the specter of the looming chronological teenage years to come, when he would no longer be as cute and cuddly as his hearing age might imply.

Shortly after the family moved to Delhi, Imran's implant processor stopped working, and his parents contacted different NGOs for financial support for a replacement. However, NGO administrators and professionals told them that they had missed out on a critical period for teaching Imran language, and that it was now too late (and funders were uninterested in paying for a new processor). In reply, his father plaintively told them, "Hamare sidhe se to kare mehanat, jitna kar paye utne kiye" (From our side, we did a lot of hard work, and whatever we could do, we did). Both he and Imran's mother stressed that they took the big step of moving from the village to Delhi and that they were doing everything they could do. Their hard work could be seen in their body language, the way that they looked at Imran, and the stories they told about the sacrifices they had made. However, the director of the NGO where they attended therapy told me that they had been doing *mehanat* only from the time that they brought Imran to the NGO. Prior to then, they did not know about, and were not engaged in, re/habilitation. The director did not recognize their moving to the city, spending large sums of money, and making material sacrifices as *mehanat*—to her, *mehanat* is the actual work of re/habilitation.[6]

Mehanat cannot be disentangled from care, although professionals emphatically consider certain kinds of care to not be *mehanat*. According to them, there are right and wrong ways of caring for one's child, specifically involving senses, modalities, and ways of relating. As the director of an institute for speech and hearing in Bangalore told me: "Psychologically, children are connected to their mothers from conception. The baby knows the mother's body, breast milk, voice, smell. The child only wants their mother and the mother has the most patience for the child." (A male administrator uttered this statement.) I also heard mothers at the training program based at the director's institute repeat the same words, emphasizing the patience that mothers have for their children and highlighting mothers' unique abilities to work hard to teach their children so that "magic would happen" and their children would start listening and talking. However, bodily knowledge and intimate familiarity can become obstacles if they prevent verbal communication.

Indeed, according to certain professionals, caring for one's child in a nonlinguistic way can be a problem, and this is where ideas about mother–child attachment such as those expressed by the above-mentioned director become fraught. In Mumbai, a passionate audiologist and speech and language pathologist who started audiology and speech and language clinics across India told me that Indian children in general have "a high EQ," or emotional quotient. According to her, mothers hug and kiss their children and offer them physical contact instead of talking to them. Such mothers "hold their babies in their arms instead of placing them in a pram." As we talked, she pointed to a family sitting in the waiting room as an example. The family, from northeast India, had traveled to Mumbai for their small child to get bilateral implants. The audiologist described the mother as someone who carefully attends to her child, but who does not talk and is very shy. "How will this child learn?" she asked, not making a distinction between what mothers do in public and what they do at home. Mothers need to focus on verbal intelligence and not emotional intelligence, she stressed, creating a binary between the two and emphasizing that Indian women and Indian society in general are good at the latter. Similarly, another professional, a bit more moderate in her approach, told me that the best place for young deaf children is sitting on their mothers' laps, facing outward; this allows for touch while maximizing the child's listening.

Professionals constantly adjudicate good and bad mothers. At a Mumbai-based NGO that was providing free cochlear implants to children through a flagship program, I sat in on the deliberations of the evaluation team, which comprised a surgeon, an audiologist, and a program administrator. As the team members were deciding which families were deserving of cochlear implants, they discussed the mothers' educational backgrounds and qualifications. In one case, a mother did not have formal education, and the team members were unsure if they could trust her to talk with the child appropriately and to commit to taking the child to therapy for the long term. In another situation, the team decided against providing a child with an implant because both parents were deaf and did not speak themselves. The NGO administrators did not see the point of implanting this child, given that the parents could not talk to the child. In cases of deaf parents with deaf children, school administrators, surgeons, and auditory verbal therapists told me that such children should be handed over to grandparents or other extended family members who are not deaf, at least until the children can talk. As one school administrator told me: "The mother should remove herself for a while and let the grandparents become the primary caregivers." Here "care" means letting go and permitting someone else to care for one's child, or, more specifically, for the child's auditory sense.

This targeted and restrictive understanding of care for and of a single sense may be contrasted with theories of care proposed by feminist scholars such as Eva Feder Kittay (1999), who argue that care involves sustaining another person and that an ethics of care is about interpersonal relationships that extend beyond capabilities and specific senses (also see Tronto 1993). I think here about Marjorie Harness Goodwin's (2017) argument that presence, proximity, and touch foster relationships; relationships are often formed and maintained through nonlinguistic practices and routines that emplace people. Emplacement is key to thinking about children displaced from their parents and what such an action does. David Howes (2019, 20) writes that the sensorium is produced through the "'emplacement' of the sensing subject in a particular environmental and cultural context." What is the connection between emplacement, displacement, and removal? A child is taken away from her mother and re-placed with hearing grandparents in order to focus on audition. Can this be a replacement for a mother? How can replacement result in emplacement? I argue, in contrast to the administrators and experts described above, that attending to multisensory engagement and multimodality, and to the whole sensorium, is a form of care.[7]

Quiet Signals

Balavidyalaya is perhaps India's most well-known early intervention program and school for deaf children. Educators and families come from across India for its training and early intervention programs. The institute has also developed parent kits, handbooks, and video materials that are widely used by families. The center is located on a quiet residential street in an upper-middle-class area of Chennai, where there is little traffic or other outside noise, beyond birds, to be heard. Children and their parents walk down a narrow leafy lane to a large and spacious house, which is the school building. The children clutch identical plastic lunch boxes and have hankies attached to their shirts with safety pins. Mothers escort their children inside if they are under three years old or are new to the program, or drop them off if they are three or older. Mothers dropping their children off might spend some time outside chatting with one another in the small playground attached to the school. Everyone who enters the school building removes their shoes outside and then is greeted at the front desk by a friendly staff person, and often by the principal as well. All of the school's rooms feature soundproofing, to minimize noise and maximize speech signals, and in each classroom, a teacher works with a small number of students, usually one to four children.

Mrs. Saraswathi, a mother of a deaf child, started the school in 1969. Up until her death in early 2020, Mrs. Saraswathi could often be found at the school, where her daughter, Dr. Meera, is the principal. Mrs. Saraswathi learned that her son was deaf in 1963, before his first birthday. At that time, there were no resources in Chennai for testing hearing or fitting hearing aids, so she traveled to Christian Medical College in Vellore, about three hours away by train, where she learned that her son was deaf. She subsequently found a dentist in Chennai who was willing to make ear molds out of denture materials, and she then purchased imported hearing aids. When her son was one year old, she visited schools in Chennai to inquire about admissions, and they told her to come back when he was five.

Mrs. Saraswathi did not want to wait another four years, so she frequented libraries in the city to find books about deafness. She chose only those books that offered clear successful trajectories, "where there was narration of how somebody was able to make a child talk and how they did it." One day, she found a book by Alexander Graham Bell, which changed everything. She told me: "It was a huge book, it had a hand-drawn picture of a girl sitting on the swing and a boy pushing. The boy was Alexander Graham Bell and the girl was Mabel. And then there was one small story written under that: 'Mabel sat on the swing, I pushed the swing, the swing went to and fro.' Some four or five sentences. That became a gospel for me. I knew how to proceed." From that point on, Mrs. Saraswathi said, she knew what to do with her child: "Everything that happened at home, I made it into a narration. I would draw a picture and I would talk about it and I would write about it and make him read." Mrs. Saraswathi created multimodal narrations featuring spoken words, images, and text. The focus on reading through sight words is a significant pedagogical component at Balavidyalaya, as is the use of images, drawings, and art projects of all kinds.

Mrs. Saraswathi told me that the school uses the auditory oral method, which differs from auditory verbal therapy in that children are allowed to read lips, although there are times when they are required to put their heads down and listen to teachers. Mrs. Saraswathi stressed that everyone else reads lips in everyday life and that lips—and faces—provide valuable information about how people are feeling. What is important in the school's methodology, however, is that no gestures or signs are used. Looking at lips is allowed, but gestures are not; there are appropriate and inappropriate visual cues and behaviors. As the current principal, Dr. Meera, firmly told me: "Nobody gestures. No finger cues. Our policy is if even a dog can understand commands, why would you not allow a deaf child, a child, to understand commands? Why do you need to help the child by giving additional cues?" Mrs. Saraswathi said that she believes that every child has a "birthright to speak," and that what is important is starting very young and as early as possible. The administration stresses that the school is unabashedly oralist. Here, being oralist means allowing lipreading, reading, and repetition, but no signs or gestures.[8] The school also does not focus heavily on speech clarity, to avoid making children self-conscious about their speech. The first priority is language; children can seek speech therapy later if they need it.

As Balavidyalaya is well known across India, I wondered about waiting lists. Dr. Meera told me that for a deaf child every day is critical, and the child's life is on the line: "If you are late, you've missed the bus." Here, missing the bus means that the child is no longer trainable in listening, reading, and speaking, and would therefore be sent to a sign language–based program (the school does occasionally make exceptions for older children, but children with additional disabilities are never admitted, regardless of age). Whenever a deaf child under the age of three arrives, the school immediately accommodates the child by moving other children around or shifting schedules as needed. Children attend from Monday through Friday. The smallest children come each day for an hour, from 9:00 a.m. to 10:00 a.m. At 10:00 a.m., older children, two and a half years old and up, arrive for their school day, which goes until 3:00 p.m. However, the children are not finished for the day at 3:00 p.m. As Dr. Meera explained: "The parents are talking to them, we tell them what to do at home, they are doing everything at home with the child. So all the waking hours, there is someone talking to the child. There is language input." (While Dr. Meera said "parents" and not "mothers," it is the mothers who are overwhelmingly present at the school and who are featured in its instructional books and videos.) Children graduate from the school when they are five years old and are then mainstreamed.

The school has developed a method called DHVANI, an acronym for Development of Hearing, Voice and Natural Integration; in Sanskrit, the word *dhvani* means sound.[9] Over a ten-year period, the school created two massive books for parents devoted to this method. Divided by age range, each weighs about five pounds and contains instructions for three hundred (mostly domestic) activities parents can do with their children. For children up to age three, these include everyday activities like copy games (in which a mother and child copy each other's movements), eating, scribbling, riding a tricycle, watching a butterfly, blowing soap bubbles, sorting clothes, and killing cockroaches. For ages three to six, the activities include cleaning the table, climbing a hill and going to a temple, packing lunch for a father going to work, and showing the child an article in the newspaper about a baby elephant being born. The description of each activity is accompanied by an illustration of people engaged in the activity, suggestions of what to talk about, sample sentences to use, and recommendations for how long the activity should last. As Dr. Meera told me: "See, one activity as simple as drinking a glass of milk, you can present twenty different sentences to explain that. So today you taught twenty sentences. Tomorrow you teach another twenty sentences." The goal is to turn every activity into an opportunity to teach language and interact, so that interacting through language is naturally integrated into all aspects of the child's life. Who knew that one could spend so much time talking about a glass of milk, a cockroach crawling up a wall, or the simple act of dusting a bicycle?

In the beginning of the first training book for parents of children up to three years old, much attention and emphasis are devoted to relationship building and getting to know the child through multisensory engagement. The book instructs mothers to watch their children carefully to get to know their moods and thoughts. Mothers are told to maintain eye contact, which helps "the child to get visual information." Similarly, they are instructed to take notice of the child's smile, to reassure the child "that you love him," and to demonstrate affection frequently with "a hug, a kiss, or a pat," through tickling and cuddling, and speaking in motherese, or in "love talk." The book advises that if "you find that you are not hugging and kissing your child often, find out what is going wrong with your life." It also emphasizes that the child should always be in the presence of an adult or older child "who keeps talking to him." Additionally, the book instructs mothers to "provide a multisensory stimulation by allowing the child to see, touch, smell, taste and hear throughout the day" and to engage in interesting conversation and activities to captivate the child and avoid boredom (Balavidyalaya 2011a, 5–16). Mothers are assured that their children are communicating with them, even if they are nonverbal (Balavidyalaya 2011a, 5). All of these instructions for mothers suggest that communication—and relationality—can come in different forms, in contrast to what professionals often tell mothers about the primacy of listening and spoken language.

The importance of multisensory engagement and affection can also be seen in the Balavidyalaya teaching videos that focus on activities such as a mother feeding her infant a bottle while the child lies snugly on her lap making eye contact, a mother spooning carrots into her child's mouth while looking closely at her, a mother walking in a garden while carrying her child and showing her flowers, and a mother and child gazing at a car together. In all of these instances, the mother holds the child closely, makes eye contact and establishes joint attention, and talks to the child constantly and with warmth. Like the mothers in these videos, teachers at the school tenderly pinch the children's cheeks and snuggle and kiss the children. This focus on affection, proximity, and multisensory stimulation is striking. Dr. Meera commented that such affection and "body language" are both "part of Indian culture" and a means of getting the children to want to communicate with their mothers and to do the difficult training work required of them. There is thus tension between proximity, affection, and multisensory engagement as ends in themselves and their use as a means to get children to do something else, specifically, to use conventionalized spoken and written language.

Attempts to cultivate connection—between people and between people and objects—permeate everything at the school, including the notes that teachers send to mothers each day in notebooks with sections titled "Tell Amma" and "Tell Teacher." In "Tell Amma," the teacher uses a pen to write a single line outlining the lesson of the day. The mother is expected to ask her child questions based on that information. In "Tell Teacher," the mother uses a pencil to write a single line about a home incident she has discussed with her child. The teacher reads this note and follows up the next day. In this way, a connection is made between school and home through talk. This connection is not to be broken or mediated by communication technologies. The school is adamantly against the use of cell phones, tablets, computers, and televisions, either in the school or at home. As Dr. Meera told me, there is no replacement for a human being; parents who want to watch television can do so after their child goes to bed. From the school's point of view, there is no place for gadgets or technology in pedagogy, mediating relations, or creating appropriately sensing children. The school is a technology-free social space that is produced and maintained through active embodied communicative work. (I recall an audiologist in Bangalore telling me about Balavidyalaya, "At that program, parents go through hell.")

To highlight the multisensory forms of care and communication that take place at Balavidyalaya, I describe two lessons that I observed there. The discussion that follows may seem repetitive and full of unnecessary details, but it is through repetition and details that engagement is created and relationships are formed.

In the first lesson, which took place in a small quiet room, a one-year-old girl named Radha sat with a teacher named Varuna and a small box of toys and other objects. Radha's mother, three education students, and I sat in a circle around Radha and Varuna. The first activity involved Radha putting plastic rings of various colors onto a post. As Radha grabbed each ring, Varuna matched its color to another object in the room. One ring was blue and so was Radha's dress. Varuna touched both the ring and Radha's dress and said with excitement, "Take the blue and put it on! Look, this is blue and it matches your dress. It is matching!" The little girl clapped after every action, and Varuna affectionately asked why she was clapping at everything. We were all moved by Radha's excitement and Varuna's scaffolding of it.

After she put the ring activity away, Varuna used her dupatta to hide her head and then she pulled Radha under the dupatta as well. She asked, "Where is Varuna? Under the dupatta! Where is Radha? Under the dupatta!" She then gave Radha a kiss. The next activity involved making a tower with plastic cups. Varuna asked Radha, "Who made a tower? It was Radha. Radha made a tower!" After cleaning up the cups, Varuna showed Radha a small plastic bus and told her to look at it while Varuna described it, saying that it was made of plastic and that it was purple in color. She also suggested that Radha should count the wheels on the bus. After finishing this activity, Varuna brought out a small plastic shoe and commented that it was black in color and made of plastic. She said that the shoe goes on a foot but it was too small for Radha's feet. Then she took a pink plastic flower from the box and asked, "Is this a real flower? No! Does it smell? No! It is made of plastic. But you can put flowers on your hair!" Radha then put the plastic shoe on her head and everyone laughed. The final activity involved a matching exercise in which two shoes, two flowers, and two buses were to be placed next to each other. This was a dynamic multisensory lesson that included student and teacher touching objects and each other, making eye contact, and narrating actions. In this setting, Radha was introduced to language through joint embodiment and intersensing with Varuna, who was also creating scaffolding for Radha's mother to do similar exercises and engage in the same kind of talk with Radha at home.

The second lesson took place in a preschool class. In a brightly decorated room, three children sat around a small low table with their teacher, who enthusiastically asked them what they had eaten for breakfast. A girl answered that she had eaten an idli (a fermented rice and lentil dumpling). The teacher asked her, "Why did you not eat two idlis? And what did you eat it with?" She instructed the child to say, "I ate one idli with chutney." The teacher then asked her, "What kind of chutney? You should say coconut, tomato, or mint." After hearing about the kind of chutney, the teacher expanded the conversation and asked her, "What did Appa [Father] eat? How many idlis did Appa eat?" The next child said that she had eaten idli with sambar for breakfast. The teacher asked her how many idlis she ate and instructed her to say, "I ate one idli with sambar." The teacher inquired if it was tasty, and the girl said, "Yes!" The teacher then followed up by asking the girl to create a full sentence: "The idli and sambar were tasty."

After the discussion of breakfast, the class examined a drawing of a man climbing a coconut tree. The teacher instructed: "Say in full sentences! The coconuts were in bunches. Uncle plucked the coconuts. The coconut tree is tall. The coconut tree has leaves. The coconut tree has a long trunk." The children took turns repeating these sentences and then wrote them out. They drew pictures of coconut trees and discussed how many coconuts were on their trees. After class, a mother came to show the teacher an experience book she had created, with immaculately drawn pictures of the family's house and of a playground that her daughter visits, as well as carefully worded text about all of the images. The teacher praised her work; it looked like the mother had spent a significant amount of time on this painstakingly drawn book, which would be a source of many discussions about daily life for the mother and her child and would help to structure narratives about their experiences.

While the classroom activities at Balavidyalaya include drawing, acting, and arts and crafts, listening is an overarching activity. Children are asked to put their heads down at various points during lessons to listen to words and sentences. These auditory training times are focused and serious. At other times, lighthearted conversations can quickly become opportunities for listening practice. During lunch, for example, everyone sits together in a circle on the floor in a classroom to eat their rice, *dosa*, or *roti* and vegetables. The lunch-duty teachers go around the room and ask what the children have for lunch or point out that a child should eat only two of her *dosas* and not the three she has, because three would be too much. During this banter, the teachers point at their ears and command the children, "Listen!" When I ate lunch with a group of children and teachers one day, I made small talk with a child sitting adjacent to me by asking her if she was eating beetroot (she had a container of shredded beetroot with coconut and curry leaves). The teacher closest to us firmly pointed to her own ear and told this little girl, "Listen! You have to listen! She has asked you a question." This exhorting or summoning to listen, to be interpellated as a listening subject who responds appropriately to a question about beetroot in a noisy room, is striking. I love beetroot and think of eating it as a multisensory experience. I wanted to talk to this child about how tasty her lunch was (I was projecting, perhaps), but she

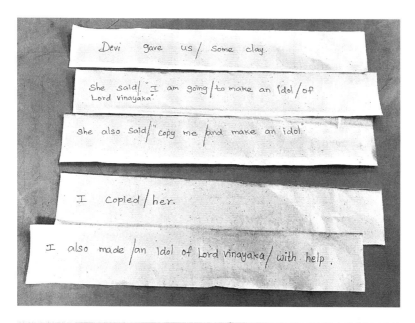

Devi gave us / Some clay.

She said / "I am going / to make an idol / of Lord vinayaka."

She also said / "copy me / and make an idol."

I copied / her.

I also made / an idol of Lord vinayaka / with help.

On strips of paper, a teacher has written sentences about the process of sculpting Lord Vinayaka (or Ganesha) idols in clay. The children then practice listening to, repeating, and ordering these sentences. After listening practice, they make the idols out of clay, lovingly attended to by their teacher. Photographs by author.

was ordered to listen to me, and in that moment, I was not sure we could have a playful conversation about delicious food. And then, a few minutes later: "Listen! The bell has rung!"

Noisy Signals

The Mothers Teaching Center is located on a busy main road in Bangalore; it occupies two large classrooms in a compound that also houses an institute that offers audiology and speech and language pathology clinics, higher education courses in these fields, and an elementary school for deaf children where signed language and spoken language are used together. The MTC's training program, however, does not interact with this school, and the children in the program are kept separate from those in the school, even though the two groups are in physical proximity and often visible to each other.

Sasikala (she preferred to be called by her first name), the founder and director of the MTC, received training from both Balavidyalaya and another flagship program in Mysore that was modeled on Balavidyalaya. Like Mrs. Saraswathi, Sasikala has a deaf son, and her pursuit of educational resources for him led her to the programs where she was trained. After her training, she started her program in Bangalore, where she carefully selected "hardworking" mothers with young deaf children who she thought would be successful. Sasikala's deaf son earned a master's degree from a university in the United States and is now an engineer working for a multinational corporation in India, as she proudly tells people who inquire about the program. Her son is held up as an example of what mothers and their deaf children can achieve if they are hardworking.

The MTC is open five days a week from 10:00 a.m. to 3:00 p.m., and the program is three years in length. Mothers commit to attending for the full duration, a significant investment of time. The two classrooms, decorated with Hindu imagery and pictures of civic leaders, are spare but feel crowded when they are filled with children and their mothers. They become noisy when many people talk at once, which happens often during the day. The rooms are structurally loud, with open windows, fans, concrete and tiled floors, and oil paint on the walls. Mothers and children sit on floor mats in these rooms and also out in the narrow corridor connecting the two rooms during dyadic and small group sessions. Mothers enroll from across south India, and I met mothers and children originally from

Bangalore, elsewhere in Karnataka, Tamil Nadu, and Andhra Pradesh as well. Mothers and their children sometimes move to Bangalore from other locations to attend the MTC, renting rooms nearby while they complete the program.

Sasikala insisted that only mothers can enroll in the MTC. She does not permit fathers because, she said, they would make the women uncomfortable. Grandmothers are not allowed either, because she cannot order them around and they are in turn unable to order their grandchildren around. Sasikala pointed out: "I can't scold the grandmother, can I? Grandmothers mollycoddle the child and the child will never learn if the grandmother is in charge." She claimed that a child attending the program with his grandmother would not learn how to do the last rites for her when it came time for her funeral. By this, she meant that the child would not be able to *speak* the last rites for his grandmother and that demonstrating relationality and showing respect through speech is of utmost importance. In foregrounding the importance of speech here—of speaking the last rites—Sasikala stressed an understanding of care, affection, and competence as attached to and manifested through the teaching and utilization of spoken language. In her comments about mollycoddling, she emphasized the need for sternness and not nurturing through touch, although tactility was a mode of engagement in this program.

Mothers and their children were loosely grouped into cohorts that spent three years together, although the MTC's open-enrollment policy meant that new mothers were constantly being admitted. Some children had cochlear implants, while others had hearing aids. There was also variation in implant processors: some children had basic models provided through government programs and others had more advanced models purchased privately. The mothers came to know each other and each other's children well, since they spent full days together. More experienced mothers provided newer mothers with lesson plans and lesson modeling, device troubleshooting, help with negotiating government programs, and emotional support and encouragement. The mothers also ate lunch together and passed the time chatting with one another during the few moments a day that they were not responsible for talking to their children.

Days started with yoga for mothers in one of the classrooms, an activity offered so that they could relax and decompress, presumably after spending all of the previous evening talking and doing therapy at home. Yoga was the only time when any of the rooms were quiet. In the other classroom, the mothers who opted not to do yoga sat with all of the children along with Sasikala and another teacher, also a mother of a deaf child. About twenty-five children sat on the floor on mats, watching and listening for their names to be called during the daily attendance ritual. After attendance, there was a discussion of the day of the week and the date. After being temporally oriented, the children recited the Ling Six sounds (see chapter 2). Sasikala wandered around the room, stepping between children, loudly voicing the sounds—"ahh," "eee," "ooo," "mmm," "shh," and "sss"—and the students copied her, collectively uttering the sounds. I recited along, too, and watched students fidget. They grabbed on to each other's arms and legs, sometimes surreptitiously gestured to each other, and tried to escape the gazes of the ever-watchful Sasikala and the diligent mothers who surrounded them.

After this period of cacophonous togetherness, mothers and children paired off and discussed a topic or a theme, such as favorite colors, recent holidays, or the weather; their conversations constituted lessons made up of small talk. Children who were newer to the program had more structured lessons involving balls, feathers, and plastic objects to be handled, identified, put into relation to each other and discussed. Sasikala taught these structured lessons to mothers, who then taught them to newer mothers. Each mother then spent two hours of the day with another mother's child, and each child spent that time with somebody else's mother. This structure exists so that the children are exposed to a range of speech patterns and voices (although it seemed to me that many of the mothers imitated Sasikala's prosody) and also to give the mothers experience relating to children who are not their own. Sasikala said that this practice makes mothers patient and confident, and it also helps them to realize that "they are not the only ones with problems." In addition, it prevents them from excessively doting on their own children. There is, however, a paradox, because mothers are supposed to have special and close bonds with their own children. Do such bonds then extend to other people's children? Mothers told me that it was rewarding to work with other children but at the same time they kept an eye on their own children and asked them after school, "What did Aunty teach you today?" A graduate of the program, now in her late teens, fondly remembers working with other mothers. She said that these periods provided a nice break from her own mother and that they prepared her well for talking with different people.

I particularly enjoyed observing one child at the MTC. He was six years

Mothers and their children sit dyadically on mats at the Mothers Teaching Center. Each mother is teaching her child a lesson. The children must attend to their own mothers and filter out the voices of the other mothers and children. Photograph by author.

old and had been implanted at the age of four. He did not speak unless he was prodded to do so. He engaged with the other children by being mischievous or "naughty," in Sasikala's words. He pulled off their implants, tapped their shoulders, stuck his tongue out at them, and stroked their faces. He oriented to them through touch and delighted in getting a reaction. When Sasikala caught him engaged in his antics, she marched over to him and hit him sharply on the shoulder with a ruler or a stick, calling him a naughty boy. The assault never seemed to faze him—in fact, he often smiled, perhaps a reaction to the touch, although I was disturbed. I wondered if somehow this communication that came on the skin and not through the ear broke up the daily monotony. Sasikala told me that this boy's auditory nerves were not up to the task of having an implant and that he had attention deficit disorder. I wondered if he was just bored. He looked at his notebook and recited words and phrases halfheartedly, and only when he was ordered to do so. Because of his poor progress, the mothers in his cohort took turns working with him after the program was over for the day. They had different private lessons with him, depending on the day: counting windows, arranging shoes, and discussing days of the week. These were repetitive call-and-response activities that could be seen as punishment, especially at the end of a long day, although the mothers' animated attunement may have offset the roteness of what they were doing. While mothers were occasionally angry about how this boy treated their children, especially when he played with their (expensive) cochlear implants, they were careful not to speak negatively about him to his mother—as they were all mothers.

I wondered about other impairments or diagnoses and how they (dis)-appeared (Titchkosky 2011) in this space. There was a four-year-old boy who came to the MTC daily. The boy and his mother sat on the floor face-to-face, with their legs crossed and sometimes touching. His mother had stacks of books containing pictures of fruits, vegetables, animals, and numbers, among other things. The boy looked around constantly, and he often rocked back and forth and flapped his hands; he also vocalized at times. One day, his mother showed him pictures of fruits and loudly ut-tered their names with exaggerated mouth movements: orange, guava, apple, pear, papaya, watermelon. He did not respond verbally and his eyes darted around widely. She tapped his hands and legs with a ruler to get his attention and then pointed to the fruits with the same ruler. She firmly pushed his face back to the page whenever he looked away. Determined to keep going, she switched from fruits to animals. She used her fingers to imitate horns on her head, moved her head back and forth, and said, "Moo moo moo," to resemble a cow. The cow, or her rocking motions, elicited a response: the boy started and smiled. His mother also smiled. Unlike other children and mothers at the MTC, rather than working separately for part of the day, this dyad was always together. Occasionally this mother led activities after lunch during more unstructured times when mothers take over, do informal lessons, and read stories to all of the children. I wondered if she compared her son to other children as mothers often told me they did. Sasikala encouraged such comparison, because she believed it made mothers work harder. This mother and her son were included in the MTC in that they shared space and time, albeit not developmental trajectories, with the other children and their mothers.

The boy had an expensive implant processor that the family had pur-chased privately. Sasikala told me that he was autistic but that his mother did not accept the diagnosis. She hoped that her child would progress and become more like the other children at the MTC, and to this end she also sought out therapy at different centers around the city: at the private clinic where he was implanted, at a school for children with intellectual disabilities, and at the adjacent institute for speech and hearing, among other places. Sasikala said that she told this mother that the MTC was not equipped to work with children with autism, but she could not stop them from coming. She asked, rhetorically, and also expressing care for this mother: "How can I disappoint her as she is a mother, no? She has hopes and dreams for her son . . . How can I deny her the fact that he smiles and is happy when they come?" (The boy did look at the other children in the program with interest.) Sasikala told me that this woman's husband was cruel and did not help her. When he was home from work, he was busy with his mobile phone and his laptop. She called him a "technology addict," engaging with his devices and not his family. This mother was with her son all day long, ferrying him to the MTC and to other appointments.

Another mother told me that while she and her son walked to and from the MTC each day, she constantly pointed out people and objects to him. She said, "Whatever we see, I will explain to him." Sasikala followed up on this mother's comment: "We want mothers to notice everything, they need to see everything." The implication of Sasikala's statement is that mothers will then talk to their children about whatever they notice and see. The focus on "seeing everything" can be jarring. One afternoon, Sasikala talked with the children about recent floods in Karnataka's Coorg district and in the neighboring state of Kerala, and she chided the mothers for not taking their children to see the flooded areas. I wondered if she was joking, but she always seemed to be serious.

Sasikala often asked the children what they had for lunch. One day, when a child said that she had eaten sambar, Sasikala followed up by asking, "Which sambar did Amma make? Which vegetable was in the sambar?" The child replied, "Radish." After checking with the child's mother to confirm that this was indeed what the child had eaten, Sasikala asked, "What color radish?" A few days prior, Sasikala had shown a radish plant to the children, and she reminded them of this. The conversation was oriented to making abstract things tangible and to showing material examples. The children had to see things and learn their names to know them; everything was a "language game" (Wittgenstein 2009). There were trips to vegetable and clothing markets during which Sasikala, mothers, and children talked about what they observed. On Teachers' Day, there was a celebration at the training center with a brightly colored cake. The students discussed the shape of the cake and the knife used to cut it—specifically, the material the knife was made of (plastic) and how sharp it was (very sharp, not dull).

A popular yearly trip for mothers and children attending the MTC is to Bangalore's Pottery Town, where they watch potters making clay Ganesha idols for the festival of Ganesh Chaturthi in September. Before each trip, Sasikala and the mothers ask their children, "Where are you going and what will you see?" and "How will you get to Pottery Town?" As they travel to Pottery Town in the institute's van, the mothers spend the time pointing out things like trees, other vehicles, and landmarks and asking their children questions about what they are seeing along the way. When they reach Pottery Town, some mothers use their phones to record the potter in action so that they can later use the video for conversation practice. On a 2018 trip, one mother narrated the potter's activities for the children:

[The potter] is making the idol with clay. He is taking clay and wetting it. This is the mold of the Ganesha. If you put clay in the mold, the clay will take the shape of the mold. He is breaking the clay and putting it in the mold. He is adding more clay. He is smoothening the clay now. He is putting clay in the other mold. He is putting some water in it. He is smoothening the clay. He is now closing the two molds together. He is putting more clay at the hollow bottom. He is making a hole in the bottom. He is smoothening the bottom part. He is now opening the mold. [The children oohed and aahed when they saw the idol come out of the mold.] Doesn't it look nice? He is now taking some clay and making the trunk of Ganesha. He is now shaping the trunk. He is now making the tusk of Ganesha. The idol is now ready. It will have to dry.

The mothers purchase a Ganesha to bring back to the classroom so that the children will have an object to look at during their follow-up discussions. Mothers spend the ride back to the program asking questions about what the children saw in Pottery Town, how they got there, and with whom they traveled.[10] Back in the classrooms, mothers sit with their children and ask them the same questions again. So many details, so much repetition, so much work to turn the trip into a language game.

At the MTC, mothers learn various skills in addition to learning how to talk to and conduct training sessions with their children. Some mothers learn to write in English because Sasikala gives them dictation in English daily, and after writing down what she narrates, they recite these passages to their children. Mothers are also given nightly writing assignments in which they are expected to write three paragraphs about things they have seen and done; they are supposed to deliver these paragraphs through dictation and discuss them with their children.[11] Some mothers begin reading newspapers and watching the news so that they can talk to their children about current events, such as the flooding in Coorg. Mothers also learn about holidays across religions: I talked to one mother who had never celebrated Ganesh Chaturthi before.

The mothers I met occasionally seemed ambivalent about their time at the center. A single mother from Chennai told me about relocating to Bangalore and struggling to perform her work as a software engineer in the evening. She had asked Sasikala if it would be possible for a family member or a hired person to bring her child to the center, and Sasikala adamantly refused the request. As such, the mother appealed to her employer, who agreed to let her work at night. When I talked to the mother during her first week at the center, she seemed overwhelmed but optimistic that she could make it all work out. Another mother from Bangalore who was enrolled at the center for the second time with her second child told me that it was difficult for her to be away from home all day and she had to do all of her housework when she got home; such compounding of responsibility is experienced by most of the mothers at the center. Another mother had a different perspective on this—she told me that her time at the MTC was the only dedicated time she had to spend with her child because at home she had to focus on her housework, although ideally she would do the housework while simultaneously talking to her child about what she was doing. Because there was always a familial and/or economic cost to being away from the home or work, mothers were often especially anxious about their children's progress. And for mothers who traveled to Bangalore alone with their deaf children and rented rooms or apartments near the MTC, their children's failures on any given day often took on outsize proportions, and they experienced mother blame, even though the mothers in the program supported each other.

In one incident, a six-year-old girl could not repeat back to Sasikala during a dictation exercise. Sasikala harshly scolded the girl's mother for not working hard enough with her, setting off a chain of events. That night, the child refused to study or do her writing. In response, her mother cried and did not eat. That evening, she talked on the phone with another mother from her cohort, who also shed tears, and the next day this other mother asked the little girl: "You don't like Mummy? Why don't you study? Why don't you obey her? See how sad she is? Your mother is always smiling and friendly but she is so sad today." She lectured the girl about how her mother was living away from her other daughter and her husband, and she asked the girl to study. The next day, this other mother sat with the girl for a two-hour lesson that was intended to prevent another scolding by Sasikala (what a weight to place on a child). Here we see the shared efforts of mothers, who often maintain their relationships even after they graduate from the program.

Relational Signals

When I left the MTC in the afternoons and walked outside, I felt a sense of relief even though the sounds of Bangalore's ever-present traffic were immediately beyond the gates. It was too noisy for me in the two classrooms with all of the children and their mothers talking. I was exhausted from the signal labor (Sterne and Rodgers 2011) associated with trying to separate speech from noise. I wondered about the children, about their listening effort, and about what it would be like for them to have classes and conversations in quieter spaces. Would it make a difference? Would it have been easier for the girl discussed above to hear Sasikala's dictation? Other program administrators, therapists, and educators with whom I spoke routinely criticized Sasikala for not being "natural" because she speaks very loudly and makes use of significant intonation and acoustic highlighting (exaggerated mouth movements and stressing of syllables and sounds). They also commented on the MTC's lack of appropriate "listening infrastructure," a problem of which Sasikala was well aware; she pleaded with the institute's director for soundproofing for her classrooms, to no avail. Indeed, she spoke the way she did to compensate for the echoes and reverberations in the rooms. Despite the noisy spaces, Sasikala provided relational infrastructure, and mothers supported each other and each other's children through sharing space and time, conversations, and aspirations day in and day out. Children became close to other mothers and learned different ways of speaking, although mothers often taught the same lessons and sounded similar to each other in that they imitated Sasikala.

In the moments when mothers peeled a *mosambi* (sweet lime) and gave slices to all of the children, touched and cared for bruises and cuts, pulled children onto their laps, shared lunches and compared cooking notes, and smoothed down children's unruly hair, there was care that transcended a focus on listening. This was evident too in lessons in which mothers blew on children's little hands, brought these same hands to their faces and necks to feel sounds, and animatedly discussed everyday life using gestures, images, and touch. How might we think about the kinds of signals that are transmitted in this space? They are communicative in nonlinguistic and often nonauditory ways, in contrast to dominant professional discourses. These signals establish relationships and enable the scaffolding of time, sociality, and trajectories.

I end with the story of a mother who found it difficult to talk all the time with her child. Ashwini grew up in a rural village in Karnataka. Her parents died when she was young, and during her late teens, she was married to a distant relative who was almost twice her age. She became pregnant soon after marriage and gave birth to one child, a boy, and then another. Ashwini said she was sure that her second child, a girl, was deaf when she was ten months of age. However, her conjugal family first ignored her and then told her that she was "psychic." They sent Ashwini to an institution where she was forcibly drugged. Still worried after returning home, she pointed out that her child did not hear any of the firecrackers during the celebration of Diwali. When Ashwini's daughter was one and a half years old, the entire family finally took her to the All India Institute of Speech and Hearing in Mysore for tests and received an official diagnosis of deafness. The family did not act because they said that the girl would be married off to another family, so what was the use of investing in her? After two years, Ashwini quickly packed a suitcase, bundled up her daughter, and left the family home, leaving her son behind. She took her daughter to Bangalore, to a speech and hearing institute that a friend had told her about. The institute director raised funds for an implant for the child, who attended three to four hours of therapy per day both before and after implantation. The director also gave Ashwini a job at the institute's library and provided her with an apartment. Ashwini had no contact with her in-laws or her husband, who refused to take her calls, and she feared that her in-laws were out to steal the parcel of land that she owned.

I asked Ashwini about talking to her child, and she said that she could not do it all the time, she was tired and had "too much tension." At night, after the cooking and housework were done, she could not and did not talk with the girl, as her mind was constantly racing. The question raised by therapists is whether "hard work" means anything if mothers are not constantly talking to their deaf children and actively engaged in re/habilitation. However, there are mothers like Ashwini who do not have the social, emotional, and economic infrastructure they need to scaffold their children's lives through talk or who experience barriers to inter-sensing and joint embodiment (let us not forget that Ashwini had been declared senseless by her family). By leaving her native place with her daughter in order to maximize the child's potential, Ashwini chose to in-vest in her daughter's future over the desires of her husband and conjugal family. Rather than looking at such mothers as failures, as many therapists do, I am interested in the forms of care, support, facilitation, and engage-ment that they provide and the signals that they apprehend and transduce. Becoming a cricket commentator is not the only way to be a mother and give and receive signals.

In this chapter I have argued that mothers and their deaf children make sense and relate to each other in multisensory and multimodal ways. Mothers do active work to produce and transduce a multitude of signals, even if these signals are not valued or occur under the radar. The question is not whether deaf children are appropriately social but how the social is produced, recognized, and stretched during carefully taught classes, thera-peutic practices, and everyday engagements in quiet and noisy rooms. Intersensing and joint embodiment can be unruly and involve affectionate acts such as patting and hugging, touching plastic objects, and gazing at imperfectly drawn pictures of grapes, body parts, and Ganeshas. Just as children ostensibly learn language in addition to developing their various senses, mothers learn new ways of relating to their children and commu-nicating in general. Care extends beyond caring for one sense. At times it also involves embracing and succumbing to noisy signals. As I discuss in the next chapter, care also extends to maintaining devices, relationships, and senses more broadly.

(Non-)Use

Maintaining Devices, Relationships, and Senses

A cochlear implant is the starting point of a journey. Speech and language behavior is the goal that you want to reach. AVT [auditory verbal therapy] is the road, and cochlear implant is a vehicle. Care and maintenance is the oiling that you need to do every time.

> —Kiran, audiologist and speech and language pathologist at the
> Ali Yavar Jung National Institute of Speech and Hearing Disabilities

I always say an individual is married to the CI. Even we [audiologists and speech and language pathologists] have married the CI as such! We need to walk together all the time. And it's a one-way. You can't—we can't divorce it also.

> —Kalpana, audiologist and speech and language pathologist in Pune

Maintenance Problems

In 2013, I read articles in the newspaper *The Hindu* about a five-year-old deaf orphan named Ashreya in Madurai, Tamil Nadu, whose case had been taken up by a Chennai-based grassroots disability rights organization. When she was around three years old, Ashreya had been found abandoned at a pilgrimage site outside Madurai and taken to an orphanage. A couple of years went by, and then a wealthy philanthropist associated with the orphanage arranged for a local otolaryngologist to examine Ashreya. This doctor referred her to a hospital in Chennai for cochlear implant surgery under the Tamil Nadu Chief Minister's Comprehensive Health Insurance Scheme. However, because Ashreya was an orphan, she did not have a birth certificate or a ration card, and the hospital was unwilling to accept her disability certificate or age proof as certified by a hospital board. The philanthropist sought help from the Office of the Chief Commissioner for Persons with Disabilities in Delhi as well as from the Chennai-based disability activist organization. It was a race against time, because Ashreya was ostensibly five and a half years old by then, and the cutoff age for cochlear implants under the Tamil Nadu state program was six years. While reading about the case, I was intrigued that a rights-based disability organization had advocated for an individual child to get an expensive surgery and device, and I was also surprised that such an organization would embrace cochlear implants, because most Indian deaf organizations were against them. I never followed up on my curiosity, however.

In the summer of 2019, I found myself in Chennai in the office of the disability organization that had advocated for Ashreya. I eagerly asked for an update and inquired about Ashreya. Landon, the organization's director, was tickled that I remembered the case from six years ago. He was happy to tell me that because of his organization's intervention, Ashreya had gotten a cochlear implant. She now lived in Chennai with the family that had taken her in when she needed to be in Chennai regularly for postoperative therapy. Serendipitously, the father of the family, Deepak, was the director of a disability trust with whom Landon shared an office, and he called Deepak over to meet me.[1] As we sipped coffee and waited for Deepak, I asked Landon what his organization was doing about cochlear implant maintenance problems, since this was a major issue that I had been hearing a lot about from families, audiologists, and speech and language pathologists. He looked at me in surprise and asked what I was talking about, exclaiming that implants are a one-time expense. I gazed back at him, also quite surprised, because I had found talk about maintenance to be ubiquitous.

At that moment, Deepak walked in. He told me that Ashreya was now twelve years old and in seventh standard, where she was an "average student." She was very close to his two biological children and also to his wife, a special educator who helped Ashreya with her schoolwork and worked with Ashreya's teacher to modify the school curriculum as needed. The family had taken an Indian Sign Language class together because signing helped them with communication. I asked Deepak about Ashreya's implant, since her surgery had taken place more than six years ago. He exclaimed that the cochlear implant "is so difficult to maintain!" and began reciting an itemized list of the money spent: Rs 7,000 (US$93) for a battery, Rs 2,500 (US$33) for a cord, and additional funds for the battery charger and the drying balls for the dry kit. (The external processor is supposed to be placed in a drying machine every night, and maintaining this machine involves consistent replacement of small balls containing moisture-absorbing silica crystals.) In a critique of how expensive these patented parts are, Deepak observed that the "coil does not really do anything and has no electronic parts," so it could or should be "some fifty-rupee [US$0.67] China-made part but it is not, it is two thousand five hundred rupees." He did not receive any replacements directly from the government, although sometimes a government hospital unofficially gave him a used rechargeable battery.

Deepak was distressed that implant maintenance costs are so prohibitive, but he was invested in continuing maintenance routines. He had no choice. Ashreya, her teachers, and the rest of the family became upset when the implant stopped working, and they pressured him to have it repaired quickly.[2] As he told me all this, I looked over at Landon, who said that he previously had no idea about these "maintenance issues." He asked Deepak why he had not shared any of this before. Deepak replied that maintenance was personal and not a political issue. In saying this, he exhibited a logic that resonated with that of the state: there is the initial implantation, the "one-time expense," and everything after that is the personal responsibility of the beneficiary. Deepak's statement that maintenance is a personal issue brings up questions about the kinds of domestic worlds that maintenance creates. How do these worlds intersect with the state, medical institutions, audiology and speech and language therapy centers, multinational cochlear implant manufacturers, and nongovernmental and charitable organizations as families seek funds to help with maintenance costs? Care for one's child means caring for the device (or the "machine," as it is called), and caring for the device means caring for the child.

In this chapter, I explore the "maintenance problems" that I heard about frequently during my research. I analyze comments such as these: "Madam, there are maintenance problems," "I am worried about how I will maintain the device because it is so costly," and "Poor people will not be able to maintain the device." I also examine statements such as this one: "It is important that we ask families to contribute and pay for accessories as otherwise they will not value the implant." In a discussion about the importance of maintenance and repair as analytic and experiential categories, Stephen Graham and Nigel Thrift (2007, 4) write: "It becomes increasingly difficult to define what the 'thing' is that is being maintained and repaired. Is it the thing itself, or the negotiated order that surrounds it, or some 'larger' entity?" As Graham and Thrift stress, concerns about maintenance are not just concerns about particular devices, here cochlear implants; rather, they index larger issues within a structuring order that are political as much as they are personal, in contrast to Deepak's view of maintenance as personal.

The phrase "maintenance problems" indexes a plethora of issues, from maintaining devices and finding funds for such devices to maintaining relationships with corporations and different kinds of professionals, and from maintaining a child's status as a hearing and speaking child to maintaining visions of a future in which the child continues to be a listening and speaking person. Mothers and teachers often talked to me about "behavior problems" and how children become despondent, agitated, and unruly when their implants stop working. "Maintenance problems" thus result in "behavior problems" through the rupturing of routines and the foreclosing of (hard-earned) channels of communication and sociality. Children who are "successful cochlear implant cases" are especially vulnerable: for them the impact of a broken or missing device is significant, because they have become dependent on the device and oriented toward being listening and speaking persons. Such children experience the loss of the cochlear implant as a loss of capacity.

Arguing that scholars and laypersons alike are overly attentive to innovation and ignore maintenance, Andrew Russell and Lee Vinsel (2018, 7) define maintenance as "all of the *work* that goes into preserving technical and physical orders." Note that while they do not include social or emotional work, or care, under this definition, I do. Care runs through discussions of maintaining devices, relationships, and infrastructures. Care also animates the sentiments that implant users (are supposed to) have toward cochlear implant companies, and users are led to believe that these companies care for them as well. Care and maintenance here are inseparable. According to María Puig de la Bellacasa (2017, 44), care can be a "concrete work of maintenance" with "ethical and affective implications"; she encourages us to look at the material, the affective, and the political as dimensions that are sometimes in tension. She poses the question: "What worlds are being maintained and at the expense of what others?" Cochlear implants are often considered to be "life changing" or to offer "a second life." However, how do the everyday lives of recipients change after implantation?[3] To answer this question, I attend to how families maintain cochlear implant "machines" in order to care for their children. I analyze this maintenance work in relation to how families are instructed to focus on caring for and maintaining one sense—the sense of audition—to ensure that their children listen and speak. I end this discussion by taking up Puig de la Bellacasa's question about what worlds are being maintained in relation to other possible (deaf) world-building and maintenance projects.

Maintaining, Repairing, and Tinkering

In attending to maintenance and repair, scholars have analyzed the emergence of informal maintenance and repair workers who creatively tinker with and fix things—particularly mobile phones (Ahmed, Jackson, and Rifat 2015) and televisions and stereos (Prasad and Kumar 2009)—using recycled and repurposed parts.[4] The *Oxford English Dictionary* defines tinkering as follows: "to mend (an item of metalware) as a tinker. More generally: to mend (any material object) in a clumsy, imperfect, or makeshift way; to attempt to repair or improve, to patch *up*." Annemarie Mol, Ingunn Moser, and Jeannette Pols (2010, 14) argue for tinkering as a form of care and care as a form of tinkering in which people figure out what works and then make do. They define "good care" as "persistent tinkering in a world full of complex ambivalence and shifting tensions." Similarly, Marianne de Laet and Mol (2000, 225) discuss their great love of the Zimbabwean bush pump, which can be tinkered with and adjusted. They find the pump endearing because of its "fluidity" and because its "boundaries are vague and moving." The pump is "tailored to local circumstances," and its "local manufacture guarantees that there will always be spare parts at hand" (236). In contrast to this body of literature on the care-full, pleasurable, sustaining, and important work of tinkering, cochlear implants represent a hard limit to this discourse, although one that is still subject to, in Mol et al.'s words, "complex ambivalence and shifting tensions." While families and individuals can maintain external processors (albeit only for so long) through daily routines, they cannot tinker with, or repair, these devices. "Spare parts" must come from the cochlear implant corporations or their licensed suppliers.

A novel field of inquiry called "crip technoscience studies" critiques how disability-related technologies have been designed *for* and not *by* disabled people. According to Aimi Hamraie and Kelly Fritsch (2019, 2), "crip technoscience" encompasses "practices of critique, alteration, and reinvention of our material-discursive world." It "braids together two provocative concepts: 'crip,' the non-compliant, anti-assimilationist position that disability is a desirable part of the world, and 'technoscience,' the co-production of science, technology, and political life." Hamraie and Fritsch write of disabled makers who have tinkered with and hacked infrastructures and technologies, engaging in acts as diverse as making curb cuts, rigging air conditioners, and repairing wheelchairs. They stress "the transformative possibilities for crip hacking, coding, and making" (5) and argue that disabled people are designers and engineers (see also Hamraie 2017, 99). Similarly, Arseli Dokumacı (2019, 493) analyzes disabled people's creation of what she calls "micro-activist affordances," or "disabled people's micro, ongoing, and (often) ephemeral acts of world-building, with which they make the world offer affordances that are otherwise unimaginable." Dokumacı attends to how her interlocutors in Quebec and Istanbul find new ways of doing difficult everyday tasks, such as putting on a shirt with small buttons and opening a jar.

Scholars have foregrounded the liberatory power of tinkering and making and point to the ways that disabled people have always made, hacked, and tinkered with ramps, curb cuts, online platforms, and kitchen aids, among other things.[5] While most of this theoretical and empirical work has taken place in the global North, it resonates with scholarship and applied and activist research concerning the emergence of low-cost and sustainable wheelchairs, prosthetics, and other disability aids and devices as a means of "improvising" (Livingston 2012) disability access. Crip technoscience, as a concept and practice, raises questions about who can hack, tinker, and design and the role of these practices in actually dismantling infrastructures of power—although it perhaps still foregrounds material infrastructure and objects. Recall that the original tinkerers were traveling repair workers who mended malleable metal utensils. In contrast, cochlear implants are literally unmalleable black boxes (it is the users who are seen as malleable). And the sledgehammers that were so useful for creating curb cuts in 1970s Berkeley, California, would simply destroy implants.

Fixing, Fixedness, Fixity, Fixation, and Fixes

There is a hard limit to what tinkering can do when it comes to cochlear implants.[6] In contrast, a focus on cochlear implantation foregrounds how technology in general has become less available to be adjusted, hacked, or manipulated through other seemingly empowering practices. Given the increasing complexity of devices and the proliferation of intellectual property regimes, the affordances of many devices are limited in that the devices are "fixed." Ruha Benjamin (2019, 137) reminds us that "to fix" can mean to repair; to make firm, stable, or stationary; or to influence actions, outcomes, or effects through improper or illegal means. As Sarah Besky (2017, 619) notes: "Fixity is less a negative correlate to freedom than a multi-dimensional condition that calls into question the sharp divide between freedom and bondage." In similarly thinking through binaries and divides, Rashmi Sadana, Tarini Bedi, and I have suggested that "fix" as a concept serves "as a means of interrupting grand and teleological notions of devel-opment in order to consider what might occur between the poles of failure and progress, brokenness and wholeness, cure and disability, and decay and generation" (Friedner, Sadana, and Bedi 2018, n.p.). Like maintenance in relation to innovation, fixing differs from tinkering, hacking, and designing in the affective register it calls forth. It exists within more ambiguous and ambivalent (and less celebratory) regimes of valuation, although it is no less agentive or important. Fixing involves maintaining and being maintained. Maintenance functions as a fix, an attempt to keep breakdowns and the need for repair in abeyance (Domínguez Rubio 2016).

The concepts of "fixing," "fixedness," "fixity," and "fixation" are produc-tive for thinking about cochlear implants and allow us to approach these devices with more ambivalence. Cochlear implants function as a "fix" for deafness. They are "fixed" in that they are unavailable to be tinkered with. They constantly need to be "fixed" as they break down, albeit by and through specialized repair processes. Furthermore, cochlear implant recipients are "fixed" in relation to cochlear implant manufacturers, sur-geons, and allied health professionals such as audiologists and speech and language pathologists as they become dependent on cochlear implants and need new parts, maintenance, and mapping. And in return the same co-chlear implant users "fix" these other actors, who desire and require good outcomes in order to continue to expand cochlear implant infrastructures. The state and the mainstream media are "fixated" on promoting stories of successful cochlear implant outcomes. With actors and objects "fixed" in relation to each other and stakeholders "fixated" on one another and co-chlear implant outcomes, an anxious and precarious order is maintained.

Madeleine Akrich (1992, 205) notes: "Machines and devices are obvi-ously composite, heterogeneous, and physically localized. Although they point to an end, a use for which they have been conceived, they also form part of a long chain of people, products, tools, machines, money, and so forth." Cochlear implants are examples of what Akrich calls "stabilized technologies that have been blackboxed" (211), and users are very much inscribed (208) by them, becoming particular kinds of listeners, attuned to whatever their maps determine to be speech and not noise, although noise will overpower speech. Users also enter into various prescribed routines of care and maintenance, to be discussed below. Akrich poses the question of whether the "composition of a technical object constrains actants in the way they relate both to the object and to one another" (206). I appreciate this focus on constraint: throughout this book I argue that implants constrain what is possible in terms of language (the child is to become a listening and spoken language person) and in terms of sociality (the child is to be social only through using specific senses and modalities). While cochlear implants are ostensibly life changing and unleash specific kinds of potential, they also constrain lives. Constraining is also a form of fixing. Inscribing is a form of fixing.

Much of the work on technology development and transfer in the realm of disability focuses on questions of accessibility, affordability, sustainability, and maintainability. In international disability and development discourse, there is a growing focus on the importance of assistive technology, which includes "hearing aids, wheelchairs, spectacles, prostheses and devices that support memory, among many others."[7] In work on wheelchairs and other assistive aids in the global South, scholars and practitioners have pointed to the importance of technology that is accessible and maintainable, and available to be tinkered with using locally sourced materials (although they do not use those words). In India, the growing field of assistive technology focuses primarily on individualized technological solutions. Incubators and accelerators funded by the Indian government and corporations encourage the development of sustainable assistive technology.

The World Health Organization, in collaboration with national government agencies and nongovernmental organizations, has produced handbooks such as *Guidelines on the Provision of Manual Wheelchairs in Less Resourced Settings* (2008) and *Preferred Profile for Hearing-Aid Technology Suitable for Low- and Middle-Income Countries* (2019), which explicitly discuss sustainable design and maintenance. The WHO, however, has not released any such guidelines for cochlear implants. While a hearing aid is considered to be a form of assistive technology, a cochlear implant processor is not. As an assistive technology engineer in India said to me, "How can a cochlear implant be DIY? It involves a surgery." Yet the same issues of affordability, access, and maintainability exist for the external processor as for a hearing aid; batteries, coils, cables, microphone covers, and magnets, among other things, must all be maintained and often replaced. The precarity of depending on a thing that you may not be able to maintain—of needing to fix a device and being fixed by it in return—creates anxiety.[8]

Maintenance Routines

In October 2019 at the annual convention of the Cochlear Implant Group of India, Kiran, an audiologist and speech and language therapist at the Ali Yavar Jung National Institute of Speech and Hearing Disabilities in Mumbai, gave a presentation devoted to the "care and maintenance" of cochlear implants.[9] In her talk, she prescriptively outlined all of the steps—both material and financial—that families should take to care for and maintain cochlear implants, starting immediately after surgery. Kiran noted that the internal electrode array does not need any "active care and maintenance practices" because it is not exposed to the outside environment. The external processor, however, requires careful daily and weekly maintenance. Every night, the external processor should be cleaned of sweat and salt deposits with a dry soft cotton cloth. After the processor is cleaned, it should be placed in a special dry box, which itself needs to be kept clean and maintained, because it functions properly only if its internal drying component is working. The processor's rechargeable batteries should be charged for two to three hours nightly, and these batteries should be labeled, because it is easy to mix them up. Every morning, or at another set time during the day, special earphones should be used to test that the processor is working. On a weekly basis, the processor's magnet and microphone should be cleaned with a cotton cloth and alcohol swabs. And every three months, the processor's microphone covers should be changed. (So many "shoulds" here.)

Kiran noted that many parents do not follow this routine "meticulously." She observed: "There is the initial period after switch-on, parents are very careful in using the device. It's like a new device, new phone, or a new car that they have. So, they're very meticulous in doing that, especially with listening checks and cleanings. Then, slowly, slowly as the time passes and the device is working fine, one day is missed, slowly one week is missed, and eventually then there is something going wrong with the processor." Kiran and other professionals at AYJNISHD stressed the importance of these routines during families' clinic visits, and they asked families to keep diaries of their maintenance work. AYJNISHD also held workshops at regular intervals to provide families with further information and maintenance protocols.

After describing the steps of material care and maintenance, Kiran

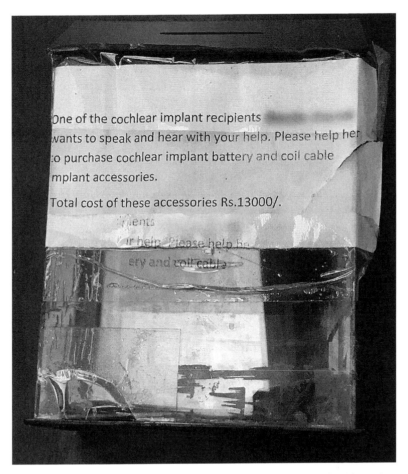

This collection box at an audiology and speech and language clinic is for donations to help pay for cochlear implant accessories for an individual child. According to the note on the box, the child "wants to speak and hear with your help," and the needed accessories (a battery and coil cable) cost Rs 13,000. This simple and empty collection box starkly demonstrates the difficulty of ongoing implant maintenance for many families. Photograph by author.

moved on to finances (inseparable from material maintenance). She stated: "The cost of accessories is huge. It is very difficult for parents to get that on a regular basis. Cost of servicing and repairs after the warranty period is also difficult for them to maintain. The replacements in case there is a loss of processor is again a huge thing. This has been a big challenge for parents to maintain the device to buy accessories; even a simple cord which costs around two thousand rupees, people take around a month to buy that. And the eventual effect is that the child is off-ear during that period." As discussed above, being "off-ear" can mean the loss of a sense, and it is associated with "behavior problems." Note that what Kiran and others call "accessories" are actually essential, contrary to the connotations of the word, which is often used to refer to things that are extra, supplemental, or additional. The cable that attaches the processor to the magnet that connects the internal and external processors is an accessory, but the implant cannot function without it. Similarly, a working battery is essential. Cochlear implant surgery and activation are just the beginning of complex maintenance routines, both material and financial.

Activating Relationships

Cochlear implant activation videos are ubiquitous on YouTube and other social media. In a typical video, the camera focuses on a small child as the child's implant is activated in a clinic. The child ostensibly hears or senses something, celebratory tears are shed, and the child is sent back out into the world—the child, the family, the implant, and the new sense. However, this is not all that happens when a cochlear implant is activated, or "switched on." At the point of activation, which typically takes place two to three weeks after surgery at an audiologist's office, the family is given a large kit in a cardboard box, a duffel bag or backpack, or a hard-plastic box, depending on the manufacturer. The kit contains individually wrapped spare magnets, cables, batteries, battery chargers, microphone covers, small tools for cleaning the processor, and a thick instruction manual, among other things. The kit is often visibly branded with the name of the cochlear implant manufacturer and can be quite jarring to see and to transport. I was overwhelmed when I received my kits for my two implants: the first was a futuristic-looking, shiny white hard-plastic briefcase that was difficult to close unless all the components inside it were stacked and aligned perfectly. It was bulky to carry home on public transportation, and I worried that I would drop it or it would be snatched out of my hands. The second was more manageable, a black nylon backpack with the yellow Cochlear label, in which all of the parts and components, some of them in hard-plastic cases, fit more easily.[10]

Most of the Indian families I met received no information about care and maintenance practices or accessories until activation. While I observed audiologists discussing the external processor with future implant recipients during orientation sessions, I never saw a discussion of cables, coils, or even batteries. Families typically did not see these things until activation day. Audiologists informed me that their practice was to activate the implant and then give the kit to the family. They would then send the family, lugging the kit, to lunch or tea "to process everything" and tell them to return to the clinic afterward. At that point, the audiologists would explain the care and maintenance processes and go through the objects in the kit with the family. Although these things are not included in the cochlear implant activation videos that circulate online, for the family, receiving the kit and learning about the different devices, cables, batteries, and spare parts is a significant part of activation. At switch-on, a new sense is activated, and the family is given instructions and objects for maintaining this sense. Maintenance routines like the one described by Kiran must be adhered to from that day onward.

The central government's cochlear implant program, the Assistance to Disabled Persons for Purchase/Fitting of Aids/Appliances scheme, provides funding for the cochlear implant surgery, the external processor, cables, and batteries that are intended to last for at least two years, as well as two years of therapy and implant mapping (see chapter 1 for an overview of the ADIP scheme). If the internal device stops working, this is considered a device failure, and another surgery is required. No records are kept concerning the numbers of device failures, and the state and corporations are not required to report these numbers. While internal device failure is a significant issue, there is much more discussion of external processor maintenance. Some state programs, notably those in Kerala and Tamil Nadu, provide lifelong maintenance support, including free replacement parts, but the processes that families must go through to get replacements and repairs involve many bureaucratic steps and are often inconsistent. Stories abound of children who have become "nonusers," or gone "off-ear," with the blame for their noncompliance placed squarely on the families for being lazy or careless, or for not saving up the money needed to maintain their children's implants (Farmer et al. 1991; Moran-Thomas 2019). This blanket use of the category of nonuser ignores the fact that people have many reasons for going off-ear and situates the category of user as an unquestioned good (Wyatt 2003).

No government agency or NGO has undertaken any systematic follow-up on the various schemes, which is ironic given that the state is diligent about recording the numbers of surgeries completed. As children and families are "lost to follow-up," neither the state nor other stakeholders actually know the number of nonusers. These previous users are not fixed in place or hearing status, after all. Government officials and other stakeholders know that going off-ear often happens because people cannot afford maintenance or repairs, but it is easier to critique parents than it is to blame political economic structures. A surgeon who previously worked with the ADIP scheme told me that 60 percent of implanted children have become nonusers, while a government employee working on the scheme itself estimated the proportion of nonusers at 20 percent. The point is, no one really knows. In a particularly vivid critique of the ADIP scheme, a deaf education expert told me about a family she had met in northeast India: "There were three deaf children in the family, all of whom had been implanted, and they were running around with the nonworking implant processors dangling off their ears."

Mary-Jo DelVecchio Good (2001) argues that biotechnology functions as a "biotechnical embrace," another example of a fix. She analyzes the tendency among medical practitioners to opt for high-technology solutions that feel good and have a certain allure attached to them; she describes these practitioners as "embracing and being embraced" by this technology because they see it as offering promise and potential (399). I find this metaphor especially apt in the case of cochlear implants, especially as the embrace is seemingly bidirectional. Consider the temporality and affectivity of the biotechnical embrace: At what point does it stop being an embrace? What happens when one embracer simply lets go? When does an embrace become a strangling? In an interview, the India-based director of a leading cochlear implant manufacturer stressed that "the cochlear implant is a lifetime device" and that "children are married to the company for life." He viewed this positively, telling me that his corporation is in the business of forming and maintaining relationships. We might also consider that the Cochlear corporation, in its marketing materials, calls Cochlear recipients "members of the Cochlear family" and that one of its slogans is "Hear Now. And Always." The failure of the embrace to "always" remain an embrace reveals that such kinship, while fixed, is always in danger of coming up short and/or failing.

In the United States, a surgeon commented that implanted patients often become more "attached" to their implant corporations than, say, people with pacemakers do to the manufacturers of those devices; he suggested there is something more relational about cochlear implants. On listservs and Facebook pages, parents of implant candidates agonize over which brand of implant to choose (if they have choices), and heated debates break out about which implant manufacturer is better (these debates are called "brand wars"). Different manufacturers have their own WhatsApp groups, Facebook pages, YouTube channels, and in-person support groups. At conferences such as the AG Bell annual conventions and the meetings of the Hearing Loss Association of America, manufacturers host breakfasts and other gatherings exclusively for their own users. Implant corporations also organize cruises and other social events for their recipients. While doing research to decide which implant corporation I should choose for myself, I observed further that it can be difficult for users to identify with one another across devices. At an implant user support group, for example, someone would bring up a problem she had—not being able to hear well in noise, for instance—and someone with a different device would comment that he did not have that problem. In the United States, choosing a brand can be especially fraught, because manufacturers' representatives are often implant users who mobilize their own personal implant stories to build rapport.

In India, the heightened role of emotions and relationships is equally present, although corporations do not employ users as marketing representatives or salespeople. They do, however, often feature users and their families in inspirational videos that they post on YouTube and other social media platforms (the families are not compensated for appearing). Implant corporations also invite users to engage in public speaking on behalf of the corporations and to give speeches at corporate events. In lieu of users as salespeople, corporations utilize other tactics: for example, in 2015 Cochlear enlisted the (hearing) cricket star Brett Lee as its first "global hearing ambassador," and when Lee travels to India, which he does often, he interacts with select successful Cochlear recipients and sometimes plays cricket with them. Corporate representatives make home visits and even "simply show up" at hospitals or clinics where families are seeking information. A marketing person for one company told me that she must often assuage concerns and fears, as families are worried about the financial investment they are making and the fact that their child is undergoing surgery. Her role is to comfort and reassure families through building relationships with them.[11] These visits and marketing efforts are directed at families purchasing implants on the private market; government programs typically contract with one manufacturer for a set period of time, leaving families without a choice.

In contrast to the biotechnical embrace, some parents describe their relationship with the cochlear implant corporation as "a hostage situation." They did not know that they would have to spend money "for life" on expensive accessories and that there is no turning back or divorce from the device or the corporation. This is true for audiologists and speech and language therapists as well, as Kalpana expressed in the statement quoted at the beginning of this chapter: speech and language therapists also cannot divorce implant corporations. A journalist told me about families who are reluctant to criticize cochlear implant manufacturers publicly because they are afraid of retaliation; they see this relationship as a potentially abusive one that they have to maintain. There is not even the possibility that they might "remarry." One cannot use one corporation's processor with another corporation's internal electrode array, and it is rare for a user to have one corporation's internal device replaced with another's. While being married to more than one company is a possibility in bilateral implantation, this is also rare, as individuals and families tend to stick with one manufacturer. The only possibility, then, is to go off-ear, or become a nonuser. It is important to note, however, that going off-ear really does mean going off-ear, as in many cases, residual hearing is not preserved. Postimplantation, an individual cannot return to using hearing aids. The embrace, the fix, includes loss as well.[12]

After my second implant surgery, I was discomfited that I could no longer hear the (low-pitched) sound of my child's footsteps coming down the stairs in the morning or the rumbles of trains on the tracks behind my house. When I discussed this loss with my surgeon, he commented that once my implant was activated, I would not miss not hearing these sounds. He suggested that once my implant was up and running, I would enter into a new relationship with environmental sounds. As Benjamin (2019, 151) writes: "If people do not have the choice to wiggle free from the suffocating embrace of techno-benevolence without repercussions, that is a sign of fixity—an innovation that constrains." As noted above, cochlear implants, in addition to fixing hearing, fix people in relationships with other people and corporations, albeit without offering stability. Perhaps if this were the case—if implants remained "firm, stable, or stationary" (Benjamin 2019, 137)—other aspects of fixity might be more palatable.

Caring for Lifelines

There is often a honeymoon phase immediately after activation when the family is anticipating or seeing some benefit. During the summer of 2018 I sat with two fathers and their two-year-old sons in an audiology and speech and language clinic in Delhi. Both of the boys were recently—in the past two months—implanted, and the fathers were brimming with optimism for their sons' futures. Each morning, they attended an early intervention program, where they learned how to talk with their sons and do auditory exercises. In addition to chatting with them about how rare it was to see fathers instead of mothers accompanying children for therapy, I asked these men how they were approaching the issue of maintenance, as their children were so young and potentially less than diligent in caring for their external processors. One father told me, "Madam, see, we take so much care of the machine, maybe more care than that of the child. I am telling you the truth. Now this is his lifeline." When I asked him what he meant by "taking care of the machine," he said, "There is a certain way of keeping it in the night, whatever was told to us we follow all the things. We keep it in its box where we are supposed to keep it. We have told [the child] that the machine should not be removed with a jerk, you have to take it out with love and care. He takes it out very slowly and gently and hands it over to us, meaning that he has also realized how valuable and important that machine is to him." While this father was joking about caring for the machine more than for his child, I am struck by his words. The implant, as a "lifeline," becomes a means of ensuring that the child has a meaningful life. Material and emotional care are entangled. An implant is a lifeline to be handled with love and care, a lifeline that sets a child on a trajectory—one that is fixed and difficult to get off of.

When I asked the fathers how else they were caring for the cochlear implants, the other one said, "I have instructed his mother to protect him from other kids. We have instructed the other kids who play with him that they should not beat him, don't push him, and if you want to tell him something tell from some distance. Don't put any pressure on him and be calm or gentle with him." Similar to this father, many mothers told me that they would not permit their children to play outside without them supervising, because they did not want the implants to get damaged.[13] (I thought about these mothers' concerns when I watched videos of Brett Lee playing cricket with implanted children on well-manicured lawns in Mumbai, as these mostly upper-class children did not seem worried about potential implant damage.) Taking care of the cochlear implant here meant observing the child (fixating on him) even more carefully than before and monitoring, sometimes restricting (fixing), his interactions with other children.

Mothers told me that they would not let their implanted children go outside in the rain for fear that their processors might be damaged. On a particularly rainy day during the summer of 2018, I went to visit an early intervention NGO and preschool program in Delhi. I had managed to find transportation to the NGO and was pleased with myself because I had even arrived early. However, the NGO director told me that most likely, very few or no children would come, because parents worried about implants getting wet. She was right—only three children showed up that morning. I also heard about situations in which, ironically, families sent their children to deaf schools rather than mainstreaming them because the normal schools told them that they would not be responsible for "taking care" of implants. This question of "who takes care of the implant" comes up quite frequently in schools. Families told me that they had engaged in complex negotiations with school administrators and classroom teachers because they were concerned about other children somehow dislodging or damaging their children's processors; they were distressed that schools refused to offer any help or support to protect their children's implants. In contrast, deaf schools had experience with hearing aids and ensuring that children wear them.

Compounding parents' anxieties about implant processors breaking or being lost is the expectation that children will wear their processors during every waking hour, from morning to night.[14] Mothers of small children must frequently adjust their processors or fix them back into place after the children pull them off or move them around; these mothers are fearful about loss, damage, and theft all the time. Audiologists and speech and language therapists stress that children should be constantly "on-ear" and listening nonstop (just as mothers are ideally talking nonstop) in order to "catch up" to their hearing peers. Therapists argue that if a child wears hearing technology for four hours a day, it will take that child six years to hear what a typically hearing child hears in one year. Therefore, a child should ideally wear hearing technology for ten to twelve hours a day. As a therapist instructed a parent during preimplant counseling at AYJNISHD: "You have to see to it that she wears the machine all the time. If she is ill, you administer the medicine forcibly, no? Why? Because you know that this is for her well-being. Similarly, the machine is also for her well-being. . . . Can you remove your ear? No, right? You hear throughout the day, till you sleep. . . . So, make it a point that she wears the machine throughout the day till she falls asleep." In regard to this pressure to be constantly "on-ear," a thoughtful audiologist commented to me: "Why do we say that individuals will not be off at any time? That creates a stress on us. Why our stress that twenty-four/seven it will be 'on' as such?" Recall the discussion in chapter 2 of the increased cognitive loads of deaf children and adults, and the effort required to hear through and with degraded signals. Constantly wearing cochlear implants causes stress for users as well.[15]

Maintaining Unequal Sensory Potential

A notable feature of the latest cochlear implant processors made by the Cochlear corporation is that they offer data tracking—audiologists and speech and language therapists can track how many hours per day implanted children are wearing their processors as well as how many hours they spend in speech and noise environments. The therapists can then use this information, easily accessed via a smartphone app, to prompt or pressure families to make sure that the children keep their processors on for longer durations and that they are provided with enough spoken language.[16] (An American speech and language therapist called this feature "better than a nanny cam.") However, only the latest versions of Cochlear's processors offer data tracking, and the majority of Indian children with cochlear implants do not have these processors.

The central government's ADIP scheme and most state government programs offer a basic cochlear implant package without sophisticated noise-cancellation features or noise programs. The corporation that wins the government contract to supply the implants is required to service the specific implant processor model provided for a set number of years. The corporations have worked to ensure that the internal components remain compatible with newer external processors, so that people do not have to undergo unnecessary and redundant surgery when their processors need to be replaced. After a certain point (the time frame differs around the world), external processors become obsolete, and users must "upgrade" because the corporations no longer support (or care for) obsolete devices and spare parts are no longer available. In her presentation at the CIGI conference described above, Kiran, the AYJNISHD audiologist and speech and language pathologist, called this replacement of an obsolete processor a "compulsory upgrade." "Compulsory" is an appropriate adjective here, in that such an upgrade is coerced. Clear class stratifications and obvious ethical (and sensorial) variability (Petryna 2005) are fixed into the global implant market. I am troubled that children need higher-end processors in order to sensorially "experience more."

Upgrades, planned and geographically stratified obsolescence, and the existence of a private market reveal deep inequalities in terms of how people hear with and experience implants. In 2016, Cochlear unveiled the Kanso, a wireless processor that sits directly on the magnet location, with nothing sitting behind the ear; it can thus be hidden entirely from view by the user's hair (if it is long enough) or a hat. The Kanso, according to professionals and families, is a status symbol because it is considered to be "discreet" and results in children being, in the words of a Cochlear India marketing video, "sound-conscious and not self-conscious." In the same video, a therapist comments that because the processor sits directly on the implanted child's head, it is integrated into the child's anatomy—a dubious yet compelling claim.[17] In another Kanso marketing video, a young college graduate who studied fashion design describes her Kanso as a "chic" fashion accessory that she can choose to either hide or reveal.[18] The Kanso and other higher-end implants come with accessories such as television streaming devices, mini-mics, and phone clips; these accessories transmit sound directly into the implant processor and make it easier for the user to hear in noisy situations. In the video featuring the fashion graduate, she drinks juice with a friend in a noisy café. Her friend wears the mini-mic, which enables the pair to chat effortlessly despite the noisy surroundings. In these marketing videos, users, parents of users, surgeons, audiologists, and speech and language pathologists extol the benefits of the Kanso and describe it as offering the absolute best and most sophisticated technology, unparalleled by anything else that has come before or that currently exists.

This representation of the Kanso and the wonders of its accessories—which allow a user to seamlessly listen to music, have effortless conversations in crowded cafés, and hear teachers' voices clearly even from the backs of classrooms—brings up questions about access and equity. Why shouldn't all children be able to hear seamlessly in their classrooms without significant listening effort, especially when professionals constantly tell us about the debilitating effects of noise on hearing and the importance of the signal-to-noise ratio for deaf and hard-of-hearing people (Iglehart 2016)? The Kanso retails in India for about Rs 14 to 18 lakh (US$18,500–$24,000); the prices of other processor models start at about Rs 6 lakh (US$8,000).[19] The Kanso and other newer implants offer programs that "read" or "scan" the environment and adjust background noise, zooming in on speech. In marketing videos such as the ones discussed above, Kanso recipients note that these programs make it is easier for them to hear, and that they experience "finer hearing." Parents who provide their children with the Kanso are complimented in these videos for wanting to do everything possible for their children and giving them the best options to maximize their potential in life. (Note that while all of the cochlear implant manufacturers produce new and upgraded processors every few years, the Kanso is unique in that it is not a behind-the-ear processor.)

When I asked an audiologist about the difference between the basic model provided under the ADIP scheme and more expensive implants, she replied that the difference was like driving a "Tata Nano versus a Mercedes-Benz. Both cars will go to the same place, but the latter might be a smoother ride." Comparing these two cars is an interesting choice, as the Nano, a largely failed experiment in creating an affordable car for the masses, will transport you from point A to point B, but it is less safe, does not have shock absorbers, and might lack sufficient air-conditioning in searing summer heat. You will most likely arrive at your destination sweaty and frazzled from road traffic and with a sore behind. According to this audiologist, the government-provided processor offers basic hearing: "It is good enough for those who can't afford better, and it enables a child to hear. It has no noise control and no scanning ability but it provides a basic need, hearing, that is taken care of." Her statement implies that this basic processor does not provide "the finer aspects of hearing." The basic Cochlear processor that is sold in India is marketed as "designed for humid and dusty climates and environments and to withstand the rough and tumble of everyday life. It is . . . tough and reliable."[20] What kind of hearing is "good enough"? What is the difference between "basic" and "finer" hearing? It seems to me, however, that being able to hear in noise and to distinguish speech is indeed a "basic need."

I am left with lingering unease. According to researchers and practitioners, newer processors yield better results in noise.[21] Of course, practitioners stress that every child is different and that some children with older technology do better than others with newer technology (although this focus on difference and diversity is at jarring odds with the certainty with which cochlear implants are seen as producing successful outcomes across the board). Cochlear implants are held up as the gold standard in treatment, often compared to (other) lifesaving devices. But while cochlear implants might be the gold standard in theory, the sensory hierarchies that exist as a result of costs within political economic systems must be acknowledged.

Deaf children are not given a "whole sense" with basic processors, and providing them with such processors sets them up to be behind in a context in which they are already working through "degraded signals." We are talking about senses, not cars. I understand that providing children with older models of processors that are obsolete in other geographic contexts does not violate international ethical guidelines or best practices. I also understand that government administrators, surgeons, audiologists, and speech and language pathologists operate under the logic that "something is better than nothing." I critically consider what this "something" is and what other "somethings" might potentially exist, even when people claim that the alternative is "nothing." In the next chapter, I discuss the analytics of becoming and potentiality and the ways that cochlear implants are held up as technologies that can make deaf children "become normal" or "become near to normal" through normative sensing. Cochlear implants are seen as offering potential, which ostensibly recedes as a child gets older and the so-called critical period is passed. However, what happens to potentiality when children are working with and through older "basic" technology, and how are children afforded different sensory potentials?

Even a processor designed to "withstand the rough and tumble of everyday life" must be maintained. Coils and cables break, magnets become dull, and batteries need to be replaced. Aruna, an AVT practitioner, told me that "providing a cochlear implant to a child through the ADIP scheme is like giving a Mercedes to a street vendor." She wondered how a street vendor would ever be able to maintain an implant processor. Other people with whom I spoke did not go that far with classist comments, although car analogies abounded, perhaps because a car is also a significant family investment and an aspirational object. Another therapist told me that while the government was providing the car (the implant), she thought it was up to the families to pay for the gas (maintenance). These analogies can go only so far, however: a car is not implanted inside a person.

Some sympathetic government officials pointed out what they saw as the irony of the ADIP scheme: it was specifically designed for families below the poverty line, families that would be unable to afford to pay for maintenance. The officials also asserted, however, that if the implants worked, the families would become "motivated" and "find a way" to fund maintenance. Therapists often counseled families to keep a piggy bank with the child's name on it and deposit Rs 500 to 1,000 (US$6.75 to $12.50) in it each month, but for many families, even this amount was prohibitive.[22] At an NGO program providing implants, families were told that they needed to keep Rs 50,000 (US$666) in a bank account to pay for implant expenses. While they did not have to pay for the implant or the surgery, the NGO told them, they had to contribute to therapy costs so that they would "value the implant." For many families, however, financially "valuing the implant" existed in competition with paying for food, educational fees, and other medical expenses. A family might have to make the impossible choice between paying for an implant cable and paying the school fees for another child, for example.

This discourse about "not getting anything for free" was ubiquitous. A surgeon at a prestigious government hospital stated: "If people get it for free they will not value it. If I give you this pen for free, will you value it? No, you won't try to keep it safe or maintain it." Another surgeon told me: "What I tell the parents is, you people have a cell phone, you have a TV, you have cable. Every month you have certain expenses. So, why can't you have an expense of a hearing implant? Why should the government do everything throughout their lifetime?" Switching to first person and taking the perspective of an imagined implant recipient, this surgeon went on: "The minute I know the government is going to give, I am not going to take care of my processor." How could he be so certain? And from another surgeon: "Just as you would do for clothing or various other things, bettering your home, you should factor in something for the maintenance. Okay, you got the car for free, but you need to take care of maintenance." Here "taking care" is entirely financial and ignores all of the other ways in which families "take care" of implants and children.

I do not know why government bureaucrats and professionals think that families would not value cochlear implants (similar arguments are made about aids and assistive devices such as wheelchairs and prosthetics).[23] Recall, for example, the father quoted above who said (only half jokingly) that he treats his son's implant more carefully than he treats his son. When surgeons and professionals tell families things such as "After the implant switch-on, your child will have a new life," or, as it is commonly put in Hindi, "Switch on ke bad dusara janam hoga," why would they think that families would not value that life, or specifically the device that can activate that life? Indeed, the implant ostensibly activates an immanent set of relations with and in the world that are valuable beyond the value of the implant as a consumer good. The rub is that these relations are fixed by and through the consumer good itself.

A Mumbai-based NGO that funds cochlear implants as one of its flagship programs recently decided to curtail the number of implants funded each year because the foundation must now also focus on maintaining the devices it has provided. The program manager told me that the foundation realized that families are unable to maintain the devices on their own, and the foundation is ethically bound to help them. The NGO started this program because it saw implants as "life changing," and so how could it allow the implants to stop working and lives to change back? The program manager said that she could not say no to families and that she recognizes that there is now a lifetime relationship between the families and the foundation (a statement similar to that made by cochlear implant manufacturers regarding their users). Although she did not say so, it is worth noting that there is also a lifetime relationship between the foundation and the cochlear implant corporations. The most important thing, the program manager emphasized, is that children do not become nonusers, or go off-ear. "Life changing" can go either way.

Becoming a Nonuser and Going off the Path

What happens when nonuse occurs? Not using something might mean not becoming or unbecoming (Ahmed 2019, 45); it might also mean becoming something else and opening up other possibilities. The use of one thing or embarking on one useful path serves to limit other (also potentially useful) options. When one starts walking along a well-used path, the path seems commonsensical or natural. As Sara Ahmed notes (2019, 42),

"The law of most paths: following a path makes a path easier to follow." In chapter 1, I discussed how the state hopes that its central government implant program will make cochlear implantation a well-trodden path. As I noted, Joint Secretary Sharma spoke of building cultures of surgery, implantation, and therapy and bringing down the costs of implants. I wonder, though: What about the work needed to maintain a path? And how do you decide not to follow a path or to seek out another path? Families are told that cochlear implantation is the only option for their deaf children, the only path they can use. It thus seems the obvious thing to do.

I think about a need for multiple paths particularly in the aftermath of India's massive lockdowns during the spring of 2021, a response to the Covid-19 pandemic by the Bharatiya Janata Party government. Many families were forced to return to their villages, where they had no access to audiology or therapy services. In extreme cases, they even left their children's implants and accessories behind as they frantically packed their belongings to leave cities before lockdowns started. The pandemic, which continues at the time of this writing, has resulted in ongoing restrictions to and disruptions of movement, medical care, education, and employment as well as significant supply chain interruptions.

Before the pandemic, during the summer of 2019, I came across an interesting object in the offices and clinics of many Indian audiology and speech and language pathologists: a small cardboard container for office supplies, made to look like a yellow-and-black ambulance. Printed across the sides, top, and back of the ambulance, in capital letters, were two sentences: "HEARING LOSS IS AN EMERGENCY" and "ACT NOW." In most cases, the professionals who occupied those offices and clinics agreed with the urgent messages (although they commented that the cardboard container was not particularly durable). This ambulance was part of the Cochlear corporation's marketing strategy designed to emphasize the importance of cochlear implantation for young children—sooner rather than later and as early as possible. The ambulance, apparently, would carry the child along unblocked roads to a hospital, where the child would undergo cochlear implant surgery. But what happens when a pandemic, an emergency like Covid-19, throws a wrench into that trajectory? And what about other complications such as supply chain breakdowns, inability to pay for maintenance, lack of qualified surgeons, audiologists, and speech and language therapists, or desires for different futures? What other trajectories are possible, and how does the discourse that "deafness is a neurological emergency" disallow other possibilities?

On March 26, 2020, the *Sydney Morning Herald* published an article headlined "Kids with Hearing Loss Will Suffer from Surgery Delays: Cochlear" (Danckert 2020), which quoted Cochlear's CEO:

> A child born with hearing loss is a neurological emergency. A child born with hearing loss isn't getting the parts of their brain that are there for hearing stimulated with sound. The quicker that gets stimulated with sound the quicker that part of the brain learns what sound is, learns what speech is and to wire itself for speech and hearing. Earlier cochlear implantation for children born with hearing loss leads to them obtaining age-appropriate speech and language faster than delayed implantation.

The article reported that because "elective surgeries" had been halted as a result of the pandemic, children who needed cochlear implants were not getting their surgeries. The message was that the longer a child waits to be implanted, the less potential that child has to become listening and speaking. And meanwhile, the families of deaf children were sitting at home and waiting for surgeries to resume. Families approved for the ADIP scheme waited to be called for surgery, not knowing what else to do. (Also at the time, Facebook and other social media platforms were filled with stories from around the world about people whose dogs had eaten their cochlear implant processors and who could not get replacements, people who could not get audiology appointments for cochlear implant mapping, and people whose surgeries were delayed indefinitely.)

I was, and remain, concerned about this representation of deafness as a neurological emergency and the urgency attached to it: "ACT NOW." Because of Covid-19, families have not been able to act now, or at least not in the ways they are supposed to act. Nor have they been given options for other paths on which to embark. Such a focus on hearing loss as an immediate emergency and crisis requiring a present response also obscures the lifelong process of implant maintenance. Since the beginning of the pandemic, many families of implanted children in India and internationally have been unable to have devices mapped or repaired and have lacked access to batteries and essential accessories.[24]

SAMAR JIT DUTTA
@SAMARJITDUTTA76

···

@narendramodi @AmitShah @drharshvardhan @TajinderBagga Sir, I am father of a child with hearing impaired. During this lockdown period my child (using a cochlear implant) facing a lot of problem regarding maintenance and supply of batteries. She needs four batteries per day.

4:10 AM · Apr 19, 2020 · Twitter for Android

SAMAR JIT DUTTA @SAMARJITDUTTA76 · Apr 19, 2020   ···
Replying to @SAMARJITDUTTA76
Please include the hearing aids related items into essential items for speed post & e-commerce courier. please take necessary action asap so that she can get it quickly.

1

SAMAR JIT DUTTA @SAMARJITDUTTA76 · Apr 19, 2020   ···

During the early days of the Covid-19 pandemic, an Indian father of an implanted child tweets to the prime minister, the minister of home affairs, the minister of health and family welfare, and a Bharatiya Janata Party–affiliated political figure to implore them to help him get batteries for his daughter's cochlear implant. Because of the ongoing pandemic, many families have been unable to access working cochlear implants, batteries, and/or essential mappings and therapy sessions. Image from Twitter.

I am reminded of a conversation that I had with an Indian cochlear implant surgeon. In addition to being an ENT practitioner and surgeon, Dr. Swarnad runs programs offering early intervention and elementary school classes for implanted children (I discuss his approach to his work in chapter 2). I asked Dr. Swarnad what he thought about the messages on the Cochlear ambulances, and he replied, in contrast to most of the other surgeons and therapists with whom I spoke, that he does not think that deafness is an emergency per se. However, he said, a young deaf child who does not feel deficient or lacking now will come to feel that she is missing something when she is old enough to enter school. This feeling of inferiority will develop when she is unable to do the same things that other children can do because of structural barriers in educational and employment institutions. Dr. Swarnad also noted that schools are not designed for children who cannot participate through listening and speaking. I appreciated his recognition of these structural issues and wondered if framing them as an emergency would also be productive. That is, what if instead of a focus on deafness as a neurological emergency, there is recognition of the existence of an (infra)structural emergency around access to education, employment, and everyday life that exceeds the boundaries of an individual deaf child and her neurology? Returning to Ahmed's (2019) provocations on use and AVT practitioners' claims that deaf children's neural pathways need to be used or they will be taken over and reorganized, I see these reorganized neural pathways as paths in and of themselves. Indeed, Ahmed ultimately calls for us to refuse instructions and get off the (narrow) path, to see misfitting as offering an opportunity to use another path (199, 204).

Families often have no idea that other possible paths exist, that there are other ways of becoming and other sensory infrastructures to engage. In an April 2020 vlog posted on Facebook, an Indian Sign Language–speaking Deaf activist, reflecting on deaf people's experiences during Covid-19, urged:

> Break down that wall and take a chance in learning sign language. It would be a great alternative for you when the batteries in your hearing aids/Cochlear Implant die. You'll be surprised at how there is a whole new world for you to join. You will realize you don't have to work so hard to "fit in" compared to trying to fit in with Hearing people.[25]

In these words, which the activist transcribed into English to accompany his ISL vlog post, we see a new paradigm: a move from "maintenance problems" to a focus on world building, or a "whole new world for you to join." Addressing not only deaf people but also parents, school administrators, audiologists and speech and language pathologists, and state officials, this activist encourages all to learn to sign and to support sign language. In doing so, he focuses on building new kinds of sensory infrastructures that include deaf and hearing signers, teachers and early intervention workers who know and teach in ISL, sign language interpreters, and audiologists and speech and language pathologists who will inform families about and encourage different kinds of outcomes. As with cochlear implants, however, this sensory infrastructure comes with issues of maintenance and sustainability, in that the state has not recognized ISL, and ISL-speaking teachers and interpreters are financially, pedagogically, and politically undervalued.

A faculty member at the Indian Sign Language Research and Training Centre argued that "ISL only requires the use of two hands and no fancy technology." While this is an overly simplistic argument that ignores that the "body is always-already technological" (Manning 2007, 117), it is provocative to consider how ISL might require fewer resources in terms of technological infrastructure and more resources in terms of human labor and human infrastructure, such as ISL teachers and interpreters. A competition is set up between ISL and cochlear implants, and when families are actually told about both, they are further instructed that they must choose one or the other. This competition is promoted by the state itself as it creates fixed categories of people. In a press release related to a September 2018 event for International Day of Sign Languages, for which the theme was "With Sign Language, Everyone Is Included," the Indian Ministry of Social Justice and Empowerment stated:

> Sign language has been used for over centuries. The language capabilities of deaf children who use sign language are better. There is no advantage to delaying exposure to sign language, and research on the development of language has found that early exposure reduces the risks of language development. Lot of intensive therapy is needed after CI, even then the success is not guaranteed. (Press Information Bureau 2018)

The state—the same ministry—offers cochlear implants as a flagship program while also denigrating implantation without investing substantial resources in the thing that it represents as an alternative. This simultaneous discursive and financial over- and underinvestment and creation of competing infrastructures reveals state ambivalence and is also a form of violence.

To be clear, the state has not invested in creating infrastructure that would enable ISL to be a visible path for families. The Indian Sign Language Research and Training Centre ran pilot ISL-based early intervention programs in four states, but none of these programs were extended or renewed, despite considerable enthusiasm. Employees at the ISLRTC are endeavoring to create (and ultimately maintain) a new ISL infrastructure, but they are doing so without funding and resources. When I observed an ISL training course for parents that was part of a pilot program, I saw parents eagerly learning ISL and expressing enthusiasm for the opportunities it offered them to (finally) have conversations with their children. As an employee at the ISLRTC told me, ISL is often the last resort for families after they have gone down many paths, but when they do find it, a new world opens up. Deaf and hearing activists are attempting to make ISL more visible through social media and are asking the state to foreground ISL in education, interpreting, and everyday life.

When I talked with Indian audiologists, speech and language pathologists, and surgeons about ISL, their response was that "it is difficult because not many people know it." Deaf activists are trying to create a world in which more people know (about) it. In one remarkable instance, they were successful: the chief orator at the 2019 CIGI conference was an experienced audiologist and speech and language pathologist who used her platform to stress the importance of ISL and to point out that both Indian disability laws and the UNCRPD mention sign language. She asked those present to stop ignoring ISL's existence and to educate themselves about it. The audience listened politely, and then subsequent presentations returned to the topics of surgical techniques and the importance of bilateral implantation.

Deaf children should not learn ISL simply because cochlear implants are difficult to maintain. Families ought to be made aware of the many paths on which they can travel, and as more paths are used, the easier they will be to embark on. As Ahmed notes (2019, 41), "The more a path is used, the more a path is used." There is always the risk, however, of going down the path of an institution like the Lady Noyce School in Delhi—a state-run school filled to the brim with deaf children from all over the National Capital Region, located on prime land close to the city center, but not maintained. The school is overcrowded and has many vacant teacher positions. Much of the time, the students are ignored as the teachers sit outside and chat. Children, many of them from families living below the poverty line, peer out through the school's broken or bare windows, and it is rare to see an implant or a hearing aid on any of their ears. What one does see is ISL being used. This use of ISL is remarkable, because, as a government administrator pointed out, the school has no language policy and teachers do not use speech, sign, or total communication; they do and use "nothing," he said, rather dramatically.

The Delhi government recently took over part of the school's land, its poorly maintained recreation grounds, for its Social Welfare Department. During the summer of 2019, I met the principal of Lady Noyce School, a newly transferred social worker who was also new to deaf education. Afterward, I went next door to the Social Welfare Department, where I met the administrators overseeing the school. They were conducting interviews to fill some of the school's empty teaching posts and permitted me to observe. I asked if the interviews included testing for sign language competency, and the interviewers, including the Indian Administrative Service officer overseeing the department, and I had a conversation about the importance of ISL. One of the interviewers was a senior teacher at the school, and he said that he knew no ISL when he first started teaching, but the students had taught him all the ISL that he now knows. The IAS officer asked me and the other interviewers, "Why are we not paying the children, since they are doing the teaching?" This school is poorly maintained and overused despite its run-down condition. It is a place where deaf children learn ISL from other deaf children and form lasting relationships; it offers formative relational infrastructure despite its lack of material and pedagogical infrastructure. How might this school become well used, I wonder?

When thinking about this Delhi-based school, I am reminded that a cochlear implant surgeon in another Indian city told me that all of the deaf schools in that city would shut down because implanted children would no longer need these schools. After he told me this, I visited the schools in question and learned that they are just as well used and underfunded as ever. They currently serve a crucial function: a principal told me that increasingly her school was enrolling deaf children, some of them with implants, who previously attended mainstream schools and learned nothing. The teachers had to do significant work to bring these children up to grade level.

Brett Lee, the famous cricket player, now retired, who serves as Cochlear's "global hearing ambassador," is quoted on the company's website: "I can't imagine cricket without sound—on the field not hearing the appeals and the crowd, off the field not hearing team mates, or at home not hearing family. I can't imagine it. A cochlear implant can change all of that. I've seen it happen. The implant takes a person from silence to sound. It is a wonderful, life changing moment."[26] This statement, and others like it, represents very clearly what Alison Kafer (2013, 4) calls "ableist failures of imagination." It is these kinds of failures of imagination that contain people to one path and keep them from expanding what is imaginable; recall the "new world" invoked by the ISL activist quoted above. (Internationally, there are many wonderful cricket players who are deaf.) How might families learn about the many paths, the many sensory infrastructures, that exist and learn that there are forms of care outside of caring for a machine and a single sense? Becoming a nonuser can be the beginning of a new path. In the next chapter, I explore tensions around becoming and argue that becoming normal constrains possibilities for being, sensing, and relating.

Becoming Normal

Potentiality beyond Passing

What becomes of norms if we are serious in saying that they are part of lived reality already? And what should we make of the dazzling plurality of configurations, of the mixtures and interferences of multiple normalities?

—Annemarie Mol

Okay, a child implanted at one and a half to two years of age with bilateral cochlear implants is normal. Definitely. And we have at least a dozen of those to prove that. I can't say this child is not normal. So if you catch them early, if we implant them at less than three years—you know the neural plasticity—and you do a bilateral cochlear implant, they are no different from so-called normals.

—Dr. Murthy, cochlear implant surgeon in Bangalore

Becoming and Potentiality

In India, discussions of cochlear implants and discussions of normality go hand in hand, often in an adverbial dance. This conjoining happens in multiple domains, including the state, the clinic, the school, the home, and popular media. A 2019 *Hindustan Times* article on the successful cochlear implantation of two children under the central government–funded Assistance to Disabled Persons for Purchase/Fitting of Aids/Appliances scheme in Pune, India, reported that Dr. Ajay Chandanwale, the dean of the hospital in which the surgeries were conducted, said that "with recent advances in medical science and technology doctors are able to help hearing impaired patients to lead a near normal life." In an interview, a cochlear implant surgeon told me that implants can make children "normal se nazdik" (near to normal), and that a child who is implanted early enough can become "bilkul normal" (perfectly normal).

Consider this additional assortment of comments from state, medical, NGO, and family representatives: A Ministry of Social Justice and Empowerment official told me that cochlear implants prevent and remove deafness. After implantation, "a child is no longer deaf and is no longer a person with a disability. Slowly, through learning how to talk, he becomes totally normal." Similarly, the director of an Indian NGO that funds cochlear implant surgery and re/habilitation decided to focus on implants because they are "truly a huge and life-changing intervention," and after implantation "the children can go to normal schools and they can participate in mainstream society, they are talking and they are part of mainstream life." He then commented that cochlear implants enable children "to live normal lives." The director of the Rehabilitation Council of India, a government institute that oversees special education teacher training and curriculum, told me that children with cochlear implants do not need special education; they can work with "normal teachers and in normal classrooms, they become normal." And a mother told me that she decided to implant her twin sons after audiologists told her that cochlear implants would make her sons "nearest to normal."

Physicians, surgeons, government bureaucrats, and family members stressed that cochlear implants create a capacity that brings someone close to or near to normal or makes someone almost normal. In this line of thought (and line of flight; Deleuze and Guattari 1987, 3), cochlear implants create conditions of possibility for proximity or approximation to normal, with "normal" meaning and modifying an array of actions and ways of being: normally speaking, normally hearing, attending a normal school, having a normal job, and living a normal life, among other things. As a result of cochlear implantation and subsequent auditory and language training, deaf children potentially have the capacity—as evidenced through their performance in a sound booth—to move through life normally. Cochlear implants activate sensory normality and create potentiality for becoming normal in other aspects of life. They activate "magic," as discussed by the mothers quoted in chapter 3. *The magic of normality.*

In another line of thought, also referenced above in some of my interlocutors' comments, this period of potentiality is finite, in that deaf children eventually become what they are supposed to be. Postimplantation, some deaf children test with (near to) typical hearing in sound booths and/or attain age- or grade-appropriate language skills, which is the goal, and they can now live normal lives. These are the children who are, as the surgeon mentioned above put it, "bilkul normal." Normal, however, is a fragile accomplishment, in that technology can fail and background noise might usurp. For such children, then, normality, once reached, is context dependent and always precarious. There is always the potential for normality to be derailed.

Gilles Deleuze (1997, 225–26) writes: "To become is not to attain a form (imitation, identification, Mimesis) but to find the zone of proximity, indiscernibility, or undifferentiation, where one can no longer be distinguished from *a* woman, *an* animal, or *a* molecule" (also see Deleuze and Guattari 1987, 238–39). In thinking about Deleuze's oft-mentioned becoming-animal, becoming-woman, becoming-man, I attend to "becoming-normal," the processes that catalyze becoming, and the possibilities opened up and foreclosed by such becoming. How might we empirically analyze becoming? As João Biehl and Peter Locke (2017a, 84) note in discussing the open-endedness and plasticity of the individuals with whom anthropologists work: "Moving away from the overdetermined and toward the unfinished, human beings intrude into reality, enlarging our sense of what is socially possible and desirable." In their introduction to their edited volume on the anthropology of becoming, they call for "new kinds of imagination" and argue that "the concept of becoming destabilizes the primacy of being and identity" (Biehl and Locke 2017b, 29, 8).

While I appreciate this (hopeful) analytic attention to becoming, I am concerned that instead of "enlarging our sense of what is socially possible and desirable," we are seeing a *narrowing* or *contraction,* because it is indeed increasingly possible—through biotechnologies such as cochlear implantation—to become normal.[1] I argue that it is productive to think of becoming normal through and in relation to the concept of potentiality, or the idea that there is a teleological path with a distinct goal and clear outcomes. In the case of cochlear implants, these narrow outcomes include, as we have seen above, normal listening, normal speaking, attending a normal school, having a normal audiogram, and more broadly living a normal life.

Consider the narrowness of the measures used to determine successful outcomes with cochlear implants, such as the Categories of Auditory Perception Scale, the Speech Intelligibility Rating Scale, and the Meaningful Auditory Integration Scale. These are used to evaluate such things as how a person responds to sound, whether a person can repeat back closed sets of words, and the intelligibility of a person's speech. David Pisoni et al. (2008, 53) point out that "the conventional battery of speech and language tests that is routinely administered to measure clinical outcome and benefit was developed by the CI manufacturers to establish efficacy as part of the clinical trials for U.S. Food and Drug Administration (FDA) approval." These tests therefore do not tell us anything about quality of life and relations outside the sound booth. Indeed, as Frank Iglehart (2016) argues, controlled sound booth results often do not reflect what audition through cochlear implants is like in noisy classrooms.

Deaf children's malleability is what gives them potentiality. Without cochlear implants, they are considered to have far less or no potentiality. They might even have the wrong kind of potentiality, in that they could potentially become sign language speakers. Karen-Sue Taussig, Klaus Hoeyer, and Stefan Helmreich (2013, S5) note that "in biomedical practices, potentiality indexes a gap between what is and what might, could, or even should be." They further suggest "that people appear to ascribe potentiality to those things they believe can be manipulated (or they desire to manipulate) and not to those perceived as being beyond human control (or seen as not in need of change)" (S7). In *becoming-normal,* the hyphen represents such a space of potentiality. In this context of cochlear implantation, deaf children are seen to have potentiality because there is a sense that they can be worked upon to become what they should be. They can become listening and speaking and thus normal.

Normal can refer to normal hearing, normal speaking, normal activities of everyday life, normal brain organization, and normal Indian Sign Language use.[2] I analyze what normality means and does to and for different interlocutors and how it is a simultaneously prized and ambivalent subject position. I explore tensions between normal as a quality or experience of being in the world that is not fixed or stable and normal as related to normative, a statistical, prescriptive, and standardized category of analysis, here specifically in relation to hearing. Normal is both fixed and a moving target. (I am concerned about fixed targets; as I discuss in chapter 4, fixing can be problematic.) Disentangling these two ways of thinking about what it means to be normal is challenging, but I argue for more value to be placed on the former: for normal as an ever-expanding quality and experience, distinct from normative understandings of the senses, communication, and social relations.[3] My argument has stakes for disability studies and deaf studies scholars as well as for lay disabled and deaf people in that they also often desire a differently normal becoming that is no less teleological: becoming-disabled or becoming-deaf in terms of identity and community formation.[4] I attend to the ways that sensory infrastructures enable certain kinds of becoming while constraining others and to the active and ambivalent work that becoming normal entails. While throughout this book I analyze the ways in which the senses are relationally produced and distributed, here I attend to how potentiality and (ideas and ideals of) normality stick to individuals, their brains, and their practices, while also being moving targets.[5] The individual person is both object and outcome.

From Passing to Becoming

On a cold winter evening in 2019, I sat with my mother in my living room in Chicago. I asked her what passed through her mind when she found out that I was deaf, all those years ago when she was a young mother in Queens, New York. She told me, plaintively, that she had wanted me to be normal. She wanted me to have a normal education and normal friends, a normal life. At that time, cochlear implants had been introduced, but they were not (yet) normalized. Thus, my mother did not mention wanting me to have normal hearing, because this was not a possibility known to her. In the absence of normal hearing, she wished for me to have a normal life. I wonder what would have been different if I had been born forty years later, what she and my father would have done, and if she might have said, when I asked about it as an adult, "I wanted you to have normal hearing"—because this could have been possible. What my mother wanted (and what she still wants) is not different from what my interlocutors in India desire, although she was able to imagine a so-called normal future in the absence of normal hearing. Imagining and creating this future took significant work, from arguing with school administrators to admit me to elementary school to pushing against an Individualized Education Plan that included a goal that I would independently use an ATM by the time I was in high school.[6]

My mother's thoughts on normality remind me of an important point that Adam Geary (2010, 340) makes in his discussion of Biehl and Locke's anthropology of becoming: "There is no necessary conflict among desire, normativity, and becoming." Geary means that people can work toward the fulfillment of normative desires that uphold existing structures and value systems. He reminds us of Saba Mahmood's (2005) discussion about how norms are learned in embodied ways, through practiced repetition, habituation, and eventual becoming. Mahmood notes: "I want to move away from an agonistic and dualistic framework—one in which norms are conceptualized on the model of doing and undoing, consolidation and subversion—and instead think about the variety of ways in which norms are lived and inhabited, aspired to, reached for, and consummated" (23). Mahmood's approach is helpful for both parsing out the enactment of norms and excavating forms of agency that are oriented toward upholding norms. Her work on ethical self-fashioning and modes of subjectivation has much to offer those of us working on re/habilitation-related practices, in that re/habilitation involves the training of the (plastic) body through repetition, motivated by desire. What happens in cases in which desires for normativity exist but there is no, or less, plasticity and/or potentiality?

While I focus on becoming, disability studies and the anthropology of disability have devoted much analytic attention to the frame of passing. How do becoming and passing have different stakes? "Passing," according to Erving Goffman ([1963] 1986, 73), refers to the ways that disabled people or people with other so-called stigmatized conditions conceal that which is stigmatized and engage in identity management in order to appear normal.[7] Importantly, a stigmatized condition, in Goffman's framing, is static and unchanging. Becoming, on the other hand, is about malleability and plasticity, about the potential to be proximate and indistinguishable, the blurring (and ultimate eradication) of the hyphen between becoming and normal. Becoming invokes and involves shifting capacities, embodiments, and identifications. Deleuze (1997, 225) differentiates becoming from "imitation, identification, [and] Mimesis," which are processes and practices that are akin to passing.

Tobin Siebers (2004, 2) points out: "To pass or not to pass—that is often the question." Analyzing passing has been productive for both disability studies scholars and disabled people in everyday life, as they negotiate concealment, fitting in, disclosure, and tensions around likeness, similitude, and proximity. Jeffrey Brune and Daniel Wilson (2013, 2) note that "passing is an act that blurs the lines between disability and normality, but those lines were not always sharp to begin with." Alongside this, they state that "passing expresses, reifies, and helps create concepts of normality." While analyzing interactions between those who are stigmatized and those who are normal, Goffman ([1963] 1986) never expands on or theorizes about what it means to be normal, and normality is an unmarked category.[8] Passing, however, always maintains difference at some level. People do not become the thing that they are passing as, even if they perform or act in a certain way.[9] Crucially, there is no potentiality with passing, at least not on what Deleuze and Guattari (1987, 248–49, 274–75) call a molecular level, the level of body plasticity and malleability.[10]

Disability studies scholars and disabled people have critiqued passing as an impossible and taxing empirical process and have emphasized passing's harmful impacts on the development of self and identity. In 1997, Brenda Jo Brueggeman wrote, in an essay aptly titled "On (Almost) Passing," about her experience negotiating the "multiply hyphenated" category of "hard-of-hearing" and how at different points in her life she had strived to inhabit the categories of "hearing" and "Deaf," failing at both. Of her childhood and teenage years in rural Kansas, she wrote: "I found myself pressured into passing and then greatly pressured by my passing. Some days I could pass; some days I could *almost* pass; some other days the 'almost' got yanked out from under me" (650). As an adult, while completing a PhD and trying to pass as "H/hearing," Brueggeman went to Gallaudet University in Washington, D.C., to conduct an ethnographic study of deaf student writers, and to experiment herself with trying to pass in another context, this time as a D/deaf person (647). As she matured, Brueggeman noted, she had become more willing to "unmask myself, my deafness, before others have the chance to" (659). In a follow-up essay titled "On (Always) Passing," published in 2019, twenty-two years after the first, Brueggeman flipped the script to write about always passing—as a deaf person. Deaf studies scholars would argue that she became deaf, which she already and always was (Ladd 2003).

In Kristen Harmon's (2013, 169) discussion about the trials of passing, she shares that her mother thought that her daughter would grow up to become hearing:

> The notion of a deaf child who effectively grows up to become hearing is a compelling cultural fantasy, one that appears in the subtext of much of the discourse surrounding educational approaches for deaf children. For one, the continuing development of ever smaller and more powerful hearing devices (surgical and

non-surgical) means that these are held out as the promise of an eternally deferred, *just about hearing without actually being hearing,* future.

Harmon argues, in an analysis of short videos of interviews with deaf children produced by an organization promoting listening and spoken language, that "passing is conditional and generally dependent on the silent practices of lip reading and observing . . . but for limited moments during the interviews, some children do look down and listen through cochlear implants and hearing aids. In those moments, the children could pass as hearing children" (175). While some of these children might have so-called normal hearing through cochlear implants, and as such might actually be hearing, Harmon points out both the impossibility of totally passing and the harms of trying—and she writes positively of her own experience when she finally stopped trying to pass and allowed herself to "become" deaf (despite and in opposition to her mother's desires).

Brueggeman's and Harmon's accounts illuminate the active and ongoing work required of those endeavoring to pass. The work is physical—straining one's eyes to read lips and reading more textbooks than required—and emotional in that one is always on guard to avoid being found out. Passing is a tenuous and impermanent achievement that can be destroyed at any time. For disability studies scholars and disabled communities there is often a teleological narrative through which one moves from passing as normal to becoming disabled. As part of this narrative, one often "comes out" as and becomes a disabled person (Samuels 2003). One realizes latent potentiality of a different sort and becomes a member of a disability community or culture.[11] This teleological becoming is a well-trodden, well-documented, and well-theorized path in disability studies (Barnes and Mercer 2001; Brown 2002; Linton 1998) as well as in deaf studies (Ladd 2003; Lane, Hoffmeister, and Bahan 1996). This is a celebratory story (and counternarrative) of pride, community, and (re)clamation; it is also a story of potentiality of a different sort. I analyze the opposite of the happy story of becoming disabled or becoming deaf, although I acknowledge that for many people, like Harmon's mother and my mother, becoming normal is also an accomplishment worthy of celebration.

Becoming normal is a process involving families as well as broader social, educational, and re/habilitative networks, although it is ultimately focused on the individual. Thinking about the stakes both reveals the paucity of audiological, identity, and experiential categories and raises questions about what we might call deaf hearers or hearing deaf people (with or without hyphens).[12] Mara Mills (2015, 45) calls for an acknowledgment of a "deaf spectrum" or "deafnesses," in the plural. As she notes: "A deaf spectrum has replaced the deaf/hearing binary in both the biomedical and cultural realms. At the same time, audiometric categories of hearing impairment do not map neatly onto deaf identities." This spectrum is largely uncharted terrain, with no clear trajectories for becoming, unlike the normal trajectories sought after by many cochlear implant proponents and unlike the fixed communication categories and outcomes set out by the Alexander Graham Bell Association in its communication spectrum (as discussed in chapter 2).[13]

In India, the people I met who had cochlear implants called themselves "a cochlear implant person" or a *machinewalla* (a machine person, said both seriously and sarcastically), in addition to identifying as both normal and deaf. People expressed significant ambivalence and confusion, and had strong opinions, about whether implanted people were still eligible for education and employment under government reservations, or quotas, for deaf and disabled people because perhaps they were no longer deaf. An administrator at a well-known school for aural and oral deaf children in Mumbai said that her students were often denied discount railway identification cards because they spoke too well. (Too well compared to whom?) An audiologist wondered, with whom should implanted people be compared—deaf people without implants or hearing people? And there was always a question about whether implanted children should have their hearing tested with or without their implants as part of the disability certificate assessment process. The difference in audiogram between an aided test and an unaided one could be as much as a hundred decibels.

On an international Facebook group dedicated to cochlear implant experiences, people routinely pose the question, "Are you deaf when you have cochlear implants?" This question generates debate and an assortment of replies, as it does among stakeholders in India. I am reminded of an American Sign Language sign and concept for a deaf person who acts like a hearing person: such a person is considered "mentally hearing" or "think hearing," and the sign for "hearing" is signed up on the forehead as opposed to on the mouth.[14] The sign is meant to index a negative concept, in that it suggests that a deaf person is behaving, thinking, communicating, or acting like a hearing person (whatever that might mean).

This American Sign Language sign for "think hearing" pejoratively refers to deaf people who act like they are "mentally hearing" and/or oriented toward hearing values, often including listening and speaking. In contrast to this negative perspective, AVT practitioners and others actively work toward creating "mentally hearing" people: this is a goal and an ideal outcome. Illustration by Adrean Clark.

It foregrounds a deaf person who is trying to be something that he or she is not, as well as the idea that deaf and hearing are the only two categories that can exist, even together at the same time.

Normal Brains

While "think hearing" is meant pejoratively, I take it seriously and consider what it might mean for someone to be mentally hearing. Advocates of auditory verbal therapy and other re/habilitation approaches work toward making children and adults become mentally hearing. The current debates around deafness and language have largely crystallized for some in neurological studies about deaf children's brains and what happens to them when they receive visual or auditory input. According to proponents of AVT (such as those discussed in chapter 2), a deaf child can have a hearing brain as long as the auditory cortex is not "taken over" by vision. The brain is always normal (or mentally hearing) but can potentially become otherwise without the right input. What does it mean to claim that a deaf child can or does have a hearing brain?

A turn to the brain, and the idea that the brain is or can "become" a hearing brain, moves a discussion about how implanted children and adults inhabit the world away from an analysis of passing to one of becoming, as discussed above. The brain, according to this line of thinking, is normal. Its normality just needs to be tapped into, trained, and protected with the support of cochlear implants or other technology. As AVT researchers Carol Flexer and Ellen Rhoades (2016, 24) note: "Historically, conversations about hearing loss have focused on the ear. But, due to neurobiological research, today's conversations about sensory input focus on the brain. For example, we see with the brain; the eyes are the entryway to the brain for visual information. We smell with the brain; the nose is the pathway to the brain for olfactory stimuli. We hear with the brain; the ears are the *doorway* to the brain for auditory information."

Surgeons, audiologists, and speech and language professionals hold up cochlear implants as an unquestioned good that the public sector should provide and families should invest in—regardless of a child's age. However, the younger a child is when implanted, the more potential there is for a normal brain. During a presentation at the Cochlear Implant Group of India's 2019 conference in Mumbai, a professional audiologist and speech and language therapist who worked for one of the major cochlear implant corporations stressed the importance of timing for maximizing this potential. She focused on critical periods for implantation and learning listening and spoken language. A chart in her PowerPoint deck clearly outlined the commonly accepted stakes: from birth to three and a half years old is the maximum critical period for a child's learning language; from four years old to seven is the open critical period; and from eight to twelve is the questionable critical period. These neatly delineated periods map onto the "hearing potential" of a child (Estabrooks et al. 2016, 10) and represent a race against time, in which at any given point, plasticity is maximally,

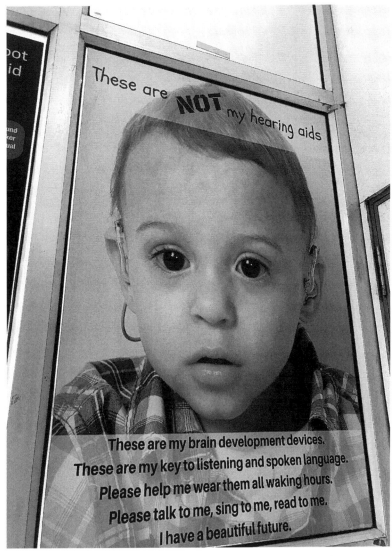

A poster on the door of a therapy room at a private audiology and speech and language clinic in India features a small boy wears hearing aids, although the caption says: "These are NOT my hearing aids. These are my brain development devices. These are my key to listening and spoken language. Please help me wear them all waking hours. Please talk to me, sing to me, read to me. I have a beautiful future." This image foregrounds the brain and the importance of language input during all waking hours. Photograph by author.

openly, or questionably present. The doorway to the brain—and to becoming normal—closes with age.

Flexer and Rhoades (2016, 27) emphasize that "identification of newborn hearing loss and other hearing differences should be considered a neurodevelopmental emergency." They go on to stress that neuroplasticity is greatest in the first three years of life, and "the younger the infant, the more neuroplasticity the child has" (30). If audition is not introduced and the brain does not stay wired for sound, "sensory deprivation" will take place, leading to cross-modal reorganization in favor of vision (30). As a result of cross-modal reorganization, the brain's "auditory neural capacity" will diminish (30). AVT advocates wish to foreclose another kind of becoming: becoming a deaf signer or someone oriented toward vision. AVT researcher and practitioner Elizabeth Rosenzweig (2011) notes, "The whole goal of the approach is that children with hearing loss should be given the skills necessary to leave and become whoever they want to be." This comment brings up questions about what kinds of becoming are encouraged and permitted.[15] Potential is pluripotent and can go or become wrong. As such, protecting potential involves being on guard against, and shutting down, the wrong pathways constantly.[16]

Like their counterparts internationally, Indian AVT practitioners and clinical audiologists increasingly focus on the brain in their marketing and other presentations, stressing that deaf children are "late" and experiencing "neurological emergencies."[17] In a presentation at the 2019 CIGI conference, Purnima, one of India's foremost AVT experts, started her PowerPoint slide deck with images of neurons firing. She stated that deaf children are born "behind" because they are supposed to begin hearing at twenty weeks in the womb. They have until seven years of age to reach their potential. After that, it "becomes too late and neural pathways are no longer available because they have become reorganized." Such comments about age, audition, and the potential of a child to utilize audition and thus to actualize a "hearing brain" are especially important in an Indian context, in which newborn hearing screening is not universal, and deaf children are typically diagnosed "late." These children are thus considered always already behind and not on an ideal developmental trajectory.[18]

When I visited Purnima at her office, she was conducting training for audiologists and speech and language pathologists from around India. Discussion topics were written on butcher paper on an easel. I zoomed in on one topic: "Older children: Is there hope?" Intrigued, I asked Purnima about this question, and she replied that, yes, there is hope, but expectations must be managed. She said that an older child can benefit from an implant and achieve some auditory discrimination, such as the ability to distinguish traffic sounds. However, the child's actual listening and speaking ability might not improve. Similarly, at a prestigious government hospital a clinician named Parvathi told me about an eight-year-old child who was just implanted, with whom she was working. She told the family: "See, your child has already crossed the age of plasticity. Though he will learn language, that will only be functional language, what he needs immediately. And if he doesn't practice it over a period of time, he is going to forget it." Purnima and Parvathi both stressed the importance of "managing expectations" while at the same time orienting families to futures for their children that would involve (limited or diminished) listening and spoken language opportunities. Potential was seen as a receding horizon as a child aged.

Why do families not intervene earlier? They might suspect that a child is not hearing but decide to wait before acting on their suspicion and seeking a hearing test; they may have a child's hearing tested and disbelieve the results, and then wait a bit before going elsewhere; they might think that a child will grow out of what appears to be a hearing impairment; or they might simply consider the child to be normal. At both the private and government speech and hearing institutes that I visited, it was not uncommon to see children five to seven years of age coming in, sometimes for the first time, for hearing tests. In many of these cases, the motivation was school admission or the need for a disability certificate. The audiologists who conducted the exams often said things like "The family is not accepting," although I had another interpretation, which was that the family was accepting but not intervening. They were not seeking diagnosis or actively trying to medicalize or change their children. Perhaps they had different ideas of their children's potential or were measuring potential in ways not predicated on listening and spoken language or language in general. Once they visited audiologists, families learned new ways of evaluating their children and thinking about goals and outcomes. Late diagnosis (although families might not feel that it is late) is also the reason the central government cochlear implant program offers funding to children up to age five and sometimes makes exceptions for six-year-olds. The age of diagnosis often dictates children's re/habilitation and treatment pathways, although these do not differ very much and always involve some focus on listening and spoken language. These different pathways index varied potential linguistic, sensory, and communicative futures for children.

Normal Hearing

According to many surgeons and re/habilitation practitioners, children are simply no longer deaf after implantation. As an engineer working on India's indigenous cochlear implant told me: "The brain is intact and not impaired, but there are connectivity problems. With an implant, deaf children do hear and they hear normally in that the CI stimulates the auditory nerve." A cochlear implant is said to feed, stimulate, and maintain the brain through a proper connection. As Stefan Timmermans and Mara Buchbinder (2013, S27) note: "Technology designers—everyone involved in bringing a technology into use—charge new technologies with potential in the sense of a not yet realized desirable future attainable with their implementation." While these scholars analyze the ways that newborn genetic screening "is thus what it does" (S29), cochlear implants work similarly. There is often a moving target in that children are said to hear normally postimplant even if they do not speak normally. However, the former ostensibly sets up the conditions of possibility for the latter—and, eventually, normal life—to happen. AVT practitioners refer to this as the "domino effect," which relies on child development neatly following a sequence.

The therapists I observed repeatedly told families to point out sounds to their children and talk about them constantly, because their children hear these sounds, even if they do not respond. Professionals refer to an auditory hierarchy (Erber 1982), and many therapists show families charts of this hierarchy. The first step is sound detection (hearing sounds). The second step is discrimination (telling the difference between sounds), and the third is identification (identifying what is making the sounds and what they mean). The fourth and final step is comprehension (being able to follow connected speech, understand directions, and participate in interactive conversation). Children are supposed to move from sound detection to comprehension with training and practice. Within this step-by-step hierarchical model, it is assumed that "learning to listen develops incrementally from simple to more difficult tasks and that auditory skills progress from sound awareness to identification/comprehension in a stepwise, linear fashion" (Gibbons and Szarkowksi 2019, 350). If only it were that easy. However, this focus on hierarchies is dependent on the conviction that children actually hear. For parents and others, speech is needed as proof of hearing and is the ultimate goal.

As a program administrator at an NGO with a flagship cochlear implant program told me: "The child actually *hears* with the help of a cochlear implant and a processor. Then that information goes to the brain. Then the child develops his language. So it's basically hearing, understanding, and then talking." She went on: "Our kids after a cochlear implant are not deaf anymore. They hear everything, it's just a matter of making them understand." She said that she instructs parents: "A cochlear implant *is* done because your child does not hear. After a cochlear implant, your child *will* hear. Even the drop of a pin your child will hear." She tells parents that their children's experience is similar to watching an English movie without subtitles: they hear everything, but they do not understand what they are hearing. In this line of thinking, children hear as long as they wear their processors. They have "normal hearing" but must learn to understand what they hear, and then they will learn to speak. The administrator told me that parents are instructed to think about it this way: "Aapke bacche ko sunna hai, samajhna hai, aur bolna hai" (Your child listens, understands, and then speaks). Again, a seamless trajectory, like dominos falling in a line, is envisioned, with the ultimate goal being listening and speaking (with the emphasis on speech).

Therapists told me that parents often do not believe that their children hear with their implants because they are unresponsive to sounds. The therapists thus counseled parents that as long as the implant battery was working and the implant processor was not broken, their children could hear. They instructed parents to look for evidence of hearing at moments such as when the pressure cooker's whistle goes off or someone rings the doorbell. Parvathi, who sees more than twenty patients a day at a large government institution, admonishes parents: "The machine is not for speaking, the machine is for listening. If your child listens well, he will *talk!*" Parvathi and other therapists ask parents to take a leap of faith, to trust that the "machine" is doing its job in the absence of indicators such as the flashing lights on battery compartments that signal the batteries are dying. Parents are directed to privilege the signals emitted by "the machine" over signals, or their lack, from their children.[19]

Normal Life

In August 2019, I sat in a trendy coffee shop in Mumbai with Mahesh, a twenty-five-year-old man with two cochlear implants who adamantly told me that he is normal. He attends a regular college and receives no accommodations (he calls them "concessions") other than extra time on tests, although he never uses the extra time. In an essay that he wrote and subsequently shared with me, titled "The Pursuit of Normal," Mahesh wrote: "For most of us, possessing normal physical faculties is a given; something we take for granted. For me, however, it was a goal, a desire, a wish, and a hope." In his family's "race to being normal," Mahesh described, "like every other child I had a normal routine of school and homework and playtime. And I had a special routine: auditory verbal therapy to learn to listen and speak . . . , one-to-one sessions at home, hearing aid fittings and trials, cochlear implant surgery, care and maintenance of my equipment all became part of my life." In addition to providing an overview of these routines, Mahesh outlined his educational and recreational accomplishments, including mastering piano and playing badminton competitively in India's deaf league. While Mahesh did not write this explicitly, his "special routine" enabled sensory normality and was a foundation for and an essential part of his normal life.

Mahesh concluded his essay with the assertion: "I struggled to reach normalcy and when I reached that, I strove for more." Becoming normal meant successfully developing "normal physical faculties." However, this was not (yet) normal life. Mahesh's "striving for more" was not to have *more* normal hearing (he already had it). Rather, his normal hearing enabled potentiality in other areas, namely, in everyday activities that are typical for children of his class position. Mahesh is an excellent example of what AVT practitioners refer to as children who are ahead of their peers socially, linguistically, and academically because of the intervention they have received. Does being ahead make him other than normal? And what happens when a path is not a typical one? How do nonnormative paths threaten ideas and ideals of enacting normality?

Mahesh participated in a deaf youth badminton league, in which he became a prize-winning player. Initially he played only in normal leagues, but he did not place competitively in them. In 2011, he was invited to play at a World Deaf Badminton League tournament in Korea. At a subsequent international tournament in Bulgaria, he won a bronze medal. As Per Koren

Solvang and Hilde Haualand (2014) point out in their analysis of the complicated politics involved in deaf international sporting competitions, players must remove all hearing aids and implant processors when they play. Thus, Mahesh and other players who use hearing technology must become deaf, at least temporarily. Mahesh's mother was upset when he joined the deaf league because she saw it as evidence of failure; she did not see deaf badminton as part of normal life, and she did not want Mahesh to become any less normal or any more deaf. Mahesh's mother had become a well-respected auditory therapist in India and internationally; in recognizing and cultivating Mahesh's potentiality, she had unleashed hers as well.

But what happens when potential is circumscribed not just by brain plasticity but also by political economic factors? I move now to experiences that surface potentiality's friction and that constrain possible becoming. In chapter 3, I introduced Imran, a friendly and intuitive twelve-year-old boy whose family lived originally in a village about five hours from Delhi; here I go into his case in greater detail.

When Imran was five years old, his parents learned about cochlear implants from an advertisement placed in a Hindi-language newspaper by a cochlear implant surgeon who practiced in Delhi. The family traveled to Delhi to meet the doctor, and he encouraged them to implant Imran but said it would cost Rs 7 lakh (US$10,000) for the necessary medical tests, surgery, implant, external processor, postoperative mapping, and speech therapy. He showed them videos of formerly deaf children now talking and told them that unless Imran was implanted, he would never be normal. The doctor then suggested that the family sell their land or take out a loan, a daunting prospect for a family in which the father was a wage laborer who sold cloth from a cart. The family saved and borrowed funds, and within a year, Imran was implanted.[20]

After one month of daily therapy that was included in the initial implant cost, the therapist said that Imran's mother had been taught how to do the therapy with Imran, and the family could return to their village, where Imran could attend a regular school. (Imran was not ready to be mainstreamed, but the family had run out of money to pay for therapy.) The boy's daily lessons with his mother would be supplemented by weekly trips to Delhi for follow-up therapy and implant mapping. After five years, during which Imran made no progress and did not learn anything in school, the family returned to Delhi to pursue more listening and spoken language–based options. There Imran was able to receive speech therapy from an NGO that a relative had told his parents about. A central government–run school admitted Imran, albeit with a falsified birth certificate identifying him as two years younger than he was (even then, Imran still lagged behind his classmates). His family established a delicate balance of schooling, therapy, and making do—although Imran was far from speaking and hearing "like normal children," as the surgeon had promised. Six years after implantation, and after the family had twice replaced implant cables and purchased batteries every six months, Imran's processor broke and needed to be replaced. The family had spent their savings and taken out loans to pay for travel, housing, and the implant. The broken processor was out of warranty, and the family could not afford a new one.

When I met the family, they were attending speech therapy twice a week, and Imran's mother was ordering him to speak different words. Instead of the *Suno!* (Listen!) that comes with AVT, she was saying *Bolo!* (Speak!) or *Bat karo!* (Talk!) and giving him different words to repeat— pencil, ball, fan, the names of fruits and vegetables, and so on (AVT practitioners would say that she was treating him like a parrot). Imran, modeling his mother's behavior, was very concerned about his missing implant— "Machine karab," he kept on saying; "The machine is broken." The broken machine was potentiality's hard limit for his mother and thus for him. It was also a convenient object on which to focus. Imran's teacher at the government school told me that he was not able to read or write although he was very social with his classmates. She said that she had fifty other children to focus on, and she could not give Imran special attention. She did not permit him to sit in the front of the noisy classroom because he was taller than the other students (she was unaware that he was older). Although mandated by the central government, a special educator was not (yet) attached to the school. The headmistress, however, was very attentive to students with disabilities and compiled a roster of them in a notebook optimistically titled "Late Bloomers." In this title she revealed her assumption that these children had potentiality and that they could and would reach grade level.

I accompanied Imran and his family to visit Aruna, a well-respected auditory verbal therapist in Delhi, for an assessment of how much Imran could hear with the hearing aid that he uses in his nonimplanted ear. As we sat in a small, colorful room, Aruna ran through different sounds with Imran before concluding that he "could not be an auditory child." She said that he was barely hearing with his hearing aid, he had never learned how to hear through his implant, and even if he had, his implant was no longer working. She stressed that Imran needed to learn language through visual and tactile cues and that he needed a working implant for environmental sounds, but the implant would not provide him with the ability to listen and speak like normal children. She said, "This hearing is good for him to get the environmental sounds, be aware of his environment, be alert about his environment . . . but it doesn't build his future." Aruna thought that it was no longer possible for Imran to become a hearing person, and she could not imagine a normal life for him (and she could tell this after an assessment of a few minutes based on how well he could hear blended consonants without visual cues). Instead, she recommended vocational training and skill development so that he could at least become independent, although she did not consider this a successful path. Because Imran could not be worked upon to become a hearing and speaking person, she could not imagine any potential successful future for him. Imran was no longer plastic in a way that was meaningful to Aruna. Note, too, that Aruna did not even consider as options that Imran could learn Indian Sign Language and attend an ISL-based school.

After the appointment with Aruna, I met Imran's surgeon. A young surgeon with a thriving practice, he proudly told me about the infrastructure he had built in Delhi for audiology and re/habilitation postimplantation (which had not existed when Imran was implanted). He said that he had told Imran's family about the importance of re/habilitation and encouraged them to stay in Delhi after implantation for a longer period of time (I do not know that I believed him). I commented that I was worried about Imran, about the fact that he was now twelve and could communicate only minimally. I mentioned that perhaps it would be good for Imran to learn ISL and to attend a deaf school (the headmistress at Imran's current school supported this idea). However, the surgeon replied, "No, actually, we don't recommend that children go for sign language after implantation. He can still learn to speak normally. It is not too late." While his words might be interpreted as naive or optimistic, it must be noted that they were also harmful. Imran was experiencing language deprivation (Hall, Hall, and Caselli 2019), and the surgeon was refusing him the possibility of a future in which he would have access to language, even if it was not spoken language. He was refusing Imran the possibility of developing a multimodal and multisensory life. For the surgeon, Imran was infinitely plastic, at least as long as this plasticity protected the doctor's practice and resonated with his goals. Potentiality existed only in relation to spoken language. The only potential future was a normal future.

A few days after we met with Aruna, Imran, his parents, and I visited an ISL-based deaf school that employed signing deaf teachers, a rarity in India. Imran and his father were excited to observe children fluently conversing in ISL as we visited classrooms. Imran's mother, however, was emphatically not happy, and she scowled at everything and everyone. At one point, a teenage boy approached us to tell us in ISL that he recognized Imran's school uniform (we had come directly from Imran's school). He wanted to tell us that he too had attended this chain of government schools. He had not learned anything there and had ultimately failed out because the school system stopped doing grace passing (automatic promotion to the next grade) in eighth class. He said that he was learning for the first time ever at this new school. Imran's mother looked at him as I interpreted what he said, and when he finished signing, she commanded him, "Bolo!" (Speak!). In spoken Hindi, he told us his name, his age, and where he lived.

When Imran's mother heard him, she said, "See, he can speak. This is what I want for my child." I gently reminded her what the boy had signed— that he had failed out of the other school and had not learned anything— but this was not of interest to her. All she wanted was for Imran to speak. Again, not hear, but speak. She said that she would do everything, that she was prepared to work hard.[21] Speech and language therapists like Aruna, however, told her it was too late, and that she had missed the window for teaching Imran language when he was younger. (In contrast, the director of the ISL-based school stressed that it was not too late to enroll Imran there, and that he would pick up ISL quickly.) Now Imran was twelve, very affectionate, and fun to snuggle and play with, but what would happen when he got older? The potential to become normal—at least in the way envisioned by Imran's mother, the surgeon, and the therapists with whom he met—was a receding horizon for Imran. Perhaps he could still pass by learning basic speech, which could provide access to (some aspects of) normal life?

Normatively Normal

And what of adults who "choose," perhaps ambivalently, to get implants? In July 2018, I took a two-hour road trip south from Delhi to Palwal, a small city in Haryana, to meet Rahul Dixit, a forty-five-year-old officer in the Indian Administrative Service.[22] Some years before, Dixit had twice passed the prestigious Civil Services Examination given by the Union Public Service Commission but each time had been refused an IAS post because there were no reservations in the service for deaf people. Under the existing reservation system, deaf people were entitled only to manual and low-level clerk positions. Rema Nagarajan, a *Times of India* reporter, became interested in Dixit's story when she filed a Right to Information Act petition to learn about what posts disabled candidates were given after passing the Civil Services Exam. She was intrigued to find out that Dixit, unlike the other successful disabled candidates at the time, had not been given a position, despite passing the exam for a third time. The documents she received in response to her petition included only an address for Dixit, no phone number, so she wrote to him and asked him to come to Delhi from his small village in Rajasthan to meet with her. He agreed to come, and brought along a neighbor who worked for Indian Railways because he had never been to Delhi before.

After meeting Dixit, Nagarajan (2009a, 2009b) wrote a series of articles about him and his attempts to better himself through education and employment. These articles were critical of the state, portraying Dixit as an innocent and hardworking young man who had faced many hardships and deserved a post that he had rightfully earned. Dixit was subsequently contacted by the Prime Minister of India's Office and was invited to meet with Manmohan Singh's personal physician, who also happened to be a renowned cochlear implant surgeon. Dixit told me:

> So, Prime Minister Doctor Manmohan Singh called me and he called [the doctor]. [The doctor] checked me and said, "He can hear with the help of cochlear implant." And this cochlear implant I did not know at that time. And I did not have a single penny at that time. Not a single penny. And this is very, very costly.

The cochlear implant surgeon and unnamed politicians raised (anonymous) funds for Dixit's implant, and Dixit was told to report for surgery at a Delhi-based hospital. He said he had no idea what the surgery would entail or how long it would last, and he did not tell his family about it. He commented that the doctor had wondered if he had any family or friends, because no one accompanied him to the hospital. After the surgery, he needed auditory re/habilitation, which he could not afford. His wife became his therapist, repeating words such as *aam, papita,* and *kela* (mango, papaya, and banana) over and over again until he recognized them. Before he was officially given an IAS post, he had to have his hearing loss (and new gain) certified, which was difficult to do, as audiologists at state hospitals claimed they did not have the equipment they needed to test cochlear implanted hearing (they were not accustomed to working with implanted people), and the state would not permit Dixit to go to a private clinic.

At the time I met him, Dixit was the deputy commissioner of Palwal district, a position he had held for three years. He had previously been posted in the northeast, where he served for a few years before he was transferred to Haryana and reunited with his family. Over coffee and Rajasthani snacks served in the lush garden adjacent to his house, where we were surrounded by his wife and two children as well as household help, Dixit told me about his journey to becoming the deputy commissioner. Dixit has a genetic condition that his mother and other relatives also had. He passed the condition on to his two children, both of whom, like him, were slowly becoming deaf. His teenage son had already gotten a cochlear implant, and his daughter was wearing hearing aids for the time being. Dixit told me about his impoverished upbringing and the hostile climate his family faced in the village because of his and his mother's deafness. Dixit studied very hard, which made some people in the village even crueler to his family, because he was one of the few residents to become literate.

Dixit ultimately left the village and studied for a master's degree and then a PhD. He became a political science professor at a Rajasthani university. He also decided to take the Civil Services Examination, which he did not pass on his first try in 1995; he took the exam again in 2005 and 2006, both times passing but not receiving a post (he finally received a post after passing the exam for a third time in 2009). Because of his deafness, Dixit had been left alone by his family and community. He had not been forced to marry as a young teenager, as his relatives and friends were. He could devote himself fully to his studies and work. By the time he married at the age of twenty-three, most of his friends and their wives already had two or three children, and the women had undergone hysterectomies; their families were "finished" when his was just beginning. Dixit emphasized that his deafness offered him potential in the form of time and space away from normative responsibilities. He told me, "Because I was deaf, I couldn't hear gossip, films, stories, nothing at all, right? So, I was completely alone with my studies."

Despite or because of the time and space that deafness offered him, Dixit ultimately found his way to sensory normality and political power. During our visit, he told me that he routinely has telephone calls with the chief minister of the state and that the chief minister does not know that he is deaf. His constituents, whom he meets when he goes out into villages for inspections or when they come to his imposing office and sit as supplicants in front of his large desk, think that his implant processor is a Bluetooth device. In Dixit's mind, his normal (and normative) capacities have afforded him power and allowed him to become an emissary and representative of the state. He stated: "I am the boss of my district and I have more than a thousand employees under my supervision, under my control. . . . If you are deaf, you cannot become a collector, magistrate, or any of these posts." Dixit believes that a representative of the state can only be hearing and that he must therefore perform state power through speech and, to a lesser degree, listening. In 2017, the *Hindustan Times* chronicled Dixit's use of insulting language to berate poor agrarian workers for not using toilets; the article included no mention of his implant or deafness.

Dixit's story, which he selectively narrated to foreground victimization, merit, chance meetings, and proud sensory normality, is a fascinating example of how a cochlear implant can seemingly change the trajectory of a life. Dixit moved from deafness to normal hearing thanks to the direct intervention of politicians and a well-connected surgeon, as well as the support of his wife, who tirelessly helped him to train his auditory sense. It is easy to be inspired by his story, as many are, but I am left with questions about why he needed a cochlear implant and his refrain that someone who is deaf cannot do his job. In addition, while Dixit did not discuss this during our interview, his pursuit of an IAS post was aided by protests held in Delhi on his behalf by a national disability rights organization. These demonstrations were attended by many deaf people from across India, the majority of them ISL speakers. (In our discussion, Dixit told me that he had no interest in ISL or disability or deaf activism, despite the fact that activists claim him as one of their own.) Dixit's becoming hearing resulted in his gaining a prestigious government post, where he is, in his own words, "very powerful." The man with the cochlear implant is, arguably, the most powerful man in the district, although Dixit believes that his power is predicated on the illegibility and inconceivability of his cochlear implant and the way that he is not recognized as deaf; he is unmarked as normal.

I now discuss an ambivalent case, all the more so because of how this person's deafness occurred, with a suddenness that reveals the tenuousness and contingencies of re/habilitation. Vandana Iyer was a twenty-nine-year-old woman from Mumbai who had recovered from severe tuberculosis during her college years and was on track to become a journalist at a prestigious news agency. However, Iyer's TB returned, in multidrug-resistant form, after she finished her postgraduate degree. She took a medication not recommended for multidrug-resistant TB, kanamycin, a known side effect of which is deafness. (There were other possible treatment regimens for Iyer's illness, but these were not available in India or were financially out of her reach.) During an afternoon nap one day, Iyer completely lost hearing in one ear, and the hearing in her other ear began to decrease. She soon became completely deaf. While she had learned about cochlear implants, she was afraid of possible side effects, and none of the surgeons with whom she met inspired confidence (she had developed an ambivalent relationship with medicine). She was fitted with hearing aids and set out to learn to lipread. She became a TB patients' rights activist and traveled to Geneva and New York to advocate for equitable access to TB medications and the removal of patent barriers. She also became a plaintiff in a lawsuit against Johnson & Johnson concerning a patent extension for which the company had applied.

Senior physicians and scientists whom Iyer met through her TB activism urged her to consider a cochlear implant and helped arrange an appointment for her with one of India's top cochlear implant surgeons. Since these were well-respected professionals, Iyer trusted them and traveled to Chennai to meet the surgeon. She crowdsourced funds for the surgery, the implants, and accommodation in Chennai for postsurgery re/habilitation. Now she is learning to hear (again) with the help of her implants. This process was recently delayed when she tripped while walking down a road and one of her processors was smashed by a car. She then needed to raise additional funds for a new processor. Iyer has become a disability activist of sorts, in addition to a TB activist. In a public talk (which I was able to view on video), she first described her journey through the ravages of TB to becoming hearing impaired. She then discussed the difficulties of hearing in noisy group settings and the importance of accessibility features such as closed captioning. Generally, when she discussed patient rights, pharmaceutical patents, and the ravages of TB, she was incredibly powerful and polished; in contrast, her remarks about disability access came across as newer and tacked on.

Iyer's story is particularly ambivalent because the roles of capital and international patent regimes are difficult to ignore. Structural violence cannot be wiped away by triumphant narratives of becoming normal, especially when, as in Iyer's case, the people affected have experienced the loss of their senses. In a video made by Iyer's surgeon and his clinic (in collaboration with a cochlear implant company) that Iyer shared with me, Iyer states: "The cochlear implant has its limitations. You'll be able to hear some things. You won't be able to hear some things. But definitely your hearing will get better." This is a surprisingly nuanced message for a cochlear implant corporation–sponsored video. (Both Dixit and Iyer are postlingually deaf—deafened—and both struggled with becoming deaf before they could ostensibly become normal again.)[23] I am interested in the ambivalences in their stories: Why did Dixit need an implant for an IAS post that he earned? Why did Iyer take kanamycin for TB, despite the known side effects?[24] I am also struck by way the media, surgeons, and cochlear implant manufacturers have seized on these cases as success stories. What kinds of political economic erasures happen when success is foregrounded?

Thinking about structural erasures and the ways that cochlear implants become fixes for political economic and other forms of violence, I was surprised to find out that Nobel Peace Prize winner Malala Yousafzai has a cochlear implant made by the Cochlear corporation; I learned this during an interview with a family in India in which one of the children, also implanted, had been invited to attend a Cochlear event with Yousafzai. Yousafzai's implant restored her hearing and seemingly enabled her to maintain her voice. How, however, might we depart from (re)building normative and violent (sexist, ableist, capitalist) structures and reconceptualize how we think of normal? How do we interrogate the roles of different infrastructures in building and collapsing sensory ways of being in the world? I think about village caste dynamics, a civil service exam, state power structures, multinational drug company patents, and the role of social and political connections in creating possibilities for sensory normativity.

Deaf as Normal

I offer a reconceptualization of what it means to be normal through the experiences of Justin, a thirteen-year-old deaf boy in Bangalore who was implanted at the age of ten; Justin's story reveals tensions between becoming and unbecoming and the importance of theorizing multiple ways of living normal life or multiple normals. Justin attended a deaf school where ISL and spoken English were used. He had become a confident signer and was doing well in school. Both his mother and the school principal said that he was creative, clever, and good at sports. His mother had also become fluent in ISL because she accompanied Justin to school when he was younger, and his teachers encouraged her to stay and learn both English and ISL (she previously knew only Kannada). Justin's father saw a TV show about cochlear implantation and decided unilaterally that Justin would be implanted. Since the father was a government employee, the implant was paid for. It cost altogether almost Rs 10 lakh (US$13,245), Justin's mother told me, smiling ruefully. After implantation, Justin went for a year of therapy but could not move past auditory discrimination and recognizing environmental sounds (he was stalled on the first step of Erber's auditory hierarchy; Erber 1982). When it was time for him to return to school, the deaf school's principal told the family to take Justin to "a normal school." However, Justin would have been lost in a normal school. His mother argued with the principal, saying that "without the implant, Justin is normal like a deaf child." With this phrase, Justin's mother asserted that deaf is normal and that normal is relationally constructed. The principal relented.

While Justin's mother and I talked in the family's apartment one afternoon, she told me that all life had gone out of Justin after the implantation. He sat at home with his arms crossed and lamented that he "was no use." He refused to play outside because he was afraid of harming his processor. For his school's annual sports day program, the students made a human pyramid, and while he wanted to participate, he did not because he was worried about banging his head. Currently, Justin wears his processor only at home. He finds everything loud and distracting with it on. While his mother and I chatted, Justin's sister came home from her job at an information technology company. I asked her what she thought about Justin's situation, and she said that "it was too late for Justin to have gotten the implant. He had gotten accustomed to having the kind of body that he had. The sounds are too much for him and it is too much for his body." She added, Justin "lost his identity and his special ability has been drained from him. Before he was more creative and now he wants to be normal." These perceptive comments reveal that becoming normal can be experienced as a constriction of the world and opportunities within it. Justin's sister said that "before, Justin had high marks and was doing very well, but the implant drained him of this focus. People have their own worlds inside of themselves, and Justin is not accepting his world. He wants to be one of us. I just want him to be him."

Justin's mother's comment that "without the implant, Justin is normal like a deaf child" and his sister's observation that "he wants to be one of us" reveal that pursuing normality (in Mahesh's words) also results in a narrowing of life and sensory worlds. In Justin's case, the introduction of the implant fragmented his world and his sensorium. It also affected his social life: he does not like to wear his processor at school or make it known that he has an implant, because children tease him and tell him that he will "become crazy" or "go mad" from the implant's impact on his brain.[25] At school he prefers to pass as a typical deaf student.

During our conversation, Justin's mother mentioned that the money spent on the implant could have been used for Justin's education, foregrounding another possible path of becoming normal. This speculation about another possible investment is something I heard from other parents and stakeholders. For example, I spoke with the principal at Justin's school about the case of seven-year-old twins who had recently been implanted. The twins had started attending the same deaf school at the late age of five years, and they were doing well, rapidly acquiring ISL. Their mother, under pressure from her family, decided to have the twins implanted—even though clinical expectations were low because of their age. The principal said that rather than spending this money on cochlear implants, the family should have put money into a fixed deposit account; then when the twins reached adulthood, they would have the money to use as they pleased. The implication was that the twins would be able to live a normal life in this way. A mother of an implanted teenage girl told me that while she was at the hospital after her child's implant surgery, a stranger came up to her and told her that she was crazy. The man scolded her: "Are you in your senses? Why did you spend so much on the surgery of this young girl? You should have kept the money aside!" She replied that her daughter was her investment at that moment: "I must invest in her, and she will look after her own future. I must make her able enough to take care of her own future." This mother saw her investment in her child's future potentiality as exceeding present monetary value.

In another case, the parents of a one-year-old girl decided to sell the gold that they had accumulated to fund their daughter's cochlear implant. The mother reasoned that she would eventually spend this money on her daughter's wedding, so why not spend it now?[26] In the view of some people, such as the principal of Justin's school, spending money on a cochlear implant is risky, as good outcomes are not guaranteed (a sentiment different from those expressed by the state, cochlear implant surgeons, and cochlear implant corporations). In contrast, money saved can buy a house or a business, or provide financial security in another way. This is a different path, then, to living a normal life. This comparison between spending on an implant now and saving small amounts in a fixed deposit account over time to yield a greater sum of money later reveals different ideas about investments in potential presents and futures—although the goal is perhaps ultimately the same. In the case of the former, the child will ostensibly become normal in terms of sensory configurations and this establishes a foundation for a normal life. In the case of the latter, while the child's senses will not become normal, access to funds will enable the child to integrate into normative life trajectories (Lloyd and Moreau 2011); the child might also be able to pass as normal.

Becoming Normal but Failing to Pass

In October 2019, I attended a CIGI-sponsored cochlear implant industry conference held in a five-star hotel close to the Mumbai International Airport. Among those present at the conference were approximately four hundred surgeons, re/habilitation professionals, audiologists, special educators, and representatives from the major cochlear implant manufacturers, along with a few government administrators. All of these participants were committed to expanding cochlear implant programs. I moved between the conference halls dedicated to surgery, audiology, and rehabilitation and took advantage of the ever-available espresso in the lobby as I exchanged pleasantries with people I knew and introduced myself to people I had not met before. In many cases, surgeons, therapists, or audiologists introduced me to others. Invariably the introduction went something like this: "This is Michele. She is an anthropologist from the University of Chicago writing a book about cochlear implants in India. She is also a bilateral implantee! Could you guess?" In one situation, a therapist named Aruna (mentioned above in relation to Imran's case) introduced me to two surgeon friends of hers. She could barely contain her excitement when she told them that I was a bilateral implant recipient. She asked them if they could tell. They were surprised, something that Aruna took great pleasure in, because it marked her expertise as an AVT practitioner—she was attuned to differences in speech and voice in ways the surgeons were not. Other audiologists and therapists told me, "I knew as soon as you said something" or "The first time you opened your mouth, I could tell."

How odd to be in a space where I no longer passed. I had seemingly become normal, at least in terms of audiograms and life trajectories, but I soon learned that normal speaking was more important to some attendees. (In this space I would have really liked to pass.)[27] A speech and language pathologist whom I met for the first time at the conference told me that she had known immediately that I was implanted; she was able to tell the first time I said something to her. She invited me to her clinic to work on my S; she enthusiastically offered to fix this sibilant along with some other speech issues. I politely demurred, telling her that I was busy, but perhaps during my next research trip. This helpful therapist also complained to me about a video that a surgeon screened during his conference presentation. Meant to demonstrate success, the video showcased an implanted child cheerfully and confidently talking with his family. However, according to the therapist, the child did not pronounce certain sounds, like Ss, normally, and this detracted from the surgeon's and the family's accomplishments. Normality can be discounted at any point.

This experience of not passing was particularly striking because I was the only implanted person and the only deaf person at the conference. When the first CIGI conference was held in 2003, implant recipients were invited to attend, as they offered "proof" that implants worked. One of the people involved in the planning of that first conference told me that CIGI needed these people's cases—both adult and pediatric—as evidence. When I asked why no implant recipients had been invited to the 2019 conference, an employee of one of the major cochlear implant companies (also a sponsor of the conference) told me: "These people are out leading normal lives and are busy in school or working. They don't have time to come to something like this." Ostensibly they were too normal to come. Confidently asserting this normality as a fact absolved surgeons and therapists of the responsibility to follow up or measure outcomes. And evidence was no longer needed.

Multiple Normals

Disability studies scholar Lennard Davis (2013, 1) has argued that "normal is being decommissioned as a discursive organizer." In contrast, I found that people pursue normality and are excited about its potential and what it is a springboard toward. If becoming normal means achieving a certain outcome on an audiogram and testing into the narrow slice of frequency and decibel range termed the speech banana, I argue that we need to consider how becoming normal limits and constrains possibilities, especially in relation to other normal ways of engaging the world, such as through ISL, lipreading, and total communication. How does becoming normal produce certain kinds of unbecoming?

At the same time, however, as someone with two implants, I am aware of how these devices enable moving through the world in both expanded and contracted sensory ways (noise has become unbearable, music is meh, but speech has become far easier). As Eric Plemons (2017, 133; emphasis added) writes: "Projects of political and philosophical imagination are vital to our collective spirit; they give us something to look forward to, a future worth working for. They help us envision possibilities that have not yet existed. *But the present isn't only a moment to be surpassed.*" The present was previously the future toward which hard work was directed. The present is also, for many, a time of successful outcomes, a time in which potentiality has been reached and is now being safeguarded through maintenance work.

I think about the mothers who invested in cochlear implants now for their children as opposed to gold or savings accounts for the future. I recognize these actions as motivated by a desire to create a more inhabitable world for their children in the present. A normal life, activated through sensory normality, seemingly means an easier path. Such a path is what Dixit and Iyer have pursued and what my mother wanted for me, although such paths were and are not easy. There is friction when a processor is run over by a car, when batteries die or need to be recharged, or when one does not pass as hearing, for example. In my Conclusion, I stress the importance of allowing for multisensory, multimodal, and multipersonal deaf presents and futures. Returning to Deleuze and Guattari (1987, 248–49, 274–75) and the scales that exist between the molecular and the molar, I argue that attending to the messiness of both the molecular (it is messier than AVT practitioners would have us believe) and the molar enables us to imagine different kinds of social, political, communicative, and sensorial becomings.

Beyond the Bad S

Making Space for Sensory Unruliness

The Persistence of the Bad S

In August 2020, my sister sent me a large manila envelope. She had found a folder of my audiograms and Individualized Education Plans from elementary and middle school and offered to mail them to me. I opened the envelope and slowly disintegrated while examining this file self, these representations and quantifications of my capacities and abilities. In addition to audiograms from different years, there were multiple copies of an IEP from 1990, when I was in sixth grade. The original was tissue-paper thin and included a number of assessments and goals for improving practices related to lipreading, auditory discrimination, and articulation. For example, one "functional description of performance" stated: "Michelle articulation skills are adequate for conversation, but she tends to omit the final [s] and has difficulty with [s] blends during reading and conversation. Auditory discrimination skills are weak." The goals in response to this assessment were "Michelle will improve her articulation of final [s] in reading and [s] blends during reading and conversation. Michelle will improve her auditory discrimination skills using blends and sibilants words." Those Ss! (Yes, my name was misspelled throughout.)

Another goal focused on my ability to use visual, facial, and contextual clues and cues and stressed that my lipreading needed to improve. And yet another goal stated that I had to develop my auditory discrimination skills and practice listening through "audition alone," without lipreading. My IEP goals were, bluntly stated, that I needed to improve my Ss and become a better lipreader and listener. After reading the IEP, I felt undone—undone for the twelve-year-old child who had to sit through IEP meetings year after year; undone for my mother, who had to engage in yearly bureaucratic dances; and undone that a system like this could exist, in which strengths

A page from my 1990 Individualized Education Plan in which my deficits and goals are outlined: "Michelle articulation skills are adequate for conversation but she tries to omit the final [s] and has difficulty with [s] blends during reading and conversation. Auditory discrimination skills are weak." The goal in response is: "Michelle will improve her articulation of final [s] in reading and [s] blends during reading and conversation. Michelle will improve her auditory discrimination skills using blends and silibants [sic] words." Image scan by author.

and weaknesses and goals and outcomes could revolve around Ss and sibilants, speechreading ability, and maximization of audition.

I wrote to my "hearing teacher" (this is what I called her, her official title was itinerant teacher of the deaf), now a dear friend, who created these goals to ask her what she thought thirty years later. She replied, "Remember, we didn't have cochlear implants that were working well," and "You actually did improve your auditory skills because you were able to take things like nasal murmurs and understand that it was an M or an N, or an acoustic burst and know it was a plosive," and "You had to work on your lipreading skills because what if your hearing aids stopped working?" Finally, and perhaps defensively: "Do you remember your goal from the last year you had hearing services? The goal for you was that you would balance a checkbook?" As I remember that goal, it was that I would successfully use an ATM—but in any case, our conversation, over text, was unsatisfying. I felt that my old teacher and dear friend was stating that I was ungrateful, not understanding that my IEP had been constructed during a time of different sensory infrastructures and more limited ideas of what deaf children's potential could be.

Goal setting establishes and enacts potential. However, goals are frequently constraining in how they frame development and enact relations; they are often unconcerned with individual children and their specific selves beyond the case file. Goals are also a key modality through which families, audiologists, and speech and language pathologists work to enable deaf children to become sensorially normal or to pass as normal. My hearing teacher reminded me that cochlear implants were not as widely available when I was a child. The future that we have now, she pointed out, was unimaginable back then, and IEPs are different in the present because of this technology. Her statement reminds me of two others that I heard often from audiologists and AVT practitioners in India and the United States: "It's not the same old deafness," and "Today, there is no reason we should not expect a deaf child to have an excellent listening and speaking outcome."[1] These statements suggest that children are making their Ss fine now. Are they? And why is this an important goal?

The case file, and the expectations and goals within it, produces and forecloses forms of life. The file self scaffolds how the world is sensed and inhabited. Consider the following case of a nearly eight-year-old girl who was implanted at two and a half years of age. I did not meet the girl, but I viewed her file at an Indian clinic in 2019, and I felt an affinity with her as I read its contents. The case notes included the girl's chronological age, her implantation age, and her developmental age in terms of listening, receptive and expressive language, cognition, and social communication. In all of these categories she was at most thirty-six months old. (As discussed in chapter 3, families must negotiate and attend to deaf children's multiple chronological and developmental ages.) The girl's provisional diagnosis was "delayed in receptive and expressive speech and language skills with cochlear implant." The case notes stated that the girl typically used gesture to communicate and she was predominantly nonverbal. Her oral articulations were "normal in appearance and function." She could repeat words such as *aam, kela, mama, papa,* and *didi* (mango, banana, mama, papa, and sister), which she understood through lipreading. The girl's short-term goals were to discriminate between different spoken words and produce utterances reflecting two-word semantic relationships, both with 80 percent accuracy. Her long-term goals were to increase discrimination of different stimuli and to develop an understanding of and produce vocabulary in diverse communicative contexts. Such goals—not so different from mine when I was a child—surface questions about whether achieving them is important for building and sustaining relations and worlds.

Open Sets

My IEP, with its focus on specific senses and ways of communicating, made me disintegrate. But scholars have argued that deaf people process and learn through multiple sensory integration. All of the senses available to a child work together and aid the child in processing the world. Scholars have moved away from a competitive model of sensory processing to one that looks at the ways that the senses complement each other and are intertwined, creating intersensory engagement.[2] Why, then, do AVT practitioners focus on a single sense, even initially? Why is becoming unisensory a desired goal? Throughout this book, I have argued that we need to look at deaf children and adults, and all people in general, as multisensory, multimodal, and engaged in multipersonal interactions. I have also argued that we must attend to desired and actual sensory infrastructure because it enables the creation of different sensory ways of being in the world. Infrastructure does more than get under the skin (Fennell 2015); it creates the actual conditions of possibility for sensing and inhabiting the world.

I think about "closed sets" and "open sets" as used in sound booth speech discrimination and perception tests. In tests with both kinds of sets, the person being tested must repeat the words, phrases, or sentences spoken, either in silence or with background noise, by disembodied voices piped into the booth. In closed sets, which are often used in studies of the efficacy of cochlear implants, there are limited sounds, words, phrases, or sentences from which to choose. The person being tested is sometimes "primed" so that he or she has a sense of what words or sentences are going to be used; there is a closed set of options. The ultimate goal for a person being tested, however, is to score well on open sets, which could be any sound, word, phrase, or sentence, with no structure or context given. Ideally, the person is able to hear what is said and repeat it without knowing from the outset what the nature of the sound, word, or conversation might be. The AzBio test, for example, which tests speech discrimination in people with hearing aids and cochlear implants, includes sentences such as "There are several types of tuxedos."

Beyond tuxedos, how might we hold on to the concept of open sets as a scaffolding or infrastructure through which deaf children and adults can interact with the world? And how might an open set ideally include (less linguistically bounded) communication that is multisensory and multimodal? I want to leave room for sensory unruliness and for not knowing what outcomes might take place. I wish to see a proliferation of outcomes, beyond the finite number of communication outcomes discussed in chapter 2. Surely there are more than four ways (listening and spoken language, a bilingual-bicultural approach using sign language, cued speech, and total communication) to communicate. I see value in total communication as a philosophy that involves all of the senses and orienting to children and others more generally based on what they need and when they need it.

Haraway (2007) argues for "becoming with" as an open-ended process that does not yield guaranteed results or harmonious wholes.[3] In this book, I have focused on the becoming that takes place through cochlear implants and the ways that such becoming always exists—and is valued—in relation to a teleological normal. I have endeavored to think about the work of multisensory, multimodal, and multipersonal engagement in enabling different kinds of becoming that might upend taken-for-granted hierarchies of sensory and communicative value. I have argued that becoming normal involves a narrowing or contraction of senses, modalities, and ways of relating to others; it constricts the social.[4] Haraway reminds us that "becoming with" is ultimately a project of "becoming worldly," which involves interaction in and through diverse sensory modes, including vision and touch (287). "Becoming worldly" moves us beyond the constraints of normative modes of engagement to thinking copresence with others differently.

"Becoming with" and "becoming worldly" offer other possibilities for unknown and emerging forms of difference that do not aim for predetermined outcomes (also see Malabou 2008, 5). Howes (2006, 382) points out that responses to multisensory signals might produce unknown outcomes and notes, "The response to the multisensory signal is new, qualitatively different from the response to either of the unisensory components, and thus demonstrates *emergence*." Emergence is similar to open-ended becoming. How might we rewrite the scripts of what it means to become deaf, hearing, normal, and disabled and not include teleological goals and conclusions? Such unknown futures are important, especially at a time when statements such as "Today, there is no reason we should not expect a deaf child to listen and speak" are routine. At the same time, we must examine our attachments to (stabilizing) these categories and the political, social, and economic forces that allow for their ongoing production and maintenance.

I call for a deaf futurism (Mills 2012) that is not teleological and open to multiple permutations of becoming. The concept of deaf futurism is appealing in that it insists that there is a place for deafness in the present and future. While Mills (2012, 336) addresses deaf futurism primarily as an investment in technology, posthumanism, and the importance of deaf people having a seat at the table to develop technologies that work for them, I am interested in an open-ended deaf futurism that enables the full range of deaf people's multisensory and multimodal engagements with the world. As I see it, deaf futurism involves a demand for sensory infrastructures that maximize potential (and not compensation) in all ways.

In 2021, I met a group of Indian young adults in their twenties who were implanted as children. They are considered "star cases" by cochlear implant corporations, which often invite them to be featured in promotional videos or to speak to prospective families. These implant users have all graduated from university and are employed or in graduate programs, and as such, they represent successful cochlear implant outcomes. However, these people refuse to be what they consider "inspirational porn," and they denounce the ableism of cochlear implant corporations and society more broadly. They have also claimed disability and identify as deaf and disabled. They value their cochlear implants while also critiquing the ways that "success" means adhering to a narrow normative path, and they foreground the significant work required to learn to listen, speak, and negotiate everyday life. They embrace captions and sign language and call for more expansive identities and social and communicative practices. They model these practices in whimsical and humorous videos using special effects in which they call for disability pride, "bling up" their hearing devices, and remind people that disability experiences are unique and valid (and they also poke fun at families who tell deaf children "never mind" instead of repeating themselves). Consider too a recent scholarly and activist project called the DeafSpace movement, headquartered at Gallaudet University, which has envisioned infrastructure modeled on deaf people's social, moral, political, and economic practices.[5] Project recommendations include circular seating in classrooms and outdoor nooks to allow for clear sight lines, pedestrian pathways that are wide enough to allow people who are signing to walk together, glass elevators and doors, and floors that allow vibrations to travel. The DeafSpace project is not concerned with disability or deaf access, but rather with deaf being and flourishing; it is a moral project, and infrastructure is a key component.[6] A commitment to deaf futurism allows us to include multiple sensory, social, and communicative orientations as normal and to see deaf as normal as well. Deaf futurism opens up possibilities for different kinds of becoming—and flourishing—beyond sensory normality.

Old Stories and New Goals

In October 2020, I attended a Zoom conference panel titled "Importance of Rehabilitation for Those with Hearing Loss in Developing Countries." The panel moderator, who was from India, stressed that rehabilitation's goal should be to restore or provide capacities and capabilities, with the spoken assumption that these were listening and spoken language capacities and capabilities. For this speaker, successful rehabilitation meant following a single path toward inserting a child into the currently existing social, sensorial, and communicative order. Indeed, all of the speakers discussed listening and spoken language, and some focused on auditory verbal therapy. However, there was a specter, a real bogeychild, haunting this panel: "the five-year-old child without language." Such a child, ostensibly diagnosed late and without any kind of appropriate intervention, was invoked but not discussed; this child could not be accommodated within the re/habilitation trajectories foregrounded. Those present at the conference could not imagine goals for this child; they were so fixed on ideas of listening and spoken language that any other way of sensing and communicating in the world was impossible.

The imaginary of this five-year-old child drove home the ways that ideas of re/habilitation, capabilities, and capacities are fixed. This five-year-old child was not seen as malleable and thus represented a hard limit to discourses about potentiality. Professional investment in cochlear implantation and auditory verbal therapy has erased a history and present of other sensory and modal possibilities to the degree that a binary is created between a "child with no language" and a "cochlear implant user who listens and speaks."[7] What, in contrast, would it mean to consider this child as possessing the most potential, in that new paths and possibilities are yet to be made? To consider this, we need to reimagine goals, potential, and re/habilitative trajectories and detach them from normative understandings of becoming and being normal.

I met many such children throughout the course of my research, children who were five and older, said to have "no language," who came to clinics for the first time or had returned after some time had elapsed since previous visits. Their parents often carried copies of medical files and school records proclaiming that their children had multiple disabilities, "low IQs," or "behavior issues." With the parents' consent, I pored over these documents and marveled at the conclusions drawn as well as the kinds of futures confidently projected and foreclosed. Audiologists and speech and language pathologists invariably responded to my curiosity and concern with comments such as "There are so many children like this. So many identical stories. We see this all the time." These flat and resigned statements unsettled me, as my observations and talks with the families always revealed unique details, even if what all the families desired was ultimately the same. Discussions about these children typically involved recommendations for vocational training and ways of ensuring financial productivity and independence. The goal was for them to be able to pass as normal and engage in normal practices, in addition to maximizing their ability to lipread and utter sounds or words. The complexity of their lives was ignored, and the possibility of open-ended becoming, or any kind of becoming beyond sensory normality, was foreclosed.

In an essay on biopolitics, Michel Foucault (2008, 229) writes of an intensified focus on human capital, or approaching humans as "abilities-machines," under neoliberal political economic regimes. Theories of human capital (Becker 1962; Becker, Murphy, and Tamura 1990) focus on ability, specifically the ability to earn an income, and are concerned with producing (certain kinds of) skilled people who can be assimilated into capital. As Foucault notes: "Ability to work, skill, the ability to do something cannot be separated from the person who is skilled and who can do this particular thing" (224). Foucault pushes us to see the boundaries of "abilities-machines" and to consider what kinds of abilities and forms of life might be illegible or unassimilable within such a machine. He asks: "What type of stimuli, form of life, and relationship with parents, adults and others can be crystallized into human capital?" (230).

This question is key: What about stimuli and signals that cannot be neatly categorized or crystallized in their unruliness? How might creating boundaries around what can and cannot be considered a signal constitute a form of violence? In this book I have argued for expanding how we think of stimuli and signals beyond listening and spoken language, and I have foregrounded the importance of relational infrastructures in moving beyond narrow definitions of ability. I have focused on relationships between mothers and children, families and devices, children and the state, and corporations and the state, in addition to others. I have examined the ongoing work and investment required to maintain senses, relationships, capacities, skills, devices, and infrastructures. I join with disability studies scholars and disability anthropologists to critique how we think of capital and its crystallization and the ways that deaf and disabled people are seen as both objects and subjects of capital.[8] A project of becoming normal is a project of becoming appropriately malleable and becoming (available to) capital.

Deaf life, and all life, is embedded within different and sometimes ideologically competing sensory infrastructures. I have argued that we must attend to the relational work required to maintain these infrastructures. What is at stake is not only a child's identity or the child's ability to become deaf, hearing, or normal; these are experiences, capacities, and categories that are constantly in flux and do not occur solely within an individual child's body or sensory configurations. Multiple normals, as a sensibility, moves us beyond categorizing people as hearing or deaf and turns our attention to the existence of diverse signals embedded and crystallized and/ or ignored and devalued within hierarchies of value. What is ultimately at stake is our ability to stretch the social to include diverse signals and stimuli, to sense the social differently. In doing so, we need to work toward infrastructure designed to cultivate different ways of sensing, communicating, and relating. This would be open-set infrastructure that is not concerned with mitigating or compensating for deficiency or lack—or with whether Ss are uttered properly.

A page from my 1991 Individualized Education Plan. My speech teacher at the time has written: "Michelle Friedner has been receiving speech and language therapy for numerous years. Michelle has shown improvement and is able to communicate with both teachers and peers adequately. Michelle is working up to her potential. It is felt at this time that Michelle's speech needs can best be addressed by HHVI [Hearing Handicapped and Visually Impaired, a specialized unit within the New York City Department of Education]. Michelle is no longer in need of speech services as a related service since she appears to be working up to her potential. I recommend that speech and language services be terminated at this time." There are no goals in this IEP, unlike all the others I had over the years. I have reached my communicative potential, and my case is closed (although, according to speech and language therapists I met in India, I do not utter my Ss properly, and therefore I have not reached my potential). Image scan by author.

Acknowledgments

Thinking about and writing acknowledgments is one of my favorite things to do, although it leaves me terrified that I will forget someone. I am also deeply aware and regretful of the fact that there are so many people in this book whom I do not and cannot name, yet my research and this book would not be possible without their willingness to share their knowledge, experiences, and passion for their work. To all the surgeons, audiologists, speech and language therapists, teachers, families, and government officials (not listed in order of importance) in this book, a huge thank you. I acknowledge that many of you might not agree with my analyses and conclusions. My sincere hope is that this work helps us imagine and bring into being many possibilities for deaf children's flourishing.

I thank the Department of Comparative Human Development at the University of Chicago, which has been an exceptionally collegial and stimulating space in which to think about development from all angles. I am grateful that I get to ask Jennifer Cole, Susan Goldin-Meadow, Eman Abdelhadi, Guanglei Hong, John Lucy, Eugene Raikhel, Marisa Casillas, and Terra Edwards questions about topics from brain plasticity to rehabilitation trajectories to turn-taking in language development. We also have the best undergraduate and graduate students to teach and think with. In our department and across the university, I am very appreciative of support from our department, grants, and financial administrators; these folks make a huge difference. Our interdisciplinary disability studies reading group/laboratory/workshop is a generative space for thinking through disability theory as well as empirical fieldwork. And my office is a particularly delightful and beautiful space in which to work—if only the coffee situation were a bit better. I also want to thank Pamela Block and Lisa Diedrich, my former colleagues and mentors at Stony Brook University, who modeled excellent collegiality and care. I continue to be in awe of Stefan Helmreich, my postdoctoral adviser at MIT, and now mentor for life, for all of his support and encouragement. To my dissertation adviser

Lawrence Cohen, who also looms large in my research and on these pages: thank you for being incredible to think with!

Throughout India, again, a huge thank you to all of the families, audiologists, therapists, surgeons, teachers, and government officials. A special thank you to the child I call Imran and his family, who granted me access to their lives; I value their friendship and support. I also thank the therapist in Pune whom I call Tanima and the surgeon in Pune whom I call Dr. Parel. The therapist in Pune whom I call Kalpana also provided sage advice and wonderful analyses. I am deeply appreciative to all of the staff in Dr. Parel's clinic: thank you for answering my questions, for allowing me to observe and hang out, and for the cups of coffee. In Mumbai, I thank the therapist I call Zahra for her perspectives and insights, and I also thank all of the therapists who work with her. In Bangalore, I thank the mother, teacher, and trainer I call Sasikala and all of the mothers at the Mothers Teaching Center, as well as the surgeon I call Dr. Murthy. In Chennai, a special thanks to two audiologists and speech and language pathologists for a very illuminating and never-ending coffee date on Chalmers Road. And to the audiologists and therapists around India who experiment with different methods and who are open to different approaches "below the radar": thank you for sharing your stories. There are some people I can name. In Delhi, I thank Sachin Singh, Vishwajit Nair, Khushboo Soni, Neha Kulshreshta, Rahul Sharma (a special debt of gratitude for driving me to Palwal and for making a meeting happen), Kasturi Shridhar, Pallavi Kulshrestha, Dorodi Sharma, Rema Nagarajan, Muralidharan, and Satendra Singh. I especially thank Rema Nagarajan for her important research and writing. Mike Morgan tends to show up in Delhi whenever I am there. In Kolkata, I thank Nandini Ghosh and Snigdha Sarkar. In Chennai, I thank the administration of Balavidyalaya, Ranjith Rameswaran, the faculty at Sri Ramachandra Institute of Higher Education and Research, Amba Salekar and the Equals team, and the Tamil Nadu Association for the Rights of All Types of Differently Abled and Caregivers (Taratdac).

I would be remiss if I did not mention dear friends who took care of my senses in all ways. In Bangalore, I love spending time with Vanita, Lydia, and Joella Thomas in "my house," even though the coconut tree is no longer there. Lydia in particular calmed my nerves and prayed for me when I was afraid to cross literal busy streets. Meenu Bhambani and her family have always welcomed me for meals and long days spent together in conversation. Padma Dasari always manages to rock my world foodwise. In

Pune, Rajani and Sanjiv Vaidya cared for my sensorium through stories, walks, food, and flowers. I clocked more hours in speech than ever before when staying with them—they should become speech and language therapists! (Shruti, thank you for sharing your parents with me.)

For research support extraordinaire, I thank Sravanthi Dasari, Deepa Palaniappan, Rajani Vaidya, and Anjali Murthy for help with fieldwork, conducting participant observation, forgoing lunch, translating in multiple directions, and visiting schools, clinics, and hospitals with me. Anjali Murthy, an incredible medical researcher, dug out a whole archive of medical, public health, and audiological research articles with genuine curiosity and interest. Kristen Busch spent time in auditory verbal therapy archives with me, figured out how to copy important documents, and found people to interview. Arya Muralidharan did great work with the ADIP data, and Elizabeth Shen read the entire manuscript and gave honest feedback (I hope) while also patiently helping with the illustrations.

For very helpful feedback and generous readings of individual chapters, I thank Eman Abdelhadi, David Ansari, Michaela Appeltova, Tarini Bedi, Kavi Bhalla, Lisa Bjorkman, Jennifer Cole, Janet DesGeorges, the University of Chicago Disability Studies Reading Group, Terra Edwards, the 2020–21 University of Chicago Franke Institute for the Humanities Fellowship cohort, E. Mara Green, Cassandra Hartblay, Stefan Helmreich, Erika Hoffman-Dilloway, David Howes, Jennifer Iverson, Alison Kafer, Annelies Kusters, Stephanie Lloyd, the Medicolegal Working Group (Lisa Davis, Amy Krauss, Kenneth MacLeish, Sameena Mulla, Sarah Pinto, Harris Solomon, Kaushik Sunder Rajan, Catherine Trundle), the Mobile Deaf Reading Group, Erin Moriarty, Vijayanka Nair, Alyson Patsavas, Eric Plemons, Christine Sargent, Bambi Schieffelin, Kristen Snoddon, Mette Sommer, James Staples, Jonathan Sterne, Bharat Venkat, and Matthew Wolf-Meyer. Tarini Bedi, Stephanie Lloyd, James Staples, and Matthew Wolf-Meyer read multiple chapters and served as enthusiastic sounding boards.

For generative comments on the research, I thank Debra Bellon, Pamela Block, Stuart Blume, Alison Bobzin, Diane Brentari, Marisa Casillas, Rama Chari, Tina Childress, the wonderful people at Child's Voice Chicago, John Lee Clark and the participants in the Spring 2020 Protactile Seminar, Lawrence Cohen, Maartje De Meulder, Suzanne Gaskins, Tina Greico-Calub, Aimi Hamraie, Michelle Havlik, Anja Hiddinga, Listening Together, Amber Martin, Laura Mauldin, Mara Mills, Amy Moran-Thomas, Anjali Murthy, Colleen Polite, Eugene Raikhel, Rebecca Sanchez, Sarah Sparks,

Dana Suskind, Benjamin Tausig, Jaipreet Virdi, Susanne Wengle, Tyler Williams, Karen Woolman, and Tyler Zoanni, as well as the participants in the 2019 University of Chicago Delhi Center conference "Disentangling Disability and Human Rights," participants in the 2018 preconference symposium "The Fix in South Asia" at the Annual Conference on South Asia, and participants in the *New England Journal of Medicine*'s 2019 "Case Studies in Social Medicine" series. I also thank Rahul Bjorn Parson and Jason Grunebaum, Hindi teachers for life, for going over Hindi words, concepts, and phrases with me.

I received generous funding for this book from the University of Chicago's Department of Comparative Human Development, an American Institute of Indian Studies Senior Short-Term Fellowship, a National Science Foundation Science, Technology, and Society standard grant (grant no. 1922066), the University of Chicago Committee on Southern Asian Studies, the University of Chicago Franke Institute for the Humanities, the Center for International Social Science Research at the University of Chicago, and the American Association of University Women. The Center for International Social Science Research at the University of Chicago made it possible for this book to be open access. The Giannino Family provided funding for preliminary research for this book. Stephanie Lloyd and I were coinvestigators on a Canadian Social Sciences and Humanities Research Council Seed Grant from 2017 to 2019. I thank Anna Brailovsky for her grant-whispering skill.

For the manuscript review process, I was fortunate to have two amazing reviewers, one of whom was Mara Mills. The people at the University of Minnesota Press, particularly Jason Weidemann and Zenyse Miller, have been encouraging, responsive, and excited about the project. I thank Adrean Clark for her wonderful illustrations created for this book and Judy Selhorst for her meticulous and careful copyediting.

For friendship and listening to me talk about this project ad nauseum, I thank Naomi Baer, Kavi Bhalla, Emilie Cassou, Mara Green, Liz Mazur, and Karen Weingarten. The very active MKM WhatsApp group (Mara Karen Michele) has provided much sustenance, encouragement, and sage advice. I thank my husband, Jamie Osborne, for his steadfast patience and commitment to the project, to the research, and to us and our child, Saffron Orly Friedner Osborne. A particular (one-sided) joy is to practice AVT techniques with Saffron. I thank them both for all the sensory joys they bring to my life, although I would prefer a bit less noise, thank you very much. I also thank my mother, Ann Friedner, for sitting down with me for an interview and for her commitment, all along, to always striving for and working toward the best possible future for me. Karen Woolman, my sister, and Shmuel Yochanan Friedner, my late father, also worked toward this future: it was a family project. Interestingly and perhaps ironically, Karen became an audiologist. Jim and Susie Osborne have inquired constantly about the state of the project and the book, and I thank them for coming along for the journey.

Appendix

Five Indian Cochlear Implant Trajectories

How does a child become an implant case, and what kind of casework is required? Indian families with deaf children often pursue identical goals—to have their children "listen and speak like normal"—but their paths differ according to class, caste, gender, geographic location, education level of the parents, ability status, and religion, among other factors. Here I provide five composite cases demonstrating different cochlear implant trajectories. These cases are ideal types, incorporating elements from both actual case notes and experiences that surgeons, audiologists, speech and language therapists, and families related to me. It should be noted that these cases, and cochlear implant trajectories in general, are overdetermined by the imperative that cochlear implants are a necessary intervention.

Private Funding, Government Hospital

Pramod is a six-year-old boy who lives with his lower-middle-class family in a town that is sixty kilometers from Pune, Maharashtra. His family noticed that he was not responding to sounds when he was about two years of age. During the Navratri holiday (which lasts for nine nights), his father observed that Pramod did not respond to the music that had been playing nonstop around the family home. The father took the child to a local pediatrician, who also observed that Pramod was not speaking. The pediatrician explained the connection between hearing and speaking to the family and suggested that they take him to an ear, nose, and throat doctor in Pune, about an hour by bus from their home.

The family visited an ENT surgeon who worked with an audiologist. Tests, including the brain-stem evoked response audiometry test, which measures the reaction of a child's nervous system to auditory stimulation, were conducted, and Pramod was found to have a severe to profound hearing impairment in both ears. The surgeon recommended a cochlear implant as soon as possible and said it would cost between Rs 15 lakh (US$19,930) and Rs 16 lakh (US$21,260). The family decided to see two other doctors, who also recommended an implant. They then went to a government hospital in Pune, where the cost of the surgery and implant were significantly cheaper at Rs 5 lakh (US$6,663). They were not given a choice of companies from which to purchase the implant because the government hospital had a contract with a particular cochlear implant corporation and access to only one device. The family was given a list of required presurgical procedures, including an MRI, a CT scan, and numerous vaccinations; all of these were expensive. They were also told that they had to purchase hearing aids for Pramod to wear in the interim, at a cost of Rs 35,000 (US$466). The audiologist counseled them to purchase only one hearing aid to save money; Pramod would need to switch that hearing aid from ear to ear.

To pay for the implant, Pramod's father arranged for funding from various sources, including Rs 2.75 lakh (US$3,664) from the Prime Minister's National Relief Fund, Rs 50,000 (US$666) from the state Chief Minister's Fund, Rs 1.25 lakh (US$1,665) from a charitable trust, and Rs 10,000 (US$133) from Being Human, a charity started by the Bollywood star Salman Khan. The father also approached the Rotary Club and the small private company where he worked; his supervisor arranged for everyone at the company to donate one day of salary. Ultimately, the family paid Rs 1.25 lakh of their own money. Approaching all of these sources and cobbling together the money took about five months. The surgery went smoothly, and Pramod's father commented on the free meals that they received in the hospital as well as the friendly workers; he did not want to talk at length about his son's surgery except to say that he, his wife, and their extended family were worried but felt that they did not have any other option besides surgery.

After the postsurgery recovery period, Pramod's mother took him to Pune for activation, mappings, and weekly therapy sessions, traveling an hour each way by bus from their home to the city. Pramod's father could not accompany them because he had to work. It was the first time that Pramod's mother had traveled extensively, into the city or anywhere else, unaccompanied by other adults. In therapy sessions, which lasted twenty to thirty minutes, the therapist taught her to talk to her child constantly—although it often seemed that she and Pramod spent more time sitting in the waiting room than they did with the therapist. In the waiting room, mothers chatted and compared notes, sharing tips with each other. Both the therapist and the audiologist who worked with Pramod and his mother had completed the standard bachelor's degree in audiology and speech and language pathology and had also received training from hearing aid and cochlear implant companies. In addition to their formal training, they had a great deal of experience because of the sheer numbers of people with different diagnoses whom they saw in their clinic.

Today, Pramod's father estimates that Pramod had twelve mappings altogether, and he is thankful that the implant has functioned well over the past three and a half years. During that period, the family spent Rs 5,000 (US$67) on a new coil and also purchased new batteries. The clinic has encouraged the family to bring the implant in for servicing (they would send it to the manufacturer), but that would cost Rs 45,000 (US$600), a significant amount for the family. The father has decided not to do this because of the expense and the fact that Pramod would need to be "off-ear" during the servicing period (the clinic does not have any loaner machines, and the hearing aid that Pramod wears in his other ear does not seem to offer him much assistance). Pramod is attending a local private school, where he is keeping up with his peers, with much help from his parents, although his teacher and the school administration are adamant that they will not give him any "special attention." His parents worry constantly that something will happen to the implant processor at school—that someone will hit him or pull it off, or that he will lose it. They are also concerned because Pramod's speech is not especially clear, and they think that not everyone will be able to understand him.

Central Government Funding, Government Hospital

Anjali is four years old and lives in Noida, outside Delhi. Her family are lower caste and class migrants from Uttar Pradesh. Her mother suspected that Anjali might have a hearing impairment when she was one year old because the child did not respond to loud sounds at home. Anjali's grandparents, with whom the family lived, told the mother not to worry. The pediatrician whom the family saw initially was also dismissive. Anjali's mother attempted to assuage her concerns by going to the local temple, but she still observed Anjali constantly and worried. Finally, when Anjali was three, the family decided that something must be wrong. They traveled to a government institute, where students performed a series of hearing tests on Anjali and, after verifying the results with their supervisor, informed the family that the child had a severe to profound hearing impairment. The supervisor told the family about the central government's Assistance to Disabled Persons for Purchase/Fitting of Aids/Appliances scheme and its provision of hearing aids and cochlear implants. She suggested that they seriously consider having Anjali implanted. The supervisor also gave the family a list of the documents they would need to complete before Anjali could receive an implant. The family was told to come back the next week for additional discussion and to pick up hearing aids—although the supervisor commented that the hearing aids might not make a difference because of the severity of Anjali's hearing loss.

The family returned the following week, and a group of audiology students gave them a twenty-minute presentation about the implant surgery and the external processor, or "machine." During the presentation, the students checked off boxes on a form that was designed to ensure that they covered critical points about the surgery, the importance of the child's wearing the external processor, and the family's responsibility to take the child for mapping and therapy after the surgery. Following this presentation, the students asked the family members about their expectations, and they responded that they wanted Anjali to be "like a normal child."

The family decided to proceed, but it took them a while to put together their package of documents for the ADIP scheme. Finding their caste certificate took some time, because they were no longer living in their native place. Like Pramod, Anjali had to undergo a battery of tests and receive a number of vaccinations, all of which put pressure on the family's already strained finances. Finally, they assembled all their documentation and went back to the institute, where the documents were uploaded to the ADIP web-based platform. About three months later, when Anjali was three and a half, they received a letter telling them to report to the Delhi-based hospital they had chosen for surgery, as a shipment of cochlear implants had just arrived. Nervously, the family did as instructed, and Anjali had her surgery, after staying overnight in the hospital the night before. At the hospital, her family met a number of other families whose children were also having implantation surgery.

Anjali's activation session, which took place three weeks after surgery, was overwhelming for the family. They were given a huge cardboard box full of plastic bags containing spare parts for the implant processor. They had not been told about maintenance costs and their responsibilities for the device until that moment.

Today, Anjali's mother still worries about the future costs of her daughter's implant, but she is trying to focus on Anjali's development and talking to her all the time in the present. She believes that the ADIP scheme targets poor people like her family and that in the future the government will adjust the scheme and cover maintenance costs. Still, she worries that if the device breaks or it needs a new battery or cable, the family will not be able to afford it. She hopes that there are NGOs that could help. As Anjali has been implanted for less than two years, the family is still traveling back and forth to the government institute for mappings and therapy sessions. Each time they go to the center, they are seen by different student therapists. Like Pramod's therapy sessions, Anjali's are about twenty-five minutes long, and Anjali's mother is given exercises to do at home. The family is encouraged by Anjali's progress, and they would like her to attend a government school near their home, but they are worried about seeking admission because of her deafness.

State Government Funding, Private Hospital

Arun is a three-year-old boy who lives outside Vellore, Tamil Nadu. He has an older brother and sister who are deaf. They wear hearing aids that help with environmental sounds. Both siblings attend a deaf school where Indian Sign Language is used, although many of the teachers do not sign fluently or even proficiently. When Arun was one year old, his family discovered that he was also deaf. They were referred to a private hospital where cochlear implant surgeries were conducted under the Tamil Nadu Chief Minister's Comprehensive Health Insurance Scheme. The surgeon at the hospital, eager to do more cochlear implant surgeries, submitted Arun's paperwork to the program's administrators in Chennai, and a few months later, his implant was approved. Both before and after implantation, Arun went for therapy at a new speech and language center at the Vellore hospital. After implantation, the state program required documentation of his therapy attendance and progress; the therapists kept meticulous records and uploaded case notes and videos of Arun's sessions. In contrast to his brother and sister, Arun began listening and speaking well with therapy, and his vocabulary was almost at age level. In addition to taking Arun for mapping and therapy appointments, Arun's parents were encouraged to undergo genetic counseling and testing. However, his mother was no longer concerned about the possibility of giving birth to another deaf child because of the existence of cochlear implants.

Recently, almost two years after implantation, Arun lost his implant processor while riding on his father's scooter. The family anxiously informed the hospital clinic and were told to wait for some time. A few weeks later, they were invited to a program in which politicians would give out replacement parts. The hospital told them that this would be the fastest way to get a replacement, as the processes for dealing with replacements, repairs, and upgrades through the Chief Minister's Insurance Program had not been fully rolled out yet; things were being done on an ad hoc basis. At the program, Arun received a new processor and was photographed shaking hands with a local politician. Arun was excited to start wearing his implant again; he had missed being able to hear, and his parents had been worried about a decline in his development.

Private Funding, Private Hospital

Karishma is a three-year-old girl from an upper-class family in Bombay. Her family discovered that she had a hearing impairment shortly after her birth because she underwent newborn hearing screening at the hospital where she was born. Her parents quickly did research and looked at many international websites, such as that of the U.S.-based Alexander Graham Bell Association, and they learned about the importance of early intervention. When Karishma was six months old, she received her first hearing aids and started attending a therapy clinic in the heart of the city. The clinic was run by a certified auditory verbal therapy practitioner who had trained under an international AVT expert. The entire family attended weekly therapy sessions that were an hour in length, and they were given structured homework to do after each session. The therapy clinic had an in-house audiologist, and in addition, the therapist had close connections with well-known cochlear implant surgeons in Mumbai. She recommended that the family make an appointment with a specific surgeon when Karishma was nine months old. The family went to see the surgeon and decided to move forward with surgery.

First the family had to decide on an implant corporation and a particular device. The surgeon arranged for representatives from the three major corporations to contact them. The representatives came to their house armed with glossy brochures and YouTube videos, as well as contact information for some of their successful recipients. Karishma's parents decided that they wanted the Cochlear corporation's newest processor, the Kanso, which is marketed as the world's smallest cochlear implant processor. The family was not concerned about money, but Karishma's mother did say that the price of the cochlear implants was comparable to the amount in gold that she would need to provide for Karishma's eventual marriage, and so why not spend the money now? Upon the urging of their therapist, audiologist, and surgeon, the family decided on bilateral implants, and Karishma was implanted when she turned one year old. After implantation, she continued with therapy weekly and also attended a music appreciation class. She currently attends preschool and has developmentally typical speech abilities. Karishma is being raised entirely in English, although her grandparents occasionally speak Sindhi to her when they are together.

Government Employee Funding, Private Hospital, Older Child

Daniel is an eleven-year-old boy from a middle-class family in Bangalore. He was diagnosed as having a severe to profound hearing impairment at the age of three, when, at the urging of his pediatrician, his family took him to be evaluated by an audiologist. After diagnosis, Daniel wore high-powered analog hearing aids and went to speech and language therapy weekly and then monthly. He attended a neighborhood nursery school and then a private school for lower kindergarten onward. His mother, who did not work outside the home, often accompanied him to school and spoke with his teachers about what he was learning in class; she then worked with him on these things at home. Daniel also went for private tutorials after school. His mother could always understand his speech, even when other people could not. When he was not working with his mother or in tutorials, Daniel loved to play cricket with the neighborhood children in the lane in front of his apartment building.

   When Daniel was nine, his family learned about cochlear implants and sought out a meeting with a surgeon at one of Bangalore's private hospitals. The surgeon told the family that Daniel was not the ideal implant candidate because of his age, but he would definitely benefit from implantation: he would be able to at least hear environmental sounds, and his listening and speaking ability would possibly, even probably, improve. According to the surgeon, cochlear implantation would only be a good thing for Daniel, although learning to use the implant would require a lot of time and effort. The surgeon also stressed that the cochlear implant would be beneficial for Daniel's safety: he would be able to cross the road with more ease, and he would be able to stay home alone because he could now hear if people knocked on the door. Daniel's mother was ambivalent about the surgery, but his father was very much in favor. As Daniel's father was a government employee, the surgery was paid for with funds available through his workplace.

After surgery and activation, Daniel and his mother went for mapping and therapy at the surgeon's private clinic. They worked on sound detection for over a year, and Daniel was able to detect some new sounds, although he was not (yet) able to identify them. The implant also did not help with his listening and spoken language, which disappointed the family. Despite the surgeon's reminders that they should manage their expectations, they had harbored secret hopes that Daniel's speech would become clearer. Today, Daniel is not sure if he likes the implant or not: he says that it is noisy, and he also worries about it getting hit with a ball when he plays cricket. However, as the surgeon, audiologist, and speech and language therapist told the family, it is possible that Daniel will continue to benefit, as he is still a very young child, only two years old, in terms of his implanted age.

What about the communicative, sensory, and relational engagements that are not included in (making up) these composite cases? There are diverse emotional, political, moral, and sensory infrastructures that scaffold trajectories and serve as connective tissue for the processes discussed in these ideal-type cases. Sensory infrastructures—both inside and outside the body—are always in flux, despite attempts to fix them as solid and finished. Even if a case file is closed, there is no finished outcome after implantation. "Becoming normal" requires constant maintenance.

Notes

Introduction

1. Sanchez (2020, 272) provides a succinct and accessible explanation of the work of the audiogram: "The near-universal measure of hearing loss is the pure tone audiogram, which registers the decibel level required for individuals to perceive a range of auditory frequencies (typically between 125 and 8,000 hertz). Levels of hearing loss are categorized from 'mild' to 'profound.' Even 'profound' hearing loss, however, is a range indicating that an individual cannot detect tones at a number of frequencies when they are played at or over 90 decibels. As this description suggests, these classifications are necessarily imprecise, often functioning to mask the individual and idiosyncratic ways individuals perceive sound. Because the audiogram plots hearing thresholds at a variety of pitches, and because hearing loss is variable, diagnostic labels are based on taking an average of the individual's performance. As a result, one might simultaneously have 'profound' and 'mild' or no hearing loss (or be both profoundly deaf and hearing) in the same ear, depending on the pitch. Deaf people, that is to say, inhabit soundscapes that are often effaced or poorly understood." Hui, Mills, and Tkaczyk (2020, 7) point out that "the modern scientific and popular understanding of hearing—and the practice of hearing itself, reinforced through standardization and training—codeveloped with such testing. Hearing no longer exists without audiometry."

2. According to the *Oxford English Dictionary,* rehabilitation is the "restoration of a person to health or normal activity after injury, illness, disablement, or addiction by means of medical or surgical treatment, physical and occupational therapy, psychological counselling, etc." Rehabilitation is seen as a way to repair and restore the body, returning it to previous states and levels of functioning; it also focuses on the reintegration and reincorporation of the individual body into the national and social body (see Stiker 1999). In contrast to *rehabilitation,* however, *habilitation,* according to the *OED,* is "the action of enabling or endowing with ability or fitness; capacitation, qualification." While rehabilitation is concerned with minimizing loss and restoring functioning, habilitation is focused on maximizing potential, on capacitating the individual child to become what they should become. If rehabilitation is about remaking or transforming, habilitation is oriented toward becoming. The concept of habilitation is typically used

to talk about work with and on children and brings up questions around what we mean by potentiality, capacitation, and possibilities for living both normative and nonnormative lives. As Mauldin (2016, 63) writes: "While rehabilitation is the process of restoring what was lost, habilitation creates an ability that never was—or in the case of dealing with children, one that has yet to be developed." In this book I use the term *re/habilitation* to stress that rehabilitation and habilitation have different albeit overlapping stakes and that while medical institutions, practitioners, and the state, among others, might speak of rehabilitation, they often mean habilitation, or the creation of capacities and qualities that do not yet exist.

3. In India, a bachelor's degree is available in audiology and speech and language pathology combined (BAASLP). This means that the majority of audiologists are also speech and language therapists and vice versa, although there is a tendency for individuals to specialize in one of the two fields. On the master's level at some institutions, students can choose to focus on audiology or speech and language therapy. In this book, when I discuss therapists with specialized certification in auditory verbal therapy, I refer to them specifically as auditory verbal therapists, AVT specialists, AVT practitioners, or the like.

4. That Neera's family learned a new language to communicate with her is ironic, as many of the arguments made internationally about not using signed languages with deaf children stress that it is unrealistic to expect parents to go through the difficult process of learning a new language to communicate with their children. See, for example, the comments of Jane Madell (2015), a well-respected U.S. audiologist and speech and language therapist.

5. In this book I move among the terms *implant recipient, implant beneficiary, implant user,* and *implantee,* each of which has its own politics and emotional register attached. I discuss the logics associated with the concepts of recipient and beneficiary in chapter 1.

6. The AzBio test is distributed by Auditory Potential, http://www .auditorypotential.com.

7. Mills (2020, 27) notes that such tests "naturaliz[e] the ambiguous concept of intelligibility as a quantifiable variable and reinforc[e] biases about what counts as average conversational spoken English."

8. Increasingly, practitioners speak about the importance of getting people into the "speech string bean," which is located at the very top of the speech banana. A person who is hearing in the string bean will hear about 90 percent of what is said. In contrast, a person who is hearing at the bottom of the banana will hear only 10 percent of what is said. See the brief video "Audiology Fruit and the String Bean," Hearing First, accessed September 15, 2021, https://www .hearingfirst.org.

9. For an engaging simulation of what hearing loss sounds like, see "Fred

Flintstone Video Hearing Loss Simulation," YouTube, posted March 11, 2016, https://www.youtube.com. For critiques of such simulations, see French (1992) and Nario-Redmond, Gospodinov, and Cobb (2017). Kafer (2013) argues that simulations locate disability in the body instead of portraying it as a relational and interactive process.

10. See Wallmark and Kendall (2018) on the difficulty of describing sound and especially timbre. Cochlear implant corporations and individual artists have recently focused on creating music that sounds good to people with cochlear implants, in some cases composing music directly for implant users' individual profiles (Helmreich 2018).

11. In describing deaf culture, Padden (1980, 93) stated: "Members of the Deaf culture behave as Deaf people do, use the language of Deaf people, and share the beliefs of Deaf people towards themselves and other people who are not Deaf."

12. I wonder about the sensory worlds of abstract rights talk and how these do and do not imprint upon the body.

13. The U.S.-based National Association of the Deaf released a position statement on cochlear implants in 1991 that was adamantly against implantation and expressed strong reservations about the ethics of implanting children. In 2000, this statement was revised to be more neutral, describing cochlear implants as just one tool among many available to deaf people. The 2000 statement was removed in 2020, and currently the association has no official position on the subject. Similarly, the World Federation of the Deaf takes no position on cochlear implants. While this lack of a position perhaps reflects ambivalence not unlike my own, I find this nonengagement disconcerting, especially in relation to the financial aspects of cochlear implant maintenance, discussed in chapter 4.

14. See Friedner (2015, 2018), Kusters (2017), and Ladd (2003). Cochlear implantation introduces fractures based on neuro-difference. For example, a deaf ISL teacher told me that he does not have much in common with a deaf child with a cochlear implant because the child has a "different brain" from his. He located their difference in neurology and not in upbringing or language modality used, thus neurologizing social relations.

15. See Carey, Block, and Scotch (2020), Rao (2006), and Vaidya (2016).

16. At the annual symposium of the Alexander Graham Bell Association for the Deaf and Hard of Hearing in 2018, I attended a session in which participants were divided into different stakeholder groups: professionals, families, and deaf adults (never mind that someone might have belonged to more than one category). We were supposed to discuss our concerns within our respective groups. I sat with the deaf adults (we were the smallest group), and we discussed how we wanted families to see us as role models with valuable knowledge and expertise to share. At one point when we were reporting back to the other two groups, a mother from the families group asked us: "What do you know about my child

and what right do you have to speak for her? She was born in a different time period and had different opportunities with newborn hearing screening and early implantation options, things that did not exist when you all were young." Some of us received these comments as a sharp slap. Similarly, Fjord (2001, 111) writes about a young deaf woman in Norway who viewed a video of an implanted deaf child and asserted kinship with the child. In response, a cochlear implant surgeon told her: "She will *never* be in *your* category. She can do whatever she likes." According to Fjord, this surgeon rejected the possibility of connection between the two. In another work, Fjord (2003, 70) notes that cochlear implants "symboliz[e] the differing forms of kinship and cultural expertise perceived to be seriously at stake."

17. Following Spivak (1999) and Chakrabarty (2008), I am interested in "provincializing" these teleologies as well as teleologies of cure and pride. See also Friedner and Zoanni (2018).

18. Consider Kafer's (2013, 1) comments about how disability/disablement has resulted in people constantly telling her what the future holds for her: "But people have been telling me my future for years" and "My future is written on my body."

19. Also see Corker (2001) on disability sensibilities and the ways that attending to sensibility allows us to move beyond identity categories.

20. See Appel, Anand, and Gupta (2018), Gupta (2018), and Khan (2006). Appel, Anand, and Gupta (2018, 20) describe infrastructure as "a material and aspirational terrain for negotiating the promises and ethics of political authority, and the making and unmaking of political subjects." They stress that infrastructure "is an intimate form of contact, presence, and potential, one that serves as an important locus for the evaluation of the morality and ethics of political leaders and the state" (22).

21. Notably, Vygotsky conducted research on disability and was an advocate for the importance of signed languages in deaf children's development. See Gindis (1999) and Zaitseva, Pursglove, and Gregory (1999).

22. Griffin and Cole (1984, 47) note that the concept of scaffolding is teleological and does not take account of children's creativity. They cite a statement made by Caryl Emerson in 1983, that the zone of proximal development is "a dialogue between the child and his future; it is not a dialogue between an adult and an adult's past" (62).

23. See Crasborn and Hiddinga (2015), Green (2014a), Holmström and Schönström (2018), Kusters et al. (2017), Moriarty Harrelson (2017), and Pennycook (2017b).

24. Also see Brueggeman, Garland-Thomson, and Kleege (2005), Duque and Lashewicz (2018), Friedner and Block (2017), and Schriempf (2012) for disability studies critiques of normative understandings of (verbal) articulateness and com-

municative competence. Anthropologists of autistic sociality have also endeavored to expand how we see communicative competence in the case of disability; for example, see Ochs and Solomon (2010).

25. Similarly, Sterne (2003, 16) observes that "the audiovisual litany renders the history of the senses as a zero-sum game, where the dominance of one sense by necessity leads to the decline of another sense." Also see Howes (2006).

26. I agree with Howes (2019, 22) that "sensory values are social values and social interaction is sensory interaction." Also see Geurts (2002).

27. Lloyd and Tremblay (2021) make the important point that neuroscience research has shifted from a competitive model to a complementary model in its approach to understanding deaf people's multimodal sensing. As Lickliter (2011, 592) points out: "It is now known that the senses function in concert even in very early infancy and that young brains are organized to use the information they derive from the various sensory systems to enhance the likelihood that objects and events will be detected rapidly, identified correctly, and responded to appropriately, even during very early development. . . . Evidence obtained from neurophysiological research over the last decade indicates that the brain is remarkably skilled at integrating input from the different sensory systems to maximize the information available for perception and action." Similarly, Gibson (1966, 47) argues that the senses should be seen as "perceptual systems," and that "they are interrelated rather than mutually exclusive." Howes (2006) writes about intersensoriality and the many dense relations that exist between the senses.

28. Brueggemann (2009, 164) perhaps would call this a focus on "little 'd' deafness" or "little 'd' deaf studies."

29. Whyte (2014) terms such collective research "polygraphy."

30. Ott (2014, 120) writes that "disability is unique in the extent to which it is bonded with technology, tools, and machines as a medium of social interaction."

31. For additional criticisms of cochlear implants, see Sparrow (2010) and Valente (2011).

32. Mauldin (2016, 4) writes about cochlear implantation as a process of "ambivalent medicalization" through which "individuals are both empowered by *and* surrendering to the process of medicalization."

33. For discussion of the ambivalence of Japanese parents in making decisions to implant their children, see Okubo, Takahashi, and Kai (2008). As these authors note, their study is the first of its kind in that it examines parents' reluctance, another mode and sentiment of engagement.

1. Disability Camps and Surgical Celebrations

1. On Indian disability rights movements, see Bhambani (2003), Friedner, Ghosh, and Palaniappan (2018), and Mehrotra (2011).

2. See Cohen (2004, 2005, 2011).

3. I thank Vijayanka Nair for this pun phrase.

4. See Chaudhry (2015), Friedner and Osborne (2015), and Hiranandani and Sonpal (2010).

5. Writing about prosthetics, Terry (2017, 91) calls a similar nexus a "bionic assemblage."

6. I think here of Roberts's (1997) provocative points about the implantation of Norplant into the arms of Black women in the United States and about sterilization efforts internationally. With cochlear implants, we are supposed to see implantation, and the exercise of state power, in a positive, productive, and benevolent light.

7. Gupta and Sharma (2006, 283) point out that such investments are concerned with "the need to invest in human capital for the development of the nation-state." See also Gupta (1998, 2012) and Sharma (2008).

8. In its pursuit of development and welfare, the Indian government has officially structured its policy toward disability based on a medical model. In order to receive benefits, entitlements, or objects intended for disabled people, an individual must be certified by a government-employed physician as possessing a certain percentage of disability within a specific category. See Kochhar (2013) on the process of disability certification.

9. I thank Kenneth MacLeish for pointing out the subtleties of these performances.

10. While this may be salacious hearsay, multiple sources told me that the Indian distributor of the Neurelec cochlear implant was responsible for "educating" the joint secretary of the Ministry of Social Justice and Empowerment about the benefits of cochlear implants. Neurelec was subsequently awarded the first government contract, a selection that caused much consternation, because this implant was not approved by the U.S. Food and Drug Administration. There were also concerns about the minimal re/habilitation and support infrastructure offered by the Indian distributor. Hearsay or not, this line of discussion offers insights into spheres of influence and complex relationships among Indian distributors, the state, and multinational corporations.

11. Sharon Alex, "Roll Back on GST on Cochlear Implants and Accessories," Change.org, accessed September 15, 2021, https://www.change.org/p/sharon-ann-alex-roll-back-on-gst-on-cochlear-implants-and-accessories.

12. Note that cochlear implant prices are not (yet) standardized. As Nagarajan (2017b) demonstrates, the amounts that individual states currently pay for the same implants may vary by Rs 100,000 or more.

13. One enrollee in the indigenous implant human trials lost his hearing as a result of taking a particular medication to treat his multidrug-resistant tuberculosis; he did not have access to safer medications because of prohibitive patent laws.

In chapter 5, I discuss the case of Vandana Iyer, another deafened TB survivor who was implanted. If successful, the indigenous cochlear implant may serve as a nationalist "fix" (Benjamin 2019) for inequalities stemming from international patent laws.

14. As Nagarajan (2017c) points out, the majority of state-funded cochlear implant surgeries are performed in private hospitals, and in Tamil Nadu, mapping and therapy are also provided by private practitioners.

15. Mazzarella (2006, 476) writes about technocratic efforts to be transparent: "E-governance is, it seems to me, one important avatar of a more general desire for what I am calling a politics of immediation—that is to say, a political practice that, in the name of immediacy and transparency, occludes the potentialities and contingencies embedded in the mediations that comprise and enable social life." The ADIP online platform and waiting lists, as well as the actual logistics involved in distributing, implanting, and activating cochlear implants, attest to immediacy as fantasy.

16. In contrast to the ADIP program's focus on numbers, scant data are available on how many cochlear implants have been done internationally or specifically in India. Cochlear implant corporations do not share precise data. This refusal to release numbers into the public domain is ironic in light of the fact that the companies do produce marketing videos that detail the private stories of individual recipients. According to its 2021 annual report, Cochlear, the company with the largest market share, has provided more than 650,000 implantable devices internationally. By way of comparison, neither MED-EL nor Advanced Bionics releases information on the numbers of its implant recipients. In response to my e-mail inquiry, a MED-EL public relations executive stated that the global number of MED-EL recipients "is something that we do not communicate on." MED-EL employees informally told me that the company has approximately 200,000 recipients internationally, and the Advanced Bionics online newsroom states that the company has 100,000 recipients around the world (https://www .advancedbionics.com). According to the U.S.-based National Institute on Deafness and Other Communication Disorders (2021), as of December 2019 there were 736,900 cochlear implant users internationally. In India, Cochlear estimates that it has approximately 15,000 recipients. MED-EL, Advanced Bionics, and Neurelec will not share their India-specific numbers. In 2019, an official in the Cochlear Implant Group of India informally estimated that 40,000 cochlear implant surgeries had been done in India up to that point.

17. When I raised the question of why people with cochlear implants are called "recipients" on an international Facebook group devoted to cochlear implant experiences, one group member said: "We are recipients because we have received the gift of hearing and the gift of sound." However, this language obscures that implant corporations are for-profit entities and that the

neuroprosthetic/bionic market is one of the fastest-growing industries in the world at the moment.

18. I see overlaps with India's Green Revolution agricultural programs (Frankel 1971): common themes are the role of multinational actors and a focus on expensive technological inputs without support for long-term maintenance.

19. For photographs of the event, see *Sakshi Post* (2021).

20. Oldani (2004, 332) writes about the pharmaceutical industry: "The actual everyday pharmaceutical economy is based on social relationships that are forged and strengthened through repetitive and *calculated* acts of giving." Similarly, there is a focus on giving here, or at least on manufacturing the illusion of giving the state an infrastructural gift.

21. The popular media perpetuate ideas of implants as exceptional. For example, in a review of 190 articles in English-language newspapers about cochlear implant surgery in India, Murthy (2019) found that the surgeons were represented as noble and that the surgery was seen as automatically resulting in "normal" or "close to normal" hearing. And while both the ADIP scheme and state schemes have complex accounting processes that require audiologists and speech and language therapists to upload reports, videos of children speaking, and lesson plans, surgeons are largely exempt from such reporting.

22. See Cohen (2004, 2011), Copeman (2009), Gupta (2012), and Tarlo (2003).

23. See Varma (2020) for discussion of state care and violence under occupation in Kashmir.

24. This focus on objects and not people is not surprising: scholars and disability activists have argued that disabled people are underrepresented in India's national census, and attempts to quantify how many disabled people live in India have been unsuccessful. See Ali (2020) and Dandona et al. (2019).

25. Copeman (2009, 108) points to India's fascination with *Guinness World Records* and, citing Lal (2002), notes that a tenth of all correspondence that Guinness receives regarding its record book comes from India.

26. For images of adorable children sitting in "one size fits all" wheelchairs distributed as part of disability camps, see "Disabled Photo Ops," Latika Roy Memorial Foundation, March 21, 2019, https://latikaroy.org.

27. Similarly, in its report to the United Nations, the government wrote that one of its accomplishments was the "provision of cochlear implant for 500 children per year with learning disability with a ceiling of 10,000 US Dollar per unit included" (Government of India 2015, 30).

28. As of October 2021, 7,029 children were registered with the ADIP scheme, and 3,601 cochlear implant surgeries had been performed, according to the ADIP cochlear implant program website, http://adipcochlearimplant.in. Numbers are updated on the site daily. Some 16 percent of ALIMCO's budget is spent on cochlear implants, a sizable amount considering that only five hundred surgeries

are allocated per year, and ALIMCO is responsible for distributing a number of other aids and appliances, from hearing aids to prosthetics to canes to wheelchairs. ALIMCO also runs camps and provides re/habilitation services.

29. On the concepts of "camp time" "surgical time," and "project time," see Appadurai (2001), Cohen (2011), and Whyte (2019).

30. The Meaningful Auditory Integration Scale is a parent-reported assessment of a child's attunement to and use of sound through the child's device(s); the Speech Intelligibility Rating Scale is a patient-reported assessment of how intelligible speech is to the person; the Categories of Auditory Perception Scale tracks what a listener can successfully perceive in a hierarchy of sounds, from environmental noise to speech on a phone call; the Parents' Evaluation of Aural/Oral Performance of Children is a parent-reported assessment of the effectiveness of hearing aids or cochlear implants based on the child's behavior and communication through speech and language. Another scale in use is the Integrated Scale of Development, which tracks development in audition, receptive language, expressive language, speech, cognition, and social communication. For information on the assessments used by the ADIP program, see "CAP & ISD Scales" on the ADIP cochlear implant website, http://adipcochlearimplant.in.

31. The Shravanadosha Mukta Karnataka program shut down in January 2019 because the Karnataka state government argued that it duplicated what was already provided through the ADIP scheme.

2. Becoming Unisensory

1. See Hall, Hall, and Caselli (2019), Lane, Hoffmeister, and Bahan (1996), and Pfister (2017).

2. See Bascom (2012), Friedner and Block (2017), Ochs and Solomon (2010), and Sterponi and Shankey (2014).

3. Croft's use of "aural" resonates with Sterne's (2015, 68) point that "the idea of the aural and its decidedly medical inflection is part of the larger historical transformation of sound over the last four hundred years. *Aural* implies ears that are objects and tools of scientific exploration." Sterne furthermore notes that "it could be argued that since the mid-nineteenth century, dominant ideas of hearing in science, technology, and medicine retreated further and further into the head, the inner ear, and the brain" (68). Here I critically interrogate such discourses and argue for a return outward as well as an understanding of how these discourses circulate and produce on-the-ground effects in the world.

4. Max Goldstein, a founder of the Central Institute for the Deaf in the United States, also proposed an acoustic method for working with deaf children, although his method appears more open to tactility. Goldstein (1933, 215) defined the method as follows: "Stimulation or education of the hearing mechanism and

its associated sense-organs by sound vibration as applied either by voice or any sonorous instrument."

5. These notecards and others referred to below are held in the Helen Hulick Beebe Papers, Penn State University Archives, Eberly Family Special Collections Library, Penn State University Libraries. "Bathing in sound" is a phrase that Doreen Pollack originated; see Pollack (1974).

6. AG Bell's mission, as stated on its website (https://www.agbell.org), is "Working globally to ensure that people who are deaf and hard of hearing can hear and talk." The association, based in Washington, D.C., became an explicitly international organization in 2019.

7. It is telling that this professional talked about deaf speech and not deaf voice. This brings to mind Weidman's (2014, 42) decoupling of voice from identity and individuality: "The assumed linking of a voice with an identity or a single person overlooks the fact that speakers may have many different kinds of relationships to their own voices or words or that a single 'voice' may in fact be collectively produced." Weidman goes on: "Voicing emphasizes the strategic and politically charged nature of the way voices are constructed in both formal and everyday performances" (42). Focusing on deaf speech as *voice,* then, might serve as a necessary corrective and a reminder of the way that deaf speech is interpersonally produced and heard.

8. The academy's website states: "The AG Bell Academy is an independently governed, subsidiary corporation of The Alexander Graham Bell Association for the Deaf and Hard of Hearing headquartered in Washington D.C." (https://agbellacademy.org).

9. A prominent AVT practitioner and expert trainer told me that the AG Bell Academy renamed and rebranded AVT as "listening and spoken language" because AVT had a negative reputation, owing to the actions of AVT practitioners who have "holier than thou" attitudes and have been known to berate other practitioners for not using AVT. "Listening and spoken language" is seen as more politically and ideologically neutral than AVT.

10. AG Bell Academy, "Principles of Certified LSLS Auditory-Verbal Therapists (LSLS Cert. AVT)," https://agbellacademy.org.

11. Rose and Abi-Rached (2013, 15–16) write: "In the age of the plastic brain, many undesirable neurobiological traits appear to be malleable by changing the ways parents deal with vulnerable children."

12. Also see Lickliter (2011) for developmental psychology research on intersensory development.

13. Audiologists and speech and language pathologists speak of generational differences between "older" and "younger" practitioners, noting that because younger therapists work with younger children, better hearing aids, and, increasingly, cochlear implants, they do not develop as great a range of skills or as much

ability to work with diverse deaf people as did the professionals who came before them. This contraction of skill range has important impacts for practitioners working in emerging contexts in which newborn hearing screening and the latest technologies are not easily found.

14. AG Bell (n.d.) offers the following definitions: "The Listening and Spoken Language approach to language development teaches infants and young children with hearing loss to listen and talk with the support of hearing technology such as hearing aids, assistive listening devices (such as an FM system) or cochlear implants." "Cued Speech is a visual communication system that is used to demonstrate phonetic information for children who may not be able to learn entirely though amplified hearing. Designed to enhance lipreading ability, cued speech combines the natural mouth movements of speech with eight hand shapes (cues) that represent different sounds of speech." "American Sign Language is a manual communication language taught as a child's primary language, with English taught as a second language." "Total Communication (TC) is a philosophy that includes various types of sign (i.e., ASL, Signing Exact English/S.E.E., and contact languages such as Pidgin Sign English or PSE), finger spelling, speech reading, speaking, and the use of amplification."

15. See Kral and Sharma (2012), Lomber, Meredith, and Kral (2010), and Sharma, Dorman, and Kral (2005).

16. One of the therapists who worked for a cochlear implant corporation was concerned about mentoring a colleague who worked for another cochlear implant corporation: she worried that her employer would frown on her mentoring across corporation lines and thus aiding another corporation.

17. Mattingly (2010, 214) observes that "heroic" characteristics are often associated with surgeons, but not with rehabilitation professionals.

18. Signing deaf communities in India have also protested the ways that speech therapists work with deaf children and argue that deaf children are treated like parrots, in that they do not learn language or the ability to communicate independently. See, for example, the 2019 online petition titled "Stop Treating Indian Deaf Children as Parrots," Change.org, https://www.change.org; or the video "Reality of Deaf Education in India," YouTube, posted June 8, 2018, https://www.youtube.com.

19. Aruna's critique of conventional speech therapy resonates with Ochs and Solomon's (2010, 83) discussion of speech therapy for autistic children: "Most clinical interventions focus on developing severely autistic children's ability to speak as an endpoint of communicative competence."

20. This "mode-switching" has parallels with "code-switching," in that there is a dominant or preferred mode, and a mode hierarchy still exists. See Auer (1998).

21. Here one might also consider the robust literature on language socialization (Garrett and Baquedano-López 2002; Ochs and Schieffelin 1984; Schieffelin

and Ochs 1986a, 1986b), as children are being socialized into becoming appropriately social members of families and communities through AVT. However, the focused and highly contextualized literal "language games" played in clinics are not easily replicated in daily life and in some cases might be at odds with family communication practices.

22. The John Tracy Center was started in 1943 by Louise Treadwell Tracy, a mother of a deaf child. The center's website states: "By encouraging parents to build a foundation of communication with their children during the critical stage for language development, JTC has enabled close to half a million children to master the challenges of listening and spoken language and communicate on par with their hearing peers by the time they reach elementary school." "Our Story," John Tracy Center, accessed September 17, 2021, https://www.jtc.org.

23. As I waited with two therapists in Mumbai for a family to arrive for a session, I asked if they thought that I was auditory. One said that she had observed that I often looked at people's faces and that she had noticed that the day before, when we rode a train together, I looked at her face when we talked. She said that this demonstrated to her that I was not a fully auditory person and that I relied on visual cues.

24. Also see Classen (2012) on touch as the deepest sense.

25. See Moore and Shannon (2009), Pals, Sarampalis, and Başkent (2013), Pals et al. (2020), and Pisoni et al. (2008).

26. AVT practitioners train deaf children to listen in noise by piping background noise into their therapy sessions, and sound booth–based hearing tests often include components in which background noise is introduced (I experience these as horrible).

27. Also see Bijsterveld (2008), Mills (2011), and Attali (1985).

28. See Rhoades et al. (2016, 287) for an overview of criticisms of the hand cue.

29. See Moore and Shannon (2009), Pals, Sarampalis, and Başkent (2013), Stenfelt and Rönnberg (2009), and Wagner et al. (2016).

30. Ray Holcomb, an educator of the deaf who was deaf himself, is credited with introducing total communication to deaf education in the 1960s. Holcomb taught classes using total communication in Santa Ana, California, and it was later also introduced in deaf schools, such as the Maryland School for the Deaf (Schlesinger 1986).

31. I think about doorways through Benjamin Bahan's (2014) argument about deaf people's unique sensory orientations. Bahan notes that signing deaf people prefer windows to doors because they can communicate and be social across distance through windows. And there are always glass doors.

32. Total communication is not without controversy or critique. Johnson, Liddell, and Erting (1989, 4–5) point out that total communication practices often privilege spoken language. De Meulder et al. (2019, 901) stress: "The use

of multiple communicative tools is not necessarily something to be valorised in a sweeping movement, when it is an attempt by someone to create meaning from an impoverished set of linguistic tools." Autistic advocates and researchers with whom I have spoken also point out that total communication can be used as an excuse for limiting engagement or for not teaching language. I share these concerns as well. While I recognize the critiques of total communication as a method, I am interested in what total communication offers as a philosophy or orientation in parsing out hierarchies of language, communication, senses, and modalities.

3. Mothers' Work

1. On Indian childhoods, see Kurtz (1992), Minturn and Kapoor (1993), Roland (1989), Seymour (1976, 1983, 1999), Sharma (2000), and Trawick (1990). Note Donner's (2008, 33–34) comments on the paucity of literature on the effects of economic liberalization on parenting: "This bias against the family, parenting and the domestic sphere also prevails in the literature on globalization and economic liberalization in India, despite a strong interest in middle-class lifestyles." Also see Tuli and Chaudhary (2010) on "elective interdependence" in middle-class households.

2. On scaffolding and choreographies of attention, see Cicourel (2013), Tulbert and Goodwin (2011), and Vygotsky (1978). Also see Bucholtz and Hall (2016), Goodwin (2017), and Schieffelin and Ochs (1986a, 1986b) on joint embodiment as a means toward socialization. Intercorporeality, as theorized by Meyer, Streeck, and Jordan (2017), is also relevant here.

3. See Bosteels, Van Hove, and Vandenbroeck (2012) and Fisher and Goodley (2007) on learning how to become parents of deaf and disabled children, albeit in a more explicitly therapeutic register.

4. Hart (2014, 290) points out that in the case of autism, many families become "therapy omnivores," utilizing a number of different therapeutic approaches simultaneously. I similarly observed parents of deaf children visiting a wide range of early intervention centers and therapists.

5. I am reminded of Kafer's (2013) analysis of the Ashley X case. Because Ashley's body was maturing at a rate that her mind never would, she was "out of time," and her family decided to intervene surgically so that her body would match her mind.

6. In thinking through this "hard work" and mothers' engagement with their deaf children, I find Arendt's (1958) distinctions among labor, work, and action to be productive. *Mehanat* includes the maintenance of biological life itself (labor); the production of children as students, workers, and citizens (work); and mothers' acquisition of new forms of expertise as well as their creation of

new relationships with other mothers (action). I see the re/habilitative work of mothers—their *mehanat*—as blurring the boundaries between work, labor, and action, even if certain NGO directors do not agree.

7. See Connor (2006, 11) on "self-conscious care and management" of the senses.

8. As Monaghan et al. (2003) point out, there are many ways to be deaf, and similarly there are many ways to be oral and oralist. It is important to analyze the specific logics and motivations driving oralism in context.

9. According to Beck (1993, 70), *dhvani* refers to nonlinguistic or prelinguistic sound and is "atomic, all-pervasive, and imperceptible." Perhaps there should indeed be more focus on *dhvani* at Balavidyalaya and other institutions like it.

10. I thank Sravanthi Dasari for her enthusiastic and engaged fieldwork on a trip to and from Pottery Town in 2018.

11. There were English, Tamil, and Kannada cohorts at the MTC while I was there. I spent most of my time with the English-speaking group, and I heard from others that the Tamil and Kannada groups were often more lively, because the mothers were using their native languages and thus were more talkative and confident.

4. (Non-)Use

1. While serendipitous for me, the fact that Landon and Deepak shared office space and that Deepak had become Ashreya's guardian demonstrates the connections among different "disability worlds" (Ginsburg and Rapp 2013) in India.

2. Note that Deepak did not express concern about other investments—of time and of learning ISL, for example—that he and his family had made in and with Ashreya.

3. I thank Christine Sargent for this question.

4. We might think about tinkering in relation to *jugaad* in Indian contexts. See Rai (2019) for a critical analysis of *jugaad* and its simultaneous deployment and denigration by multinational capital.

5. See Hamraie and Fritsch (2019), Hamraie (2017), Hendren (2020), and Williamson (2019).

6. See Mills (2011) for an analysis of how even implant users with advanced computer science training are unable to tinker with their devices.

7. "Health Topics: Assistive Technology," World Health Organization, accessed September 22, 2021, https://www.who.int. The United Nations Convention on the Rights of Persons with Disabilities advocates for state parties to ensure the provision of assistive technology for everyday life (Article 20) and in rehabilitation (Article 26). It also stresses that assistive technology can be

a leveler in empowering people with disabilities and that nation-states should share technical and scientific research related to the development of such technology (Article 32). However, as Borg, Larsson, and Östergren (2011, 162) point out, despite this emphasis on the importance of assistive technology, "except for personal mobility, the CRPD seems not to give persons with disabilities the right—or legal support—to approach their government to demand necessary assistive technologies at affordable cost, which for many may be at no or very little cost."

8. See Moran-Thomas (2019) and Hamdy (2012) on other forms of maintenance work—in relation to diabetes—in resource-constrained locations.

9. Kiran's focus on mundane physical and financial maintenance routines was perhaps out of place in a conference hall where surgeons and the representatives of cochlear implant corporations discussed the benefits of "going bilateral" (implanting both ears), different kinds of electrode insertion, and the eventual creation of cochlear implants that will be fully implanted, with no external processors.

10. Each of the three major companies uses particular colors as part of its branding: MED-EL uses red and black, Advanced Bionics uses blue and silver, and Cochlear uses black and yellow. At international conferences, representatives of each company are easily identifiable based on their color-coded uniforms. They always remind me of flight attendants, and, coincidentally, they also perform emotional labor similar to that performed by the airline workers that Hochschild (1983) wrote about.

11. This marketing representative said that most of the cochlear implant industry's marketing people are women because women are better suited than men to the emotional work required. Also see Oldani (2004) on the relationships established by marketing representatives.

12. See Salehomoum (2020) for a study on nonuse among cochlear implanted U.S. adults with a range of communication and identification preferences. Salehomoum points out that "individuals who stop using their CI may be small in number, ranging from 1 to 10 percent of the population of recipients, but they add an important dimension to our concept of CI outcome" (1–2).

13. See Okubo, Takahashi, and Kai (2008, 2441) regarding similar concerns and fears in Japanese parents.

14. AVT practitioners in the United States often say that, unlike our eyes, which have eyelids, our ears do not have earlids to close them, and as such, typically hearing people hear all the time.

15. See Marsella et al. (2017), Meister et al. (2016), and Pisoni et al. (2008). I know implant users who choose not to wear their processors at times—especially on weekends and in the evenings—in order to have "peace and quiet" or because their surroundings are "too noisy." Unlike smaller children, older children and

adult implant users can be strategic about what they want to attune to and work to reduce their cognitive loads.

16. I have occasionally used this guilt-inducing tactic with my family, showing my husband and child the data from the Cochlear app on my iPhone to point out to them that they do not talk to me enough. Interestingly, I logged the most time in speech while I was conducting research for this book!

17. "Kanso Stories—Vainavi Dassani," YouTube, posted August 28, 2017, https://www.youtube.com.

18. "Kanso Stories—Dewanshi Tamudia," YouTube, posted November 8, 2017, https://www.youtube.com.

19. Many Indian audiologists and speech and language therapists recommend that families consider purchasing bilateral implants that are lower in cost instead of one Kanso. These professionals argue that a child will get more benefit from two basic processors than from one high-end processor.

20. "Nucleus CP 802 Sound Processor," Shravani Speech and Hearing Centre, May 17, 2019, http://www.shravaniclinic.com/latest-update/-shravani-speeh -he/111.

21. See De Ceulaer et al. (2015) and Mauger et al. (2017).

22. In an India-based study on quality of life one year postimplantation, Singh, Vahist, and Ariyaratne (2015) found that families noted increased worry about their responsibility to maintain the implant processor. They note: "The crucial need for auditory verbal training and mapping, the need to maintain an external and internal bionic device, the costs associated with paying for initial treatment and later maintaining it for life, raise the question if it will remain an effective option for life, for all who receive it" (62–63). Also see Vaid et al. (2015) and Dutta, Dey, and Malakar (2020) for additional research on cochlear implant maintenance in India and the need to inform and educate families about costs.

23. A 2005 study found that 60 percent of wheelchair users involved in community-based rehabilitation programs in India stopped using their (donated) wheelchairs because of poor fit, physical strain, and the unsuitability of the wheelchairs for rural environments. In addition, and similar to cochlear implant recipients, wheelchair recipients were not informed in advance about the need for regular maintenance (Mukherjee and Samanta 2005).

24. During the Covid-19 crisis, Cochlear unveiled a "remote check" app that allows audiologists to troubleshoot processors remotely. This app works only with the latest processors, however, and so the vast number of recipients in India cannot benefit from it.

25. Alim Chandani, Facebook post, April 28, 2020, https://www.facebook .com/drjahan/videos/10103772676433225.

26. "Announcing Our First Hearing Ambassador," Cochlear, August 18, 2015, https://hearandnow.cochlearamericas.com.

5. Becoming Normal

1. While I do not discuss them here, there are other technologies such as pre-natal screening and CRISPR gene editing that have the potential to affect/effect what is possible both in terms of bringing new life into the world and in terms of editing life as it exists. See Garland-Thomson (2012) and Kafer (2013) on prenatal testing and the case for conserving and selecting for disability.

2. I thank Michaela Appeltova for this insight.

3. Lloyd and Moreau (2011, 596) note tensions in different definitions of normal and write that "individuals have learned to put their faith in medicine and medical practices in order to have their bodies and behaviors normalized, but on the other hand they continually run up against the fact that clinicians are ultimately concerned with normality, that is, symptom reduction and not normativity or a normal day-to-day life." They point out that ideas of re/habilitated normal lives are often "part of a larger project of self-improvement via social, personal, and professional normalization in its most idealized form." As I discuss in this chapter as well, normality does and does not map onto, and is often a larger life project than, successful medical outcomes.

4. See Erevelles (2011, 28) for a critical take on becoming-disabled that calls for an analysis of the roles of differential histories, material access, and power dynamics.

5. Kafer (2013), Mialet (2012), and Wolf-Meyer (2020) call our attention to the ways in which qualities such as autonomy and independence are distributed and to the ways in which disabled people exist within interdependent relationships.

6. This IEP goal is perhaps why I am so shitty when it comes to budgeting and saving money.

7. But see Samuels (2003) for a critique of how the analytic of passing depends on disability being visible; also see Wendell (1996).

8. Brune et al. (2014) curated an excellent critical and engaged forum examining Goffman's impact on and legacy in disability studies on the fiftieth anniversary of the publication of Goffman's *Stigma*.

9. See Plemons (2017, 91) on how attending to a binary of "pass/no pass" obscures important questions about what specific self-making projects do on the ground.

10. I thank Matthew Wolf-Meyer for directing me toward the molecular and the molar.

11. Scholars have critiqued disability-as-identity and called for other categories, such as debility (Livingston 2005; Puar 2017) and crip (Kafer 2013; McRuer 2006; Sandahl 2003). In her research on chronicity, Wendell (2001) critiques celebratory identity-based models, as do Soldatic and Grech (2014) in their call for a

return to the concept of impairment. Deaf studies scholars and deaf anthropologists have moved away from ideas of deaf identity and community to consider deaf networks, spaces, and worlds (Friedner and Kusters 2020).

12. The question of how audiological and diagnostic labels map onto identity categories has been taken up by anthropologists and deaf studies scholars (Friedner 2010; Kusters, De Meulder, and O'Brien 2017) and resonates with discussions of the "many ways to be deaf" (Monaghan et al. 2003), although most of this work does not attend to questions of diagnosis and the specificities of degrees of hearing loss.

13. In fall 2019, I participated in a podcast for a Chicago-based early intervention center during which two deaf education professionals and I collectively wondered what to call implanted children. The consensus was to let the children and their families decide for themselves.

14. Full disclosure: I have been called "mentally hearing" by ASL speakers at various points in my life.

15. This is the "precarious plasticity" that Mauldin (2016, 131) writes about, under which "the 'wrong' stimulus (visual language) could derail [the brain's synaptic connections], and thus parents are told not to use sign for fear of causing their child (future) neural harm."

16. I thank Eric Plemons for pointing out the pluripotency of potentiality.

17. I observed class-based distinctions in what families were told about their children's diagnoses in terms of the brain versus the ears. Audiologists and speech and language pathologists told me that lower-class families would not understand "brain talk" because "it is too abstract" and "they can't see the brain or understand what is happening inside"; these professionals thus privileged visuality in a different domain.

18. This discourse around lateness has resonance with postcolonial scholarship on teleologies of progress (Chakrabarty 2008). However, instead of sitting in a "waiting room," these children are sitting at home without any intervention, according to professionals, who have a particular view of what intervention is. Professionals hope that families will come to a (clinic's) waiting room. And note that the "late-implanted child" occupies a particularly vexed position in cochlear implant and neuroscience research (Boons et al. 2012; Fitzpatrick, Ham, and Whittingham 2015; Holt and Svirsky 2008), as does the "late signer" in sign language and neuroscience research (Hall 2017; Mayberry 1993; Mayberry and Eichen 1991).

19. While Indian therapists often focus on the fact that implanted deaf children have normal brains and normal hearing, many told me that increasingly they discover that implanted children have other disabilities, specifically intellectual disabilities, that make it difficult for them to process what they are hearing.

In India, awareness of intellectual disabilities is growing, as are allied medical fields and diagnostic tools. Therapists exhibit a classist nostalgic bent in referring to the "good old days" when deaf children were seemingly less complicated and implanted children came from "good" families. These learning disabilities and class issues, according to therapists, block children from harnessing the full potential of their implants.

20. The surgeon, according to the family, was eager to implant Imran and pressured them through phone calls. As I discuss in chapter 1, surgeons are often concerned with increasing the numbers of surgeries that they do. My understanding is that this family encountered the surgeon early in his career, while he was trying to grow his practice.

21. Imran's mother constantly said that she was doing everything possible. However, as I note in chapter 3, she was often criticized by program administrators for not doing enough. According to this line of critique, she was considered not plastic enough and not capable of being molded into an ideal (therapeutically talking) mother.

22. The Indian Administrative Service is one of the highest-level civil service posts in India.

23. I thank Carsten Mildner for discussions about "deafening" and for introducing me to this way of thinking about "becoming deaf."

24. See Sunder Rajan (2017) on access to pharmaceuticals and the intersections of pharmaceutical development, patent law, statecraft, and citizen activism.

25. See Finlay and Molano-Fisher (2008) on feelings of loss and disorientation postimplantation.

26. Gender is important. As noted in chapter 1, the central government had wanted its first cochlear implant beneficiary to be a girl. In interviews and discussions, I did not see families eschewing implanting girls, although I met a father who declined to implant his daughter because she would ultimately be given away to another family in marriage, and he could not ensure that her new family would maintain her implant. In another situation, I learned about a young woman who was implanted and then immediately married. After marriage, she had to focus on marital and household duties and did not attend therapy; her hearing and speech did not improve. In still another case, however, I was told that implantation could increase a young woman's marriageability if she could listen, talk, and hear a baby crying.

27. Robinson (1994, 715) writes that passing is often a triangular process, with an "in-group clairvoyant" who is able to recognize the pass. In this case, the "in-group" was made up of surgeons, audiologists, and speech and language pathologists, and not other deaf people. Indeed, I often depend on hearing people to tell me whether someone has "deaf speech" or a "deaf accent."

Conclusion

1. Helen Beebe, one of the founders of auditory verbal therapy, wrote on a notecard in the 1980s: "Difference between 1890 or 1930 is that now we have the electronic technique to make all waking hours a participation in hearing world." Beebe was referring to hearing aids. Fast forward to the 2020s, when cochlear implants are considered a standard intervention. What a difference forty years makes.

2. See Lewkowicz and Kraebel (2004), Lewkowicz and Lickliter ([1994] 2013), Lickliter (2011), and Murray et al. (2016). On multisensory perception and cochlear implantation, see Rouger et al. (2007) and Stevenson et al. (2017).

3. I thank Stephanie Lloyd for introducing me to the importance of "becoming with."

4. I am reminded of McRuer's critique of the often-uttered platitude that sooner or later we will all become disabled. McRuer (2006, 198), building on Garland-Thomson's (1997) concept of the normate, writes: "Sooner or later, if we all live long enough, we will become normate." He urges us to resist becoming normate. By "normate," Garland-Thomson (1997, 8) means "the constructed identity of those, who by way of bodily configurations and cultural capital they assume, can step into a position of authority and wield the power it grants them." Writing more than fifteen years later, McRuer anticipates a different future that includes the assimilation of disability within neoliberal political economic regimes. This future perhaps also includes the proliferation of bionic devices, such as cochlear implants, that enable the creation of normative capacities.

5. On DeafSpace, see Bauman (2014), Edwards (2018), and Edwards and Harold (2014).

6. Relatedly, Edwards (2018, 286) discusses DeafBlind efforts at Gallaudet University and elsewhere to "re-channel" language and environment, approaching infrastructure as playing a significant role: "DeafBlind people at Gallaudet treated the material environment and modifications to it as capable of facilitating or inhibiting residence." Infrastructure is thus essential for DeafBlind becoming, specifically for becoming a tactile person oriented toward touch as a meaningful mode of engagement with the world.

7. I thank Mara Mills and Annelies Kusters for pointing out this erasure of oralism, lipreading, and hearing aids in the service of a new binary in which cochlear implants loom large as the "only option."

8. On disability, capital, and value, see Friedner (2015), Fritsch (2013, 2015), and Mitchell and Snyder (2010, 2015).

Bibliography

Ahmed, Sara. 2019. *What's the Use? On the Uses of Use.* Durham, N.C.: Duke University Press.

Ahmed, Syed Ishtiaque, Steven Jackson, and Mohammad Rashidujjaman Rifat. 2015. "Learning to Fix: Knowledge, Collaboration and Mobile Phone Repair in Dhaka, Bangladesh." In *ICTD Singapore 2015: Proceedings of the Seventh International Conference on Information and Communication Technologies and Development,* 1–10. New York: Association for Computing Machinery.

Akrich, Madeleine. 1992. "The De-Scription of Technical Objects." In *Shaping Technology/Building Society: Studies in Sociotechnical Change,* edited by Wiebe E. Bijker and John Law, 205–24. Cambridge: MIT Press.

Alexander Graham Bell Association for the Deaf and Hard of Hearing. n.d. "Evaluating Communication Options for Your Child." Accessed August 22, 2020. https://www.agbell.org.

Ali, Arman. 2020. "Census 2011 Ignored 60 Million Disabled People. Will Census 2021 Be Any Better?" DailyO, February 10, 2020. https://www.dailyo.in.

Ali Yavar Jung National Institute of Speech and Hearing Disabilities (Divyangjan). 2018. *Thirty Sixth Annual Report, 2017–2018.* Mumbai: AYJNISHD (D). http://ayjnihh.nic.in.

Anand, Nikhil, Akhil Gupta, and Hannah Appel, eds. 2018. *The Promise of Infrastructure.* Durham, N.C.: Duke University Press.

Appadurai, Arjun. 1986. "Introduction: Commodities and the Politics of Value." In *The Social Life of Things: Commodities in Cultural Perspective,* edited by Arjun Appadurai, 3–63. Cambridge: Cambridge University Press.

Appadurai, Arjun. 2001. "Deep Democracy: Urban Governmentality and the Horizon of Politics." *Environment and Urbanization* 13 (2): 23–43.

Appel, Hannah, Nikhil Anand, and Akhil Gupta. 2018. "Introduction: Temporality, Politics, and the Promise of Infrastructure." In Anand, Gupta, and Appel 2018, 1–38.

Arendt, Hannah. 1958. *The Human Condition.* Chicago: University of Chicago Press.

Attali, Jacques. 1985. *Noise: The Political Economy of Music.* Minneapolis: University of Minnesota Press.

Auer, Peter, ed. 1998. *Code-Switching in Conversation: Language, Interaction and Identity.* London: Routledge.

Bahan, Benjamin. 2014. "Senses and Culture: Exploring Sensory Orientations." In Bauman and Murray 2014, 233–54.

Balavidyalaya. 2011a. *DHVANI Parent Kit Stage 1.* Chennai, India: Balavidyalaya.

Balavidyalaya. 2011b. *DHVANI Parent Kit Stage 2.* Chennai, India: Balavidyalaya.

Banda González, Rosa Isela, Salvador Castillo Castillo, and Graciela Roque Lee. 2017. "Fitting Parameters for Cochlear Implant." *Boletín Médico Del Hospital Infantil de México* (English ed.) 74 (1): 65–69.

Barnes, Colin, and Geof Mercer. 2010. *Exploring Disability.* Cambridge: Polity Press.

Bascom, Julia, ed. 2012. *Loud Hands: Autistic People, Speaking.* Washington, D.C.: Autistic Self Advocacy Network.

Bateson, Gregory. (1972) 2000. *Steps to an Ecology of Mind: Collected Essays in Anthropology, Psychiatry, Evolution, and Epistemology.* Chicago: University of Chicago Press.

Bauman, Hansel. 2014. "DeafSpace: An Architecture toward a More Livable and Sustainable World." In Bauman and Murray 2014, 375–401.

Bauman, H-Dirksen L., ed. 2008. *Open Your Eyes: Deaf Studies Talking.* Minneapolis: University of Minnesota Press.

Bauman, H-Dirksen L., and Joseph J. Murray, eds. 2014. *Deaf Gain: Raising the Stakes for Human Diversity.* Minneapolis: University of Minnesota Press.

Bauman, Zygmunt. 1991. *Modernity and Ambivalence.* Malden, Mass.: Polity Press.

Beck, Guy L. 1993. *Sonic Theology: Hinduism and Sacred Sound.* Columbia: University of South Carolina Press.

Becker, Gary S. 1962. "Investment in Human Capital: A Theoretical Analysis." *Journal of Political Economy* 70 (5, pt. 2): 9–49.

Becker, Gary S., Kevin M. Murphy, and Robert Tamura. 1990. "Human Capital, Fertility, and Economic Growth." *Journal of Political Economy* 98 (5, pt. 2): S12–37.

Beebe, Helen. 1976. "Deaf Children Can Learn to Hear." In *Mainstream Education of Hearing Impaired Children and Youth,* edited by Gary W. Nix, 239–46. New York: Grune & Stratton.

Benjamin, Ruha. 2019. *Race after Technology: Abolitionist Tools for the New Jim Code.* Cambridge: Polity Press.

Benton, Adia. 2015. *HIV Exceptionalism: Development through Disease in Sierra Leone.* Minneapolis: University of Minnesota Press.

Berlant, Lauren. 1998. "Intimacy: A Special Issue." *Critical Inquiry* 24 (2): 281–88.

Berlant, Lauren. 2011. *Cruel Optimism.* Durham, N.C.: Duke University Press.

Besky, Sarah. 2017. "Fixity: On the Inheritance and Maintenance of Tea Plantation Houses in Darjeeling, India." *American Ethnologist* 44 (4): 617–31.

Bhambani, Meenu. 2003. "From Charity to Self-Advocacy: The Emergence of Disability Rights Movement in India." MA thesis, University of Illinois at Chicago.

Biehl, João, and Peter Locke. 2017a. "The Anthropology of Becoming." In *Unfinished: The Anthropology of Becoming,* edited by João Biehl and Peter Locke, 41–92. Durham, N.C.: Duke University Press.

Biehl, João, and Peter Locke. 2017b. "Introduction: Ethnographic Sensorium." In *Unfinished: The Anthropology of Becoming,* edited by João Biehl and Peter Locke, 1–40. Durham, N.C.: Duke University Press.

Bijsterveld, Karin. 2008. *Mechanical Sound: Technology, Culture, and Public Problems of Noise in the Twentieth Century.* Cambridge: MIT Press.

Blommaert, Jon, and Ad Backus. 2013. "Superdiverse Repertoires and the Individual." In *Multilingualism and Multimodality,* edited by Ingrid de Saint-Georges and Jean-Jacques Weber, 11–32. Rotterdam: Sense.

Boons, Tinne, Jan P. L. Brokx, Ingeborg Dhooge, Johan H. M. Frijns, Louis Peeraer, Anneke Vermeulen, Jan Wouters, and Astrid van Wieringen. 2012. "Predictors of Spoken Language Development Following Pediatric Cochlear Implantation." *Ear and Hearing* 33 (5): 617–39.

Borg, Johan, Stig Larsson, and Per-Olof Östergren. 2011. "The Right to Assistive Technology: For Whom, for What, and by Whom?" *Disability & Society* 26 (2): 151–67.

Bosteels, Sigrid, Geert Van Hove, and Michel Vandenbroeck. 2012. "The Roller-Coaster of Experiences: Becoming the Parent of a Deaf Child." *Disability & Society* 27 (7): 983–96.

Boster, Dea H. 2013. "'I Made Up My Mind to Act Both Deaf and Dumb': Displays of Disability and Slave Resistance in the Antebellum American South." In *Disability and Passing: Blurring the Lines of Identity,* edited by Jeffrey A. Brune and Daniel J. Wilson, 71–98. Philadelphia: Temple University Press.

Bowen, Zazie, and Jessica Hinchy. 2015. "Introduction: Children and Knowledge in India." *South Asian History and Culture* 6 (3): 317–29.

Brown, Steven. 2002. "What Is Disability Culture?" *Disability Studies Quarterly* 22 (2). https://doi.org/10.18061/dsq.v22i2.343.

Brueggemann, Brenda Jo. 1997. "On (Almost) Passing." *College English* 59 (6): 647–60.

Brueggemann, Brenda Jo. 2009. *Deaf Subjects: Between Identities and Places.* New York: New York University Press.

Brueggemann, Brenda Jo. 2019. "On (Always) Passing." In *Deaf Identities: Exploring New Frontiers,* edited by Irene W. Leigh and Catherine A. O'Brien, 336–48. New York: Oxford University Press.

Brueggemann, Brenda Jo, Rosemarie Garland-Thomson, and Georgina Kleege. 2005. "What Her Body Taught (Or, Teaching about and with a Disability): A Conversation." *Feminist Studies* 31 (1): 13–33.

Brune, Jeffrey A., and Daniel J. Wilson. 2013. "Introduction." In *Disability and Passing: Blurring the Lines of Identity*, edited by Jeffrey A. Brune and Daniel J. Wilson, 1–12. Philadelphia: Temple University Press.

Brune, Jeffrey, Rosemarie Garland-Thomson, Susan Schweik, Tanya Titchkosky, and Heather Love. 2014. "Forum Introduction: Reflections on the Fiftieth Anniversary of Erving Goffman's *Stigma*." *Disability Studies Quarterly* 34 (1). https://doi.org/10.18061/dsq.v34i1.4014.

Buch, Elana D. 2013. "Senses of Care: Embodying Inequality and Sustaining Personhood in the Home Care of Older Adults in Chicago." *American Ethnologist* 40 (4): 637–50.

Bucholtz, Mary, and Kira Hall. 2016. "Embodied Sociolinguistics." In *Sociolinguistics: Theoretical Debates*, edited by Nikolas Coupland, 173–98. Cambridge: Cambridge University Press.

Burch, Susan, and Alison Kafer, eds. 2010. *Deaf and Disability Studies: Interdisciplinary Perspectives*. Washington, D.C.: Gallaudet University Press.

Butler, Judith. 2018. *Notes toward a Performative Theory of Assembly*. Cambridge, Mass.: Harvard University Press.

Calvert, Gemma A., Charles Spence, and Barry E. Stein, eds. 2004. *The Handbook of Multisensory Processes*. Cambridge: MIT Press.

Carey, Allison C., Pamela Block, and Richard K. Scotch. 2020. *Allies and Obstacles: Disability Activism and Parents of Children with Disabilities*. Philadelphia: Temple University Press.

Chakrabarty, Dipesh. 2008. *Provincializing Europe: Postcolonial Thought and Historical Difference*. Princeton, N.J.: Princeton University Press.

Chaudhry, Vandana. 2015. "Neoliberal Disorientations: Changing Landscapes of Disability and Governance in India." *Disability & Society* 30 (8): 1158–73.

Cicourel, Aaron V. 2013. "Origin and Demise of Socio-cultural Presentations of Self from Birth to Death: Caregiver 'Scaffolding' Practices Necessary for Guiding and Sustaining Communal Social Structure throughout the Life Cycle." *Sociology* 47 (1): 51–73.

Classen, Constance. 2012. *The Deepest Sense: A Cultural History of Touch*. Urbana: University of Illinois Press.

Cochlear Limited. 2021. *Annual Report 2021*. Sydney: Cochlear Limited. https://www.cochlear.com.

Cohen, Lawrence. 1999. "Where It Hurts: Indian Material for an Ethics of Organ Transplantation." *Daedalus* 128 (4): 135–65.

Cohen, Lawrence. 2001. "The Other Kidney: Biopolitics beyond Recognition." *Body & Society* 7 (2–3): 9–29.

Cohen, Lawrence. 2004. "Operability: Surgery at the Margin of the State." In *Anthropology in the Margins of the State*, edited by Veena Das and Deborah Poole, 165–90. New Mexico: School of American Research Press, 2004.

Cohen, Lawrence. 2005. "Operability, Bioavailability, and Exception." In *Global Assemblages: Technology, Politics, and Ethics as Anthropological Problems,* edited by Aihwa Ong and Stephen J. Collier, 79–90. Malden, Mass.: Blackwell.

Cohen, Lawrence. 2011. "Accusations of Illiteracy and the Medicine of the Organ." *Social Research* 78 (1): 123–42.

Connor, Steven. 2006. "The Menagerie of the Senses." *Senses & Society* 1 (1): 9–26.

Copeman, Jacob. 2009. *Veins of Devotion: Blood Donation and Religious Experience in North India.* New Brunswick, N.J.: Rutgers University Press.

Corker, Mairian. 2001. "Sensing Disability." *Hypatia* 16 (4): 34–52.

Cox, Peta. 2013. "Passing as Sane, or How to Get People to Sit Next to You on the Bus." In *Disability and Passing: Blurring the Lines of Identity,* edited by Jeffrey A. Brune and Daniel J. Wilson, 99–110. Philadelphia: Temple University Press.

Crasborn, Onno, and Anja Hiddinga. 2015. "The Paradox of International Sign: The Importance of Deaf–Hearing Encounters for Deaf–Deaf Communication across Sign Language Borders." In *It's a Small World: International Deaf Spaces and Encounters,* edited by Michele Friedner and Annelies Kusters, 59–69. Washington, D.C.: Gallaudet University Press.

Creadick, Anna G. 2010. *Perfectly Average: The Pursuit of Normality in Postwar America.* Amherst: University of Massachusetts Press.

Croft, Ginny, and John Croft. 1978. "Overcoming the Obstacles to Five-Sensed Normality." Unpublished essay. Articles, Poems, Papers, 1943–98, Helen Hulick Beebe Papers, 1927–98 (97). Penn State University Archives, Eberly Family Special Collections Library, Penn State University Libraries.

Croft, John. 1974. "The Third Way." Unpublished essay and lecture. Articles, Poems, Papers, 1943–98, Helen Hulick Beebe Papers, 1927–98 (97). Penn State University Archives, Eberly Family Special Collections Library, Penn State University Libraries.

Croft, John. 1977. "No Longer Deaf! A Dilemma of Classification." Talk delivered to United Parents of Hearing Impaired in Louisiana, October 8, 1977. Articles, Poems, Papers, 1943–98, Helen Hulick Beebe Papers, 1927–98 (97). Penn State University Archives, Eberly Family Special Collections Library, Penn State University Libraries.

Danckert, Sarah. 2020. "Kids with Hearing Loss Will Suffer from Surgery Delays: Cochlear." *Sydney Morning Herald,* March 26, 2020. https://www.smh.com.au.

Dandona, Rakhi, Anamika Pandey, Sibin George, G. Anil Kumar, and Lalit Dandona. 2019. "India's Disability Estimates: Limitations and Way Forward." *PLOS One* 14 (9). https://doi.org/10.1371/journal.pone.0222159.

Dara, Gopi. 2021. "Andhra Pradesh CM Jagan Mohan Reddy Bats for Cochlear Implants, Deaf-Free State." *Times of India,* February 21, 2021. https://timesofindia.indiatimes.com/india.

Das, Veena. 1989. "Voices of Children." *Daedalus* 118 (4): 262–94.

Davis, Lennard J. 1995. *Enforcing Normalcy: Disability, Deafness, and the Body.* London: Verso.

Davis, Lennard J. 2013. *The End of Normal.* Ann Arbor: University of Michigan Press.

De Ceulaer, Geert, Freya Swinnen, David Pascoal, Birgit Philips, Matthijs Killian, Chris James, Paul J. Govaerts, and Ingeborg Dhooge. 2015. "Conversion of Adult Nucleus® 5 Cochlear Implant Users to the Nucleus® 6 System." *Cochlear Implants International* 16 (4): 222–32.

Decoteau, Claire Laurier. 2013. *Ancestors and Antiretrovirals: The Biopolitics of HIV/AIDS in Post-Apartheid South Africa.* Chicago: University of Chicago Press.

Deleuze, Gilles. 1997. "Literature and Life." *Critical Inquiry* 23 (2): 225–30.

Deleuze, Gilles, and Félix Guattari. 1987. *A Thousand Plateaus: Capitalism and Schizophrenia.* Translated by Brian Massumi. Minneapolis: University of Minnesota Press.

De Meulder, Maartje, Annelies Kusters, Erin Moriarty, and Joseph J. Murray. 2019. "Describe, Don't Prescribe: The Practice and Politics of Translanguaging in the Context of Deaf Signers." *Journal of Multilingual and Multicultural Development* 40 (10): 892–906.

De Meulder, Maartje, Joseph J. Murray, and Rachel L. McKee. 2019. *The Legal Recognition of Sign Languages: Advocacy and Outcomes around the World.* Clevedon, England: Multilingual Matters.

Denworth, Lydia. 2014. *I Can Hear You Whisper: An Intimate Journey through the Science of Sound and Language.* New York: Dutton.

Desjarlais, Robert. 2013. "The Look: An Afterword." In *Senses and Citizenship: Embodying Political Life,* edited by Susanna Trnka, Christine Dureau, and Julie Park, 262–74. New York: Routledge.

Dokumacı, Arseli. 2019. "A Theory of Microactivist Affordances: Disability, Disorientations, and Improvisations." *South Atlantic Quarterly* 118 (3): 491–519.

Domínguez Rubio, Fernando. 2016. "On the Discrepancy between Objects and Things: An Ecological Approach." *Journal of Material Culture* 21 (1): 59–86.

Donner, Henrike. 2008. *Domestic Goddesses: Maternity, Globalization and Middle-Class Identity in Contemporary India.* Aldershot, England: Ashgate.

Duque, Camille, and Bonnie Lashewicz. 2018. "Reframing Less Conventional Speech to Disrupt Conventions of 'Compulsory Fluency': A Conversation Analysis Approach." *Disability Studies Quarterly* 38 (2). https://doi.org/10.18061/dsq.v38i2.5821.

Dutta, Palash, Sanghamitra Dey, and Iman Malakar. 2020. "Parental Knowledge and Understanding of Monitoring and Maintenance of Cochlear Implant under ADIP Scheme." *Journal of Indian Speech Language & Hearing Association* 34 (1): 17–23.

Edwards, Claire, and Gill Harold. 2014. "DeafSpace and the Principles of Universal Design." *Disability and Rehabilitation* 36 (16): 1350–59.

Edwards, Terra. 2018. "Re-channeling Language: The Mutual Restructuring of Language and Infrastructure among DeafBlind People at Gallaudet University." *Journal of Linguistic Anthropology* 28 (3): 273–92.

Emerson, Caryl. 1983. "The Outer Word and Inner Speech: Bakhtin, Vygotsky, and the Internalization of Language." *Critical Inquiry* 10 (2): 245–64.

Emmett, Susan D., Chad Sudoko, Debara L. Tucci, Wenfeng Gong, James E. Saunders, Nasima Akhtar, Mahmood F. Bhutta, et al. 2019. "Expanding Access: Cost-Effectiveness of Cochlear Implantation and Deaf Education in Asia." *Otolaryngology—Head and Neck Surgery* 161 (4): 672–82.

Erber, Norman. 1982. *Auditory Training.* Washington, D.C.: Alexander Graham Bell Association for the Deaf and Hard of Hearing.

Erevelles, Nirmala. 2011. *Disability and Difference in Global Contexts: Enabling a Transformative Body Politic.* New York: Palgrave Macmillan.

Estabrooks, Warren, Karen MacIver-Lux, Ellen A. Rhoades, and Stacey R. Lim. 2016. "Auditory-Verbal Therapy: An Overview." In *Auditory-Verbal Therapy for Young Children with Hearing Loss and Their Families, and the Practitioners Who Guide Them,* edited by Warren Estabrooks, Karen MacIver-Lux, and Ellen A. Rhoades, 1–22. San Diego, Calif.: Plural.

Evans, Lionel. 1982. *Total Communication: Structure and Strategy.* Washington, D.C.: Gallaudet College Press.

Fanon, Frantz. (1967) 1994. *A Dying Colonialism.* New York: Grove Press.

Farmer, P., S. Robin, S. L. Ramilus, and J. Y. Kim. 1991. "Tuberculosis, Poverty, and 'Compliance': Lessons from Rural Haiti." *Seminars in Respiratory Infections* 6 (4): 254–60.

Fein, Elizabeth. 2020. *Living on the Spectrum: Autism and Youth in Community.* New York: New York University Press.

Fennell, Catherine. 2015. *Last Project Standing: Civics and Sympathy in Postwelfare Chicago.* Minneapolis: University of Minnesota Press.

Finlay, Linda, and Patricia Molano-Fisher. 2008. "'Transforming' Self and World: A Phenomenological Study of a Changing Lifeworld Following a Cochlear Implant." *Medicine, Health Care and Philosophy* 11 (3): 255–67.

Fisher, Pamela, and Dan Goodley. 2007. "The Linear Medical Model of Disability: Mothers of Disabled Babies Resist with Counter-narratives." *Sociology of Health & Illness* 29 (1): 66–81.

Fitzpatrick, Elizabeth M., Julia Ham, and JoAnne Whittingham. 2015. "Pediatric Cochlear Implantation: Why Do Children Receive Implants Late?" *Ear and Hearing* 36 (6): 688–94.

Fjord, Lakshmi. 1999. "'Voices Offstage': How Vision Has Become a Symbol to Resist in an Audiology Lab in the U.S." *Visual Anthropology Review* 15 (2): 121–38.

Fjord, Lakshmi. 2001. "Ethos and Embodiment: The Social and Emotional Development of Deaf Children." *Scandinavian Audiology* 30 (2): 110–15.

Fjord, Lakshmi. 2003. "Contested Signs: Discursive Disputes in the Geography of the Pediatric Cochlear Implant, Language, Kinship, and Expertise." PhD diss., University of Virginia.

Flexer, Carol, and Ellen A. Rhoades. 2016. "Hearing, Listening, the Brain, and Auditory-Verbal Therapy." In *Auditory-Verbal Therapy for Young Children with Hearing Loss and Their Families, and the Practitioners Who Guide Them,* edited by Warren Estabrooks, Karen MacIver-Lux, and Ellen A. Rhoades, 23–34. San Diego, Calif.: Plural.

Foucault, Michel. 2008. *The Birth of Biopolitics: Lectures at the Collège de France, 1978–1979.* Edited by Michel Senellart. Translated by Graham Burchell. New York: Palgrave Macmillan.

Frankel, Francine R. 1971. *India's Green Revolution: Economic Gains and Political Costs.* Princeton, N.J.: Princeton University Press.

French, Sally. 1992. "Simulation Exercises in Disability Awareness Training: A Critique." *Disability, Handicap & Society* 7 (3): 257–66.

Friedner, Michele. 2010. "Biopower, Biosociality, and Community Formation." *Sign Language Studies* 10 (3): 336–47.

Friedner, Michele. 2015. *Valuing Deaf Worlds in Urban India.* New Brunswick, N.J.: Rutgers University Press.

Friedner, Michele. 2018. "Sign Language as Virus: Stigma and Relationality in Urban India." *Medical Anthropology* 37 (5): 359–72.

Friedner, Michele. 2019. "Disability, Anonymous Love, and Interworldly Socials in Urban India." *Current Anthropology* 61 (S21): S37–45.

Friedner, Michele, and Pamela Block. 2017. "Deaf Studies Meets Autistic Studies." *Senses & Society* 12 (3): 282–300.

Friedner, Michele, Nandini Ghosh, and Deepa Palaniappan. 2018. "'Cross-Disability' in India? On the Limits of Disability as a Category and the Work of Negotiating Impairments." *South Asia Multidisciplinary Academic Journal,* freestanding article. https://doi.org/10.4000/samaj.4516.

Friedner, Michele, and Annelies Kusters. 2014. "On the Possibilities and Limits of 'DEAF DEAF SAME': Tourism and Empowerment Camps in Adamorobe (Ghana), Bangalore and Mumbai (India)." *Disability Studies Quarterly* 34 (3). https://doi.org/10.18061/dsq.v34i3.4246.

Friedner, Michele, and Annelies Kusters. 2020. "Deaf Anthropology." *Annual Review of Anthropology* 49: 31–47.

Friedner, Michele, and Jamie Osborne. 2015. "New Disability Mobilities and Accessibilities in Urban India." *City & Society* 27 (1): 9–29.

Friedner, Michele, Rashmi Sadana, and Tarini Bedi. 2018. "The Fix in South Asia: A Concept Note for Pre-Conference Symposium of 2018 Conference on South

Asia, Madison, Wisconsin." Prepared for the 47th Annual Conference on South Asia, University of Wisconsin–Madison.

Friedner, Michele, and Tyler Zoanni. 2018. "Disability from the South: Toward a Lexicon." Somatosphere, December 17, 2018. http://somatosphere.net.

Fritsch, Kelly. 2013. "The Neoliberal Circulation of Affects: Happiness, Accessibility and the Capacitation of Disability as Wheelchair." *Health, Culture and Society* 5 (1): 135–49.

Fritsch, Kelly. 2015. "Gradations of Debility and Capacity: Biocapitalism and the Neoliberalization of Disability Relations." *Canadian Journal of Disability Studies* 4 (2): 12–48.

Gale, Elaine. 2011. "Exploring Perspectives on Cochlear Implants and Language Acquisition within the Deaf Community." *Journal of Deaf Studies and Deaf Education* 16 (1): 121–39.

Garland-Thomson, Rosemarie. 1997. *Extraordinary Bodies: Figuring Physical Disability in American Culture and Literature.* New York: Columbia University Press.

Garland-Thomson, Rosemarie. 2012. "The Case for Conserving Disability." *Journal of Bioethical Inquiry* 9 (3): 339–55.

Garretson, Mervin D. 1976. "Total Communication." *Volta Review* 78 (4): 88–95.

Garrett, Paul B., and Patricia Baquedano-López. 2002. "Language Socialization: Reproduction and Continuity, Transformation and Change." *Annual Review of Anthropology* 31: 339–61.

Geary, Adam. 2010. "Comment on 'Deleuze and the Anthropology of Becoming,' by João Biehl and Peter Locke." *Current Anthropology* 51 (3): 340–41.

Geurts, Kathryn Linn. 2002. *Culture and the Senses: Bodily Ways of Knowing in an African Community.* Berkeley: University of California Press.

Gibbons, Pauline. 2014. *Scaffolding Language, Scaffolding Learning: Teaching English Language Learners in the Mainstream Classroom.* 2nd ed. Portsmouth, N.H.: Heinemann.

Gibbons, Susan Mumby, and Amy Szarkowski. 2019. "One Tool in the Toolkit Is Not Enough: Making the Case for Using Multisensory Approaches in Aural Habilitation of Children with Reduced Hearing." *Perspectives of the ASHA Special Interest Groups* 4 (2): 345–55.

Gibson, James Jerome. 1966. *The Senses Considered as Perceptual Systems.* Boston: Houghton Mifflin.

Gindis, Boris. 1999. "Vygotsky's Vision: Reshaping the Practice of Special Education for the 21st Century." *Remedial and Special Education* 20 (6): 333–40.

Ginsburg, Faye, and Rayna Rapp. 2013. "Disability Worlds." *Annual Review of Anthropology* 42: 53–68.

Goffman, Erving. (1963) 1986. *Stigma: Notes on the Management of Spoiled Identity.* New York: Simon & Schuster.

Goldstein, Max A. 1933. *Problems of the Deaf.* St. Louis: Laryngoscope Press.

Good, Mary-Jo DelVecchio. 2001. "The Biotechnical Embrace." *Culture, Medicine and Psychiatry* 25 (4): 395–410.

Goodley, Dan, and Katherine Runswick-Cole. 2010. "Emancipating Play: Dis/Abled Children, Development and Deconstruction." *Disability & Society* 25 (4): 499–512.

Goodwin, Charles. 2017. *Co-operative Action.* Cambridge: Cambridge University Press.

Goodwin, Marjorie Harness. 2017. "Haptic Sociality: The Embodied Interactive Constitution of Intimacy through Touch." In Meyer, Streeck, and Jordan 2017, 73–102.

Government of India. 2015. *Initial Report Submitted by India under Article 35 of the Convention* (report to the United Nations Committee on the Rights of Persons with Disabilities). https://www.ecoi.net/en/file/local/1416045/1930_1508417772_g1729386.pdf.

Government of India. 2017. *Scheme of Assistance to Disabled Persons for Purchase/Fitting of Aids/Appliances (ADIP Scheme).* New Delhi: Ministry of Social Justice and Empowerment. http://disabilityaffairs.gov.in.

Graham, Stephen, and Nigel Thrift. 2007. Out of Order: Understanding Repair and Maintenance." *Theory, Culture & Society* 24 (3): 1–25.

Green, Mara. 2014a. "Building the Tower of Babel: International Sign, Linguistic Commensuration, and Moral Orientation." *Language in Society* 43 (4): 445–65. https://doi.org/10.1017/S0047404514000396.

Green, Mara. 2014b. "The Nature of Signs: Nepal's Deaf Society, Local Sign, and the Production of Communicative Sociality." PhD diss., University of California, Berkeley.

Griffin, Peg, and Michael Cole. 1984. "Current Activity for the Future: The Zo-Ped." *New Directions for Child and Adolescent Development* 23 (March): 45–64.

Groce, Nora Ellen. 1996. "Parent Advocacy for Disabled Children and the Disability Rights Movement: Similar Movements, Different Trajectories." PONPO working paper no. 237, ISPS working paper no. 2237. https://discovery.ucl.ac.uk.

Gupta, Akhil. 1998. *Postcolonial Developments: Agriculture in the Making of Modern India.* Durham, N.C.: Duke University Press.

Gupta, Akhil. 2012. *Red Tape: Bureaucracy, Structural Violence, and Poverty in India.* Durham, N.C.: Duke University Press.

Gupta, Akhil. 2018. "The Future in Ruins: Thoughts on the Temporality of Infrastructure." In Anand, Gupta, and Appel 2018, 62–79.

Gupta, Akhil, and Aradhana Sharma. 2006. "Globalization and Postcolonial States." *Current Anthropology* 47 (2): 277–307.

Hacking, Ian. 1982. "Biopower and the Avalanche of Printed Numbers." *Humanities in Society* 5: 279–95.

Hall, Matthew L., Wyatte C. Hall, and Naomi K. Caselli. 2019. "Deaf Children Need Language, Not (Just) Speech." *First Language* 39 (4): 367–95.

Hall, Wyatte C. 2017. "What You Don't Know Can Hurt You: The Risk of Language Deprivation by Impairing Sign Language Development in Deaf Children." *Maternal and Child Health Journal* 21 (5): 961–65.

Hamdy, Sherine. 2012. *Our Bodies Belong to God: Organ Transplants, Islam, and the Struggle for Human Dignity in Egypt.* Berkeley: University of California Press.

Hamraie, Aimi. 2017. *Building Access: Universal Design and the Politics of Disability.* Minneapolis: University of Minnesota Press.

Hamraie, Aimi, and Kelly Fritsch. 2019. "Crip Technoscience Manifesto." *Catalyst: Feminism, Theory, Technoscience* 5 (1): 1–33.

Haraway, Donna J. 2007. *When Species Meet.* Minneapolis: University of Minnesota Press.

Harmon, Kristen C. 2013. "Growing Up to Become Hearing: Dreams of Passing in Oral Deaf Education." In *Disability and Passing: Blurring the Lines of Identity,* edited by Jeffrey A. Brune and Daniel J. Wilson, 167–98. Philadelphia: Temple University Press.

Hart, Brendan. 2014. "Autism Parents and Neurodiversity: Radical Translation, Joint Embodiment and the Prosthetic Environment." *BioSocieties* 9 (3): 284–303.

Hartblay, Cassandra. 2017. "Good Ramps, Bad Ramps: Centralized Design Standards and Disability Access in Urban Russian Infrastructure." *American Ethnologist* 44 (1): 9–22.

Helmreich, Stefan. 2015. "Transduction." In *Keywords in Sound,* edited by David Novak and Matt Sakakeeny, 222–31. Durham, N.C.: Duke University Press.

Helmreich, Stefan. 2018. "Music for Cochlear Implants." In *The Oxford Handbook of Timbre,* edited by Emily I. Dolan and Alexander Rehding. New York: Oxford University Press.

Hendren, Sara. 2020. *What Can a Body Do? How We Meet the Built World.* New York: Penguin.

Herzfeld, Michael. 2001. *Anthropology: Theoretical Practice in Culture and Society.* Malden, Mass.: Wiley-Blackwell.

Higgins, Paul C. 1980. *Outsiders in a Hearing World: A Sociology of Deafness.* Beverly Hills, Calif.: SAGE.

The Hindu. 2012. "DRDO Develops a New Indigenous Affordable Cochlear Implant." February 5, 2012. https://www.thehindu.com.

Hindustan Times. 2017. "Haryana IAS Officer Doesn't Mind His Language, Says

8 out of 10 Words He Speaks Are Abuses." June 16, 2017. https://www
.hindustantimes.com.

Hindustan Times. 2019. "2 Kids under ADIP Get Rs 10 Lakh Cochlear Implants
Surgery for Free at Sassoon Hospital." December 17, 2019. https://www
.hindustantimes.com.

Hiranandani, Vanmala, and Deepa Sonpal. 2010. "Disability, Economic Globalization and Privatization: A Case Study of India." *Disability Studies Quarterly*
30 (3–4). https://doi.org/10.18061/dsq.v30i3/4.1272.

Hochschild, Arlie Russell. 1983. *The Managed Heart: Commercialization of
Human Feeling.* Berkeley: University of California Press.

Holmström, Ingela, and Krister Schönström. 2018. "Deaf Lecturers' Translanguaging in a Higher Education Setting: A Multimodal Multilingual Perspective." *Applied Linguistics Review* 9 (1): 90–111.

Holt, Rachael Frush, and Mario A. Svirsky. 2008. "An Exploratory Look at Pediatric Cochlear Implantation: Is Earliest Always Best?" *Ear and Hearing* 29 (4):
492–511.

Howes, David. 2006. "Cross-Talk between the Senses." *Senses & Society* 1 (3):
381–90.

Howes, David. 2019. "Multisensory Anthropology." *Annual Review of Anthropology* 48: 17–28.

Howes, David, and Constance Classen. 2014. *Ways of Sensing: Understanding the
Senses in Society.* London: Routledge.

Hui, Alexandra, Mara Mills, and Viktoria Tkaczyk. 2020. "Testing Hearing: An
Introduction." In *Testing Hearing,* edited by Alexandra Hui, Mara Mills, and
Viktoria Tkaczyk, 1–22. New York: Oxford University Press.

Hunt, Nancy Rose. 2016. *A Nervous State: Violence, Remedies, and Reverie in
Colonial Congo.* Durham, N.C.: Duke University Press.

Iglehart, Frank. 2016. "Speech Perception in Classroom Acoustics by Children
with Cochlear Implants and with Typical Hearing." *American Journal of
Audiology* 25 (2): 100–109.

International Disability Alliance. 2020. *What an Inclusive, Equitable, Quality Education Means to Us: Report of the International Disability Alliance.*
Geneva: International Disability Alliance. https://www.internationaldisability
alliance.org.

Johnson, Robert E., Scott K. Liddell, and Carol J. Erting. 1989. "Unlocking the
Curriculum: Principles for Achieving Access in Deaf Education." Gallaudet
Research Institute working paper no. 89-3. https://files.eric.ed.gov/fulltext/
ED316978.pdf.

Jones, Caroline A. 2005. *Eyesight Alone: Clement Greenberg's Modernism and the
Bureaucratization of the Senses.* Chicago: University of Chicago Press.

Kafer, Alison. 2013. *Feminist, Queer, Crip.* Bloomington: Indiana University Press.

Kaufman, Sharon R. 2015. *Ordinary Medicine: Extraordinary Treatments, Longer Lives, and Where to Draw the Line.* Durham, N.C.: Duke University Press.

Keating, Elizabeth, and R. Neill Hadder. 2010. "Sensory Impairment." *Annual Review of Anthropology* 39: 115–29.

Kenny, Katherine E. 2015. "The Biopolitics of Global Health: Life and Death in Neoliberal Time." *Journal of Sociology* 51 (1): 9–27.

Khan, Naveeda. 2006. "Flaws in the Flow: Roads and Their Modernity in Pakistan." *Social Text,* no. 89, 24 (4): 87–113.

Kierans, Ciara, and Kirsten Bell. 2017. "Cultivating Ambivalence: Methodological Considerations for Anthropology." *HAU: Journal of Ethnographic Theory* 7 (2): 23–44.

Kim, Eunjung. 2017. *Curative Violence: Rehabilitating Disability, Gender, and Sexuality in Modern Korea.* Durham, N.C.: Duke University Press.

Kittay, Eva Feder. 1999. *Love's Labor: Essays on Women, Equality and Dependency.* New York: Routledge.

Kleinman, Arthur. 1999. "Moral Experience and Ethical Reflection: Can Ethnography Reconcile Them? A Quandary for 'the New Bioethics.'" *Daedalus* 128 (4): 69–97.

Kochhar, Rijul. 2013. 'The Analytics of Disability: Bodies, Documents, and the Order of the State." MA thesis, University of Delhi.

Kohrman, Matthew. 2005. *Bodies of Difference: Experiences of Disability and Institutional Advocacy in the Making of Modern China.* Berkeley: University of California Press.

Komesaroff, Linda, ed. 2007. *Surgical Consent: Bioethics and Cochlear Implantation.* Washington, D.C.: Gallaudet University Press.

Kos, Maria-Izabel, Marielle Deriaz, Jean-Philippe Guyot, and Marco Pelizzone. 2009. "What Can Be Expected from a Late Cochlear Implantation?" *International Journal of Pediatric Otorhinolaryngology* 73 (2): 189–93.

Kral, Andrej, and Anu Sharma. 2012. "Developmental Neuroplasticity after Cochlear Implantation." *Trends in Neurosciences* 35 (2): 111–22.

Kurtz, Stanley N. 1992. *All the Mothers Are One: Hindu India and the Cultural Reshaping of Psychoanalysis.* New York: Columbia University Press.

Kusters, Annelies, Maartje De Meulder, and Dai O'Brien. 2017. "Innovations in Deaf Studies: Critically Mapping the Field." In *Innovations in Deaf Studies: The Role of Deaf Scholars,* edited by Annelies Kusters, Maartje De Meulder, and Dai O'Brien, 1–56. Oxford: Oxford University Press.

Kusters, Annelies, and Sujit Sahasrabudhe. 2018. "Language Ideologies on the Difference between Gesture and Sign." *Language & Communication* 60: 44–63.

Kusters, Annelies, Massimiliano Spotti, Ruth Swanwick, and Elina Tapio. 2017. "Beyond Languages, beyond Modalities: Transforming the Study of Semiotic Repertoires." *International Journal of Multilingualism* 14 (3): 219–32.

Kusters, Marieke. 2017. "Intergenerational Responsibility in Deaf Pedagogies." In *Innovations in Deaf Studies: The Role of Deaf Scholars,* edited by Annelies Kusters, Maartje De Meulder, and Dai O'Brien, 241–64. Oxford: Oxford University Press.

Ladd, Paddy. 2003. *Understanding Deaf Culture: In Search of Deafhood.* Clevedon, England: Multilingual Matters.

Ladd, Paddy. 2007. "Cochlear Implantation, Colonialism, and Deaf Rights." In Komesaroff 2007, 1–29.

Laet, Marianne de, and Annemarie Mol. 2000. "The Zimbabwe Bush Pump: Mechanics of a Fluid Technology." *Social Studies of Science* 30 (2): 225–63.

Lal, Vinay. 2002. "Indians and the Guinness Book of Records: The Political and Cultural Contours of a National Obsession." In *Of Cricket, Gandhi and Guinness: Essays in Indian History and Culture.* Calcutta: Seagull Books.

Lane, Harlan. 2007. "Ethnicity, Ethics, and the Deaf-World." In Komesaroff 2007, 42–69.

Lane, Harlan, Robert Hoffmeister, and Ben Bahan. 1996. *A Journey into the Deaf-World.* San Diego, Calif.: DawnSignPress.

Larkin, Brian. 2013. "The Politics and Poetics of Infrastructure." *Annual Review of Anthropology* 42: 327–43.

Larsen, Nella. (1929) 2011. *Passing.* Mansfield Centre, Conn.: Martino.

Latour, Bruno. 2004. "Why Has Critique Run Out of Steam? From Matters of Fact to Matters of Concern." *Critical Inquiry* 30 (2): 225–48.

Lewkowicz, David. J., and Kimberly S. Kraebel. 2004. "The Value of Multisensory Redundancy in the Development of Intersensory Perception." In Calvert, Spence, and Stein 2004, 655–78.

Lewkowicz, David J., and Robert Lickliter. (1994) 2013. *The Development of Intersensory Perception: Comparative Perspectives.* New York: Routledge.

Lickliter, Robert. 2011. "The Integrated Development of Sensory Organization." *Clinics in Perinatology* 38 (4): 591–603.

Linton, Simi. 1998. *Claiming Disability.* New York: New York University Press.

Livingston, Julie. 2005. *Debility and the Moral Imagination in Botswana.* Bloomington: Indiana University Press.

Livingston, Julie. 2012. *Improvising Medicine: An African Oncology Ward in an Emerging Cancer Epidemic.* Durham, N.C.: Duke University Press.

Lloyd, Stephanie, and Nicolas Moreau. 2011. "Pursuit of a 'Normal Life': Mood, Anxiety, and Their Disordering." *Medical Anthropology* 30 (6): 591–609.

Lloyd, Stephanie, and Alexandre Tremblay. 2021. "No Hearing without Signals: Imagining and Reimagining Transductions through the History of the Cochlear Implant." *Senses & Society* 16 (3).

Lomber, Stephen G., M. Alex Meredith, and Andrej Kral. 2010. "Cross-Modal

Plasticity in Specific Auditory Cortices Underlies Visual Compensations in the Deaf." *Nature Neuroscience* 13 (11): 1421–27.

Madan, Ankur, Rajashree Srinivasan, and Kinnari Pandya. 2018. "Parent–Child Relations: Changing Contours and Emerging Trends." In *Childhoods in India: Traditions, Trends and Transformations,* edited by T. S. Saraswathi, Shailaja Menon, and Ankur Madan, 109–29. London: Routledge.

Madell, Jane. 2015. "It's Not the Same Old Deafness." Hearing Health & Technology Matters, March 24, 2015. https://hearinghealthmatters.org.

Mahmood, Saba. 2005. *Politics of Piety: The Islamic Revival and the Feminist Subject.* Princeton, N.J.: Princeton University Press.

Malabou, Catherine. 2008. *What Should We Do with Our Brain?* Translated by Sebastian Rand. New York: Fordham University Press.

Manning, Erin. 2007. *Politics of Touch: Sense, Movement, Sovereignty.* Minneapolis: University of Minnesota Press.

Marsella, Pasquale, Alessandro Scorpecci, Giulia Cartocci, Sara Giannantonio, Anton Giulio Maglione, Isotta Venuti, Ambra Brizi, and Fabio Babiloni. 2017. "EEG Activity as an Objective Measure of Cognitive Load during Effortful Listening: A Study on Pediatric Subjects with Bilateral, Asymmetric Sensorineural Hearing Loss." *International Journal of Pediatric Otorhinolaryngology* 99 (1): 1–7.

Martin, Emily. 2007. *Bipolar Expeditions: Mania and Depression in American Culture.* Princeton, N.J.: Princeton University Press.

Matthijs, Liesbeth, Stefan Hardonk, Jasmina Sermijn, Martine Van Puyvelde, Greg Leigh, Mieke Van Herreweghe, and Gerrit Loots. 2018. "Mothers of Deaf Children in the 21st Century: Dynamic Positioning between the Medical and Cultural-Linguistic Discourses." *Journal of Deaf Studies and Deaf Education* 23 (2): 365–77.

Mattingly, Cheryl. 2010. *The Paradox of Hope: Journeys through a Clinical Borderland.* Berkeley: University of California Press.

Mauger, Stefan J., Marian Jones, Esti Nel, and Janine Del Dot. 2017. "Clinical Outcomes with the Kanso™ Off-the-Ear Cochlear Implant Sound Processor." *International Journal of Audiology* 56 (4): 267–76. https://doi.org/10.1080/14992027.2016.1265156.

Mauldin, Laura. 2014. "Precarious Plasticity: Neuropolitics, Cochlear Implants, and the Redefinition of Deafness." *Science, Technology, & Human Values* 39 (1): 130–53.

Mauldin, Laura. 2016. *Made to Hear: Cochlear Implants and Raising Deaf Children.* Minneapolis: University of Minnesota Press.

Mauss, Marcel. 1973. "Techniques of the Body." *Economy and Society* 2 (1): 70–88.

Mayberry, Rachel I. 1993. "First-Language Acquisition after Childhood Differs from Second-Language Acquisition." *Journal of Speech, Language, and Hearing Research* 36 (6): 1258–70.

Mayberry, Rachel I., and Ellen B. Eichen. 1991. "The Long-Lasting Advantage of Learning Sign Language in Childhood: Another Look at the Critical Period for Language Acquisition." *Journal of Memory and Language* 30 (4): 486–512.

Mazzarella, William. 2006. "Internet X-Ray: E-Governance, Transparency, and the Politics of Immediation in India." *Public Culture* 18 (3): 473–505.

McDaniel, Jena, and Stephen Camarata. 2017. "Does Access to Visual Input Inhibit Auditory Development for Children with Cochlear Implants? A Review of the Evidence." *Perspectives of the ASHA Special Interest Groups* 2 (9): 10–24.

McRuer, Robert. 2006. *Crip Theory: Cultural Signs of Queerness and Disability.* New York: New York University Press.

Mead, Margaret. (1964) 1972. "Vicissitudes of the Study of the Total Communication Process." In *Approaches to Semiotics: Cultural Anthropology, Education, Linguistics, Psychiatry, Psychology,* edited by Thomas A. Sebeok, Alfred S. Hayes, and Mary Catherine Bateson, 277–88. The Hague: Mouton.

Mehrotra, Nilika. 2011. "Disability Rights Movements in India: Politics and Practice." *Economic and Political Weekly* 46 (6): 65–72.

Mehus, Siri. 2011. "Creating Contexts for Actions: Multimodal Practices for Managing Children's Conduct in the Childcare Classroom." In *Embodied Interaction: Language and Body in the Material World,* edited by Jürgen Streeck, Charles Goodwin, and Curtis LeBaron, 123–36. New York: Cambridge University Press.

Meister, Hartmut, Stefan Schreitmüller, Magdalene Ortmann, Sebastian Rählmann, and Martin Walger. 2016. "Effects of Hearing Loss and Cognitive Load on Speech Recognition with Competing Talkers." *Frontiers in Psychology* 7, art. 301. https://doi.org/10.3389/fpsyg.2016.00301.

Merleau-Ponty, Maurice. 1962. *Phenomenology of Perception.* New York: Routledge.

Meyer, Christian, Jürgen Streeck, and J. Scott Jordan, eds. 2017. *Intercorporeality: Emerging Socialities in Interaction.* New York: Oxford University Press.

Mialet, Hélène. 2012. *Hawking Incorporated: Stephen Hawking and the Anthropology of the Knowing Subject.* Chicago: University of Chicago Press.

Mills, Mara. 2010. "Deaf Jam: From Inscription to Reproduction to Information." *Social Text,* no. 102, 28 (1): 35–58.

Mills, Mara. 2011. "Deafening: Noise and the Engineering of Communication in the Telephone System." *Grey Room* 43: 118–43.

Mills, Mara. 2012. "Do Signals Have Politics? Inscribing Abilities in Cochlear Implants." In *The Oxford Handbook of Sound Studies,* edited by Trevor Pinch and Karin Bijsterveld, 320-44. New York: Oxford University Press.

Mills, Mara. 2015. "Deafness." In *Keywords in Sound,* edited by David Novak and Matt Sakakeeny, 45–54. Durham, N.C.: Duke University Press.

Mills, Mara. 2020. "Testing Hearing with Speech." In *Testing Hearing,* edited by Alexandra Hui, Mara Mills, and Viktoria Tkaczyk, 23–48. New York: Oxford University Press.

Minturn, Leigh, and Swaran Kapoor. 1993. *Sita's Daughters: Coming Out of Purdah; The Rajput Women of Khalapur Revisited.* Oxford: Oxford University Press.

Mitchell, David T., and Sharon L. Snyder. 2010. "Disability as Multitude: Reworking Non-productive Labor Power." *Journal of Literary & Cultural Disability Studies* 4 (2): 179–93.

Mitchell, David T., and Sharon L. Snyder. 2015. *The Biopolitics of Disability: Neoliberalism, Ablenationalism, and Peripheral Embodiment.* Ann Arbor: University of Michigan Press.

Mol, Annemarie, Ingunn Moser, and Jeannette Pols. 2010. "Care: Putting Practice into Theory." In *Care in Practice: On Tinkering in Clinics, Homes and Farms,* edited by Annemarie Mol, Ingunn Moser, and Jeannette Pols, 7–26. Bielefeld: Transcript.

Monaghan, Leila Frances, Karen Nakamura, Constanze Schmaling, and Graham H. Turner. 2003. *Many Ways to Be Deaf: International Variation in Deaf Communities.* Washington, D.C.: Gallaudet University Press.

Moore, David R., and Robert V. Shannon. 2009. "Beyond Cochlear Implants: Awakening the Deafened Brain." *Nature Neuroscience* 12 (6): 686–91.

Moran-Thomas, Amy. 2019. *Traveling with Sugar: Chronicles of a Global Epidemic.* Oakland: University of California Press.

Moriarty Harrelson, Erin. 2017. "Deaf People with 'No Language': Mobility and Flexible Accumulation in Languaging Practices of Deaf People in Cambodia." *Applied Linguistics Review* 10 (1): 55–72.

Morris, Rosalind C., ed. 2010. *Can the Subaltern Speak? Reflections on the History of an Idea.* New York: Columbia University Press.

Mukherjee, Goutam, and Amalendu Samanta. 2005. "Wheelchair Charity: A Useless Benevolence in Community-Based Rehabilitation." *Disability and Rehabilitation* 27 (10): 591–96.

Muñoz, José Esteban. 2006. "Feeling Brown, Feeling Down: Latina Affect, the Performativity of Race, and the Depressive Position." *Signs: Journal of Women in Culture and Society* 31 (3): 675–88.

Murray, Micah M., David J. Lewkowicz, Amir Amedi, and Mark T. Wallace. 2016. "Multisensory Processes: A Balancing Act across the Lifespan." *Trends in Neurosciences* 39 (8): 567–79.

Murthy, Anjali. 2019. "Discourse of Deafness in India: A Critical Analysis." BA thesis, University of Chicago.

Nagarajan, Rema. 2009a. "Govt Deaf to Maniram's Cry for Justice." *Times of India,* July 26, 2009. https://timesofindia.indiatimes.com/india.

Nagarajan, Rema. 2009b, June 4. "How Maniram Beat His Disability and the System." *Times of India,* June 4, 2009. https://timesofindia.indiatimes.com/blogs.

Nagarajan, Rema. 2017a. "Absence of Regulator Leads to 'Cartelisation' in Ear Implants." *Times of India,* September 11, 2017. https://timesofindia.indiatimes.com/india.

Nagarajan, Rema. 2017b. "TN Fights Deafness the Costly Way, Then Turns Wiser." *Times of India,* September 28, 2017. https://timesofindia.indiatimes.com/blogs.

Nagarajan, Rema. 2017c. "Why Government Hospitals Need to Up Their Share of Ear Implants." *Times of India,* September 30, 2017. https://timesofindia.indiatimes.com/blogs.

Napoli, Donna Jo. 2014. "A Magic Touch: Deaf Gain and the Benefits of Tactile Sensation." In Bauman and Murray 2014, 211–32.

Nario-Redmond, Michelle R., Dobromir Gospodinov, and Angela Cobb. 2017. "Crip for a Day: The Unintended Negative Consequences of Disability Simulations." *Rehabilitation Psychology* 62 (3): 324–33.

National CRPD Coalition–India. 2019. *CRPD Alternate Report for India.* http://accessability.co.in.

National Institute on Deafness and Other Communication Disorders. 2021. "Cochlear Implants." Last updated March 24, 2021. https://www.nidcd.nih.gov.

Nishida, Akemi. 2017. "Relating through Differences: Disability, Affective Relationality, and the U.S. Public Healthcare Assemblage." *Subjectivity* 10 (1): 89–103.

Novak, David. 2015. "Noise." In *Keywords in Sound,* edited by David Novak and Matt Sakakeeny, 125–38. Durham, N.C.: Duke University Press.

Ochs, Elinor, and Bambi B. Schieffelin. 1984. "Language Acquisition and Socialization: Three Developmental Stories and Their Implications." In *Culture Theory: Essays on Mind, Self and Emotion,* edited by Richard A. Shweder and Robert A. LeVine, 276–320. Cambridge: Cambridge University Press.

Ochs, Elinor, and Olga Solomon. 2010. "Autistic Sociality." *Ethos* 38 (1): 69–92.

Ochs, Elinor, Olga Solomon, and Laura Sterponi. 2005. "Limitations and Transformations of Habitus in Child-Directed Communication." *Discourse Studies* 7 (4–5): 547–83.

Okubo, Suguru, Miyako Takahashi, and Ichiro Kai. 2008. "How Japanese Parents of Deaf Children Arrive at Decisions Regarding Pediatric Cochlear Implantation Surgery: A Qualitative Study." *Social Science & Medicine* 66 (12): 2436–47.

Oldani, Michael. 2004. "Thick Prescriptions: Toward an Interpretation of Pharmaceutical Sales Practices." *Medical Anthropology Quarterly* 18 (3): 325–56.

Ott, Katherine. 2014. "Disability Things: Material Culture and American Disability History, 1700–2010." In *Disability Histories,* edited by Susan Burch and Michael Rembis, 119–35. Urbana: University of Illinois Press.

Oudshoorn, Nelly, and Trevor Pinch. 2003. "Introduction: How Users and Nonusers Matter." In *How Users Matter: The Co-construction of Users and Technology,* edited by Nelly Oudshoorn and Trevor Pinch, 1–24. Cambridge: MIT Press.

Padden, Carol. 1980. "The Deaf Community and the Culture of Deaf People." In *Sign Language and the Deaf Community: Essays in Honor of William C. Stokoe,* edited by Charlotte Baker and Robbin Battison, 89–103. Silver Spring, Md.: National Association of the Deaf.

Palaniappan, Deepa. 2019. "May I Dare to State the Obvious? Rights Based Approach Is Failing Us—Urgent Lessons from Rural Poor Disabled Communities of Bihar." Paper presented at the conference "Disentangling Disability and Human Rights," University of Chicago Delhi Center, Delhi.

Pals, Carina, Anastasios Sarampalis, and Deniz Başkent. 2013. "Listening Effort with Cochlear Implant Simulations." *Journal of Speech, Language, and Hearing Research* 56 (4): 1075–84.

Pals, Carina, Anastasios Sarampalis, Andy Beynon, Thomas Stainsby, and Deniz Başkent. 2020. "Effect of Spectral Channels on Speech Recognition, Comprehension, and Listening Effort in Cochlear-Implant Users." *Trends in Hearing* 24. https://doi.org/10.1177/2331216520904617.

Patsavas, Alyson. 2013. "Disabilities Studies Gains Cultural Capital? And Now What?" The Feminist Wire, November 22, 2013. https://thefeministwire.com.

Pennycook, Alastair. 2017a. *Posthumanist Applied Linguistics.* London: Routledge.

Pennycook, Alastair. 2017b. "Translanguaging and Semiotic Assemblages." *International Journal of Multilingualism* 14 (3): 269–82.

Pentcheva, Bissera V. 2006. "The Performative Icon." *Art Bulletin* 88 (4): 631–55.

Petryna, Adriana. 2005. "Ethical Variability: Drug Development and Globalizing Clinical Trials." *American Ethnologist* 32 (2): 183–97.

Pfister, Anne E. 2017. "Forbidden Signs: Deafness and Language Socialization in Mexico City." *Ethos* 45 (1): 139–61.

Pisoni, David B., Christopher M. Conway, William G. Kronenberger, David L. Horn, Jennifer Karpicke, and Shirley C. Henning. 2008. "Efficacy and Effectiveness of Cochlear Implants in Deaf Children." In *Deaf Cognition: Foundations and Outcomes,* edited by Marc Marschark and Peter C. Hauser, 52–101. New York: Oxford University Press.

Plemons, Eric. 2017. *The Look of a Woman: Facial Feminization Surgery and the Aims of Trans- Medicine.* Durham, N.C.: Duke University Press.

Pollack, Doreen. 1974. "Denver's Acoupedic Program." *Peabody Journal of Education* 51 (3): 180–85.

Power, Desmond John, and Mervyn Bruce Hyde. 1997. "Multisensory and Unisensory Approaches to Communicating with Deaf Children." *European Journal of Psychology of Education* 12 (4): 449–64.

Prahlada N.B. 2017. "Faulty Policies Are Curbing Hearing-Disabled Children's Access to Cochlear Implants." The Wire, September 26, 2017. https://thewire.in.

Prasad, Bhagwati, and Amitabh Kumar. 2009. *Tinker.Solder.Tap: A Graphic Novel.* Translated by Shveta Sarda. Delhi: Sarai-CSDS.

Press Information Bureau. 2017. "Highest Number of Divyangjan Given Aids and Appliances in the Presence of Prime Minister Modi at Rajkot Samajik Adhikarta Shivir." Press release, December 18, 2017. https://pib.gov.in/PressReleasePage.aspx?PRID=1512969.

Press Information Bureau. 2018. "DEPwD Celebrates 'International Day of Sign Languages.'" Press release, September 23, 2018. https://pib.gov.in/PressReleasePage.aspx?PRID=1546995.

Press Information Bureau. 2019. "Shri Thaawarchand Gehlot Inaugurates 'National Conference on Deendayal Disabled Rehabilitation Scheme.'" Press release, March 1, 2019. https://pib.gov.in/PressReleaseIframePage.aspx?PRID=1566887.

Price, Margaret. 2015. "The Bodymind Problem and the Possibilities of Pain." *Hypatia* 30 (1): 268–84.

Puar, Jasbir K. 2017. *The Right to Maim: Debility, Capacity, Disability.* Durham, N.C.: Duke University Press.

Puig de la Bellacasa, María. 2017. *Matters of Care: Speculative Ethics in More Than Human Worlds.* Minneapolis: University of Minnesota Press.

Rabinow, Paul. 2005. "Artificiality and Enlightenment: From Sociobiology to Biosociality." In *Anthropologies of Modernity: Foucault, Governmentality, and Life Politics,* edited by Jonathan Xavier Inda, 179–93. New York: John Wiley.

Rai, Amit S. 2019. *Jugaad Time: Ecologies of Everyday Hacking in India.* Durham, N.C.: Duke University Press.

Rao, Shridevi. 2006. "Parameters of Normality and Cultural Constructions of 'Mental Retardation': Perspectives of Bengali Families." *Disability & Society* 21 (2): 159–78.

Rhoades, Ellen A., Warren Estabrooks, Stacey R. Lim, and Karen MacIver-Lux. 2016. "Strategies for Listening, Talking, and Thinking in Auditory-Verbal Therapy." In *Auditory-Verbal Therapy for Young Children with Hearing Loss and Their Families, and the Practitioners Who Guide Them,* edited by Warren Estabrooks, Karen MacIver-Lux, and Ellen A. Rhoades, 285–326. San Diego, Calif.: Plural.

Roberts, Dorothy. 1997. *Killing the Black Body: Race, Reproduction, and the Meaning of Liberty.* New York: Vintage Books.

Robinson, Amy. 1994. "It Takes One to Know One: Passing and Communities of Common Interest." *Critical Inquiry* 20 (4): 715–36.

Roland, Alan. 1989. *In Search of Self in India and Japan.* Princeton, N.J.: Princeton University Press.

Rose, Nikolas, and Joelle M. Abi-Rached. 2013. *Neuro: The New Brain Sciences and the Management of the Mind.* Princeton, N.J.: Princeton University Press.

Rosenzweig, Elizabeth. 2011. "The Hand Cue." Auditory Verbal Therapy (blog), January 29, 2011. https://auditoryverbaltherapy.net.

Rouger, J., S. Lagleyre, B. Fraysse, S. Deneve, O. Deguine, and P. Barone. 2007. "Evidence That Cochlear-Implanted Deaf Patients Are Better Multisensory Integrators." *Proceedings of the National Academy of Sciences* 104 (17): 7295–300.

Rudnyckyj, Daromir. 2011. "Circulating Tears and Managing Hearts: Governing through Affect in an Indonesian Steel Factory." *Anthropological Theory* 11 (1): 63–87.

Russell, Andrew L., and Lee Vinsel. 2018. "After Innovation, Turn to Maintenance." *Technology and Culture* 59 (1): 1–25.

Sakshi Post. 2021. "Andhra CM YS Jagan Interacts with Kids Who Underwent Cochlear Implant." January 29, 2021. https://english.sakshi.com.

Salehomoum, Maryam. 2020. "Cochlear Implant Nonuse: Insight from Deaf Adults." *Journal of Deaf Studies and Deaf Education* 25 (3): 270–82.

Samuels, Ellen. 2003. "My Body, My Closet: Invisible Disability and the Limits of Coming-Out Discourse." *GLQ: A Journal of Lesbian and Gay Studies* 9 (1–2): 233–55.

Sanchez, Rebecca. 2020. "Deafness and Sound." In *Sound and Literature,* edited by Anna Snaith, 272–86. Cambridge: Cambridge University Press.

Sandahl, Carrie. 2003. "Queering the Crip or Cripping the Queer? Intersections of Queer and Crip Identities in Solo Autobiographical Performance." *GLQ: A Journal of Lesbian and Gay Studies* 9 (1–2): 25–56.

Sandahl, Carrie, and Philip Auslander. 2005. *Bodies in Commotion: Disability and Performance.* Ann Arbor: University of Michigan Press.

Sassen, Saskia. 2005. "The Global City: Introducing a Concept." *Brown Journal of World Affairs* 11 (2): 27–43.

Scherer, Patricia. 1972. "Audition, Speech, and Methodology." *Volta Review* 74 (9): 552–53, 559–60.

Schieffelin, Bambi B., and Elinor Ochs. 1986a. "Language Socialization." *Annual Review of Anthropology* 15: 163–91.

Schieffelin, Bambi B., and Elinor Ochs, eds. 1986b. *Language Socialization across Cultures.* New York: Cambridge University Press.

Schlesinger, Hilde. 1986. "Total Communication in Perspective." In *Deafness in Perspective,* edited by David M. Luterman, 87–116. London: Taylor & Francis.

Schriempf, Alexa. 2012. "Hearing Deafness: Subjectness, Articulateness and Communicability." In *Embodied Selves,* edited by Stella Gonzalez-Arnal, Gill Jagger, and Kathleen Lennon, 160–79. London: Palgrave Macmillan.

Schultz, Theodore W. 1961. "Investment in Human Capital." *American Economic Review* 51 (1): 1–17.

Schwenkel, Christina. 2015. "Sense." Theorizing the Contemporary, Fieldsights, September 24, 2015. https://culanth.org.

Seaver, Leeanne, ed. 2010. *The Book of Choice: Support for Parenting a Child Who Is Deaf or Hard of Hearing.* Boulder, Colo.: Hands & Voices. https://www.handsandvoices.org.

Sequenzia, Amy, and Elizabeth J. Grace, eds. 2015. *Typed Words, Loud Voices: A Collection.* N.p.: Autonomous Press.

Seymour, Susan C. 1976. "Caste/Class and Child-Rearing in a Changing Indian Town." *American Ethnologist* 3 (4): 783–96.

Seymour, Susan C. 1983. "Household Structure and Status and Expressions of Affect in India." *Ethos* 11 (4): 263–77.

Seymour, Susan C. 1999. *Women, Family, and Child Care in India: A World in Transition.* Cambridge: Cambridge University Press.

Shakespeare, Tom. 2010. "The Social Model of Disability." In *The Disability Studies Reader,* edited by Lennard Davis, 266–73. New York: Routledge.

Sharma, Anu, Michael F. Dorman, and Andrej Kral. 2005. "The Influence of a Sensitive Period on Central Auditory Development in Children with Unilateral and Bilateral Cochlear Implants." *Hearing Research* 203 (1–2): 134–43.

Sharma, Aradhana. 2008. *Logics of Empowerment: Development, Gender, and Governance in Neoliberal India.* Minneapolis: University of Minnesota Press.

Sharma, Dinesh. 2000. "Infancy and Childhood in India: A Critical Review." *International Journal of Group Tensions* 29 (3): 219–51.

Siebers, Tobin. 2004. "Disability as Masquerade." *Literature and Medicine* 23 (1): 1–22.

Simone, AbdouMaliq. 2004. "People as Infrastructure: Intersecting Fragments in Johannesburg." *Public Culture* 16 (3): 407–29.

Singh, Shomeshwar, Shashank Vahist, and Thathya Ariyaratne. 2015. "One-Year Experience with the Cochlear™ Paediatric Implanted Recipient Observational Study (Cochlear P-IROS) in New Delhi, India." *Journal of Otology* 10 (2): 57–65.

Smelser, Neil J. 1998. "The Rational and the Ambivalent in the Social Sciences: 1997 Presidential Address." *American Sociological Review* 63 (1): 1–15.

Snoddon, Kristin. 2014. "Baby Sign as Deaf Gain." In Bauman and Murray 2014, 146–58.

Soldatic, Karen, and Shaun Grech. 2014. "Transnationalising Disability Studies: Rights, Justice and Impairment." *Disability Studies Quarterly* 34 (2). https://doi.org/10.18061/dsq.v34i2.4249.

Solomon, Olga. 2010. "Sense and the Senses: Anthropology and the Study of Autism." *Annual Review of Anthropology* 39: 241–59.

Solvang, Per Koren, and Hilde Haualand. 2014. "Accessibility and Diversity: Deaf Space in Action." *Scandinavian Journal of Disability Research* 16 (1): 1–13.

Sparrow, Robert. 2010. "Implants and Ethnocide: Learning from the Cochlear Implant Controversy." *Disability & Society* 25 (4): 455–66.

Spivak, Gayatri Chakravorty. 1999. *A Critique of Postcolonial Reason.* Cambridge, Mass.: Harvard University Press.

Spivak, Gayatri Chakravorty. 2006. *In Other Worlds.* New York: Routledge.

Staples, James. 2018. "Doing Disability through Charity and Philanthropy in Contemporary South India." *Contributions to Indian Sociology* 52 (2): 129–55.

Star, Susan Leigh. 1999. "The Ethnography of Infrastructure." *American Behavioral Scientist* 43 (3): 377–91.

Stenfelt, Stefan, and Jerker Rönnberg. 2009. "The Signal–Cognition Interface: Interactions between Degraded Auditory Signals and Cognitive Processes." *Scandinavian Journal of Psychology* 50 (5): 385–93.

Sterne, Jonathan. 2003. *The Audible Past: Cultural Origins of Sound Reproduction.* Durham, N.C.: Duke University Press.

Sterne, Jonathan. 2015. "Hearing." In *Keywords in Sound,* edited by David Novak and Matt Sakakeeny, 65–77. Durham, N.C.: Duke University Press.

Sterne, Jonathan, and Tara Rodgers. 2011. "The Poetics of Signal Processing." *Differences* 22 (2–3): 31–53.

Sterponi, Laura, Kenton de Kirby, and Jennifer Shankey. 2014. "Rethinking Language in Autism." *Autism* 19 (5): 517–26.

Sterponi, Laura, and Jennifer Shankey. 2014. "Rethinking Echolalia: Repetition as Interactional Resource in the Communication of a Child with Autism." *Journal of Child Language* 41 (2): 275–304.

Stevenson, Lisa. 2014. *Life beside Itself: Imagining Care in the Canadian Arctic.* Berkeley: University of California Press.

Stevenson, Ryan A., Sterling W. Sheffield, Iliza M. Butera, René H. Gifford, and Mark T. Wallace. 2017. "Multisensory Integration in Cochlear Implant Recipients." *Ear and Hearing* 38 (5): 521–38.

Stiker, Henri-Jacques. 1999. *A History of Disability.* Ann Arbor: University of Michigan Press.

Sunder Rajan, Kaushik. 2017. *Pharmocracy: Value, Politics, and Knowledge in Global Biomedicine.* Durham, N.C.: Duke University Press.

Talbot, Pamela. 2016. *Topics in Auditory Verbal Therapy: A Collection of Parent Handouts.* N.p.: Language Launchers. https://www.teacherspayteachers.com.

Tarlo, Emma. 2003. *Unsettling Memories: Narratives of the Emergency in Delhi.* Berkeley: University of California Press.

Taussig, Karen-Sue, Klaus Hoeyer, and Stefan Helmreich. 2013. "The Anthropology of Potentiality in Biomedicine: An Introduction to Supplement 7." *Current Anthropology* 54 (S7): S3–14.

Terry, Jennifer. 2017. *Attachments to War: Biomedical Logics and Violence in Twenty-First-Century America.* Durham, N.C.: Duke University Press.

Thompson, Marie. 2017. *Beyond Unwanted Sound: Noise, Affect and Aesthetic Moralism.* New York: Bloomsbury.

Times News Network. 2016. "Guinness Record of 600 Hearing Aids Fitted in 8 Hours." *Times of India,* September 19, 2016. https://timesofindia.indiatimes.com.

Timmermans, Stefan, and Mara Buchbinder. 2013. "Potentializing Newborn Screening." *Current Anthropology* 54 (S7): S26–35.

Titchkosky, Tanya. 2011. *The Question of Access: Disability, Space, Meaning.* Toronto: University of Toronto Press.

Trawick, Margaret. 1990. *Notes on Love in a Tamil Family.* Berkeley: University of California Press.

Tronto, Joan C. 1993. *Moral Boundaries: A Political Argument for an Ethic of Care.* New York: Routledge.

Tulbert, Eve, and Marjorie H. Goodwin. 2011. "Choreographies of Attention: Multimodality in a Routine Family Activity." In *Embodied Interaction: Language and Body in the Material World,* edited by Jürgen Streeck, Charles Goodwin, and Curtis LeBaron, 79–92. New York: Cambridge University Press.

Tuli, Mila, and Nandita Chaudhary. 2010. "Elective Interdependence: Understanding Individual Agency and Interpersonal Relationships in Indian Families." *Culture & Psychology* 16 (4): 477–96.

United News of India. 2019. "Deaf Kashmiri Girls Get New Lease of Life at Katra Hospital." *Brighter Kashmir,* December 15, 2019. http://brighterkashmir.com/news-archive/15-12-2019.

Vaid, Neelam, Shweta Deshpande, Kalyani Salve, Rajesh Nikam, and Sanjay Vaid. 2015. "Fuel for the Processor: Our Experience." *Journal of Indian Speech Language & Hearing Association* 29 (1): 1–7.

Vaidya, Shubhangi. 2016. *Autism and the Family in Urban India: Looking Back, Looking Forward.* New Delhi: Springer.

Valente, Joseph Michael. 2011. "Cyborgization: Deaf Education for Young Children in the Cochlear Implantation Era." *Qualitative Inquiry* 17 (7): 639–52.

Varma, Saiba. 2020. *The Occupied Clinic: Militarism and Care in Kashmir.* Durham, N.C.: Duke University Press.

Vygotsky, Lev S. 1978. *Mind in Society: The Development of Higher Psychological Processes.* Cambridge, Mass.: Harvard University Press.

Wagner, Anita, Carina Pals, Charlotte M. de Blecourt, Anastasios Sarampalis, and Deniz Başkent. 2016. "Does Signal Degradation Affect Top-Down Processing of Speech?" *Advances in Experimental Medicine and Biology* 894: 297–306.

Wallmark, Zachary, and Roger A. Kendall. 2018. "Describing Sound." In *The Ox-

ford Handbook of Timbre, edited by Emily I. Dolan and Alexander Rehding. New York: Oxford University Press.

Weidman, Amanda. 2014. "Anthropology and Voice." *Annual Review of Anthropology* 43: 37–51.

Wendell, Susan. 1996. *The Rejected Body: Feminist Philosophical Reflections on Disability.* New York: Routledge.

Wendell, Susan. 2001. "Unhealthy Disabled: Treating Chronic Illnesses as Disabilities." *Hypatia* 16 (4): 17–33.

Wheeler, Alexandra, Sue M. Archbold, Tim Hardie, and Linda M. Watson. 2009. "Children with Cochlear Implants: The Communication Journey." *Cochlear Implants International* 10 (1): 41–62.

Whyte, Susan Reynolds, ed. 2014. *Second Chances: Surviving AIDS in Uganda.* Durham, N.C.: Duke University Press.

Whyte, Susan Reynolds, ed. 2019. "In the Long Run: Ugandans Living with Disability." *Current Anthropology* 61 (S21): S132–40.

Williamson, Bess. 2019. *Accessible America: A History of Disability and Design.* New York: New York University Press.

Wittgenstein, Ludwig. 2009. *Philosophical Investigations.* Rev. 4th ed. Translated by G. E. M. Anscombe, P. M. S. Hacker, and Joachim Schulte. West Sussex: Blackwell.

Wolf-Meyer, Matthew J. 2020. *Unraveling: Remaking Personhood in a Neurodiverse Age.* Minneapolis: University of Minnesota Press.

Wood, David, Jerome S. Bruner, and Gail Ross. 1976. "The Role of Tutoring in Problem Solving." *Journal of Child Psychology and Psychiatry* 17 (2): 89–100.

Woodward, James. 1975. "How You Gonna Get to Heaven If You Can't Talk with Jesus: The Educational Establishment vs. the Deaf Community." Paper presented at the annual meeting of the Society for Applied Anthropology, Amsterdam.

Wool, Zoë H. 2015. *After War: The Weight of Life at Walter Reed.* Durham, N.C.: Duke University Press.

World Health Organization. 2008. *Guidelines on the Provision of Manual Wheelchairs in Less Resourced Settings.* Geneva: World Health Organization. https://www.who.int.

World Health Organization. 2019. *Preferred Profile for Hearing-Aid Technology Suitable for Low- and Middle-Income Countries.* Geneva: World Health Organization. https://www.who.int.

World Health Organization. 2021. "Deafness and Hearing Loss." Last updated April 1, 2021. https://www.who.int.

Wyatt, Sally. 2003. "Non-users Also Matter: The Construction of Users and Non-users of the Internet." In *How Users Matter: The Co-construction of Users and*

Technology, edited by Nelly Oudshoorn and Trevor Pinch, 67–80. Cambridge: MIT Press.

Zaitseva, Galina, Michael Pursglove, and Susan Gregory. 1999. "Vygotsky, Sign Language, and the Education of Deaf Pupils." *Journal of Deaf Studies and Deaf Education* 4 (1): 9–15.

Index

Page numbers in italic refer to illustrations.

MICHELE ILANA FRIEDNER is associate professor in the Department of Comparative Human Development at the University of Chicago.